THE RE-DISCOVERY
OF THE OLD TESTAMENT

The

RE-DISCOVERY

of the

OLD TESTAMENT

HAROLD HENRY ROWLEY

Essay Index Reprint Series

BOOKS FOR LIBRARIES PRESS

FREEPORT, NEW YORK

STANDARD BOOK NUMBER:

8369-1154-7

LIBRARY OF CONGRESS CATALOG CARD NUMBER:

75-76912

PRINTED IN THE UNITED STATES OF AMERICA

To the Reverend Principal
H. WHEELER ROBINSON

*Whose profound and penetrating scholar-
ship has put all who love the Old Testament
under an enduring debt—this volume is inscribed in token of high esteem.*

PREFACE

In some quarters there is to-day an impatience with Old
Testament scholarship. This is partly due to the complexity of the world it has opened up, and the difficulty of plac-
ing the varied contents of the Old Testament in the setting
of that world. It is also partly due to the backward look
which has naturally and necessarily characterized so much
of its study. The world out of which Israel and her literature arose, and the processes by which that literature grew
up, and the development of its religious ideas, have occupied the focus of interest. And they will still occupy a great
deal of its attention. Yet increasingly are men turning their
thought to the deeper message of the Old Testament, and
finding richer meaning in the light of all the work that has
been done. The Old Testament need not be buried beneath
the weight of scholarship, but may rather stand on the
foundation of scholarship, sustained by it and firmly upheld
before men.

It is clear that no one can grasp all the many-sided work
that has been done on this Book without much toil. But this
is no matter for reproach. For the fruits of scholarship that
are gained by infinite toil can in no sphere be appropriated
without toil. And few spheres are more complex than that
of the Old Testament. Yet the Old Testament specialist —
who cannot himself be completely acquainted with every
side of his vast field — can serve others by offering some of

the fruits of his study, not as an end in themselves, but related to the message of the Old Testament.

Such a task is attempted here. Into the minutiae of scholarship I do not enter, not because I regard them as meaningless, but because their study lies behind, rather than in, this book. Elaborate documentation, which is rightly found in work intended for scholars, is here dispensed with, and the focus of interest is in the edifice of Old Testament thought rather than in the foundations of its study. Yet it is my hope that the edifice stands squarely on the foundations. For only so is it secure. If these pages can help any reader to a fuller apprehension of the religious meaning of this most wonderful Book, they will have fulfilled their purpose.

For Biblical quotations I have kept largely to familiar words, though I have frequently modified the translation to some extent for reasons which are not stated, since they would distract the general reader. In no case has a change been introduced for *a priori* or dogmatic reasons, but only where philological or textual support could be provided to justify the change.

It is a deep grief to me that while this book has been in the press Principal H. Wheeler Robinson has passed from our midst. I have left the Dedication unchanged.

I have to thank Professor A. R. Johnson for his help in reading the proofs, and for his stimulating friendship, which has yielded many suggestions embodied in this book. I have also to thank Professor T. W. Manson for reading my work in proof — and for many other kindnesses.

H. H. ROWLEY

BANGOR, NORTH WALES
July, 1945

CONTENTS

I. THE ABIDING VALUE
OF THE OLD TESTAMENT

THE OLD TESTAMENT would be of abiding value to men, if only because three great religions have sprung out of it, and those the three great monotheistic faiths of the world. It is not a part of the Scriptures of Islam, but through both Christians and Jews the Old Testament exercised a considerable influence on Muhammad, and it belongs very definitely to the background of Islam. Of Judaism the Old Testament is the sole Scripture, though it is a mistake, as Father Lev Gillet has reminded us in his recent book, *Communion in the Messiah,* to forget that Judaism to-day is not merely the religion of the Old Testament, but has developed in many ways since the Canon of the Old Testament was closed. But it is more particularly the abiding value of the Old Testament to the Christian Church that is in mind here, and it is relevant to remember that it has belonged to the Bible of the Church from the days of its foundation. In the second century there was an experiment at dispensing with it, and in modern times there have been some who have advocated its elimination from the Bible of the Church, while many have adopted the simpler expedient of tacitly ignoring it.[1] Against this we are now witnessing a healthy reaction, and the rise of a new sense of the meaning and worth of the Old Testament.

This great collection formed the Bible of our Lord, and the early Christians found it to testify of Christ. When the books of the New Testament were written, they were in no sense intended to replace the Old Testament. They every-

1 For a careful study of these attitudes, Godfrey Phillips' *The Old Testament in the World Church* may be warmly commended.

where take it for granted, and would be difficult to understand without it. Many things did not need to be said in the New Testament, just because they were already so magnificently said in the Old. The loss of the Old Testament could therefore only be an impoverishment of the Church. It is not the case, as is so often supposed, that the Old Testament was merely the preparation for the New. Many who have so regarded it have supposed that just as the Old Testament was the tutor unto Christ for the Jewish people, so the sacred Scriptures of other faiths may be tutors unto Christ for other peoples, and their sacred books may well replace the Old Testament in the Bibles of the Christians of other lands.

This is wholly to misunderstand the meaning of the Old Testament and its place in our Bible. Few missionaries would to-day advocate an unsympathetic approach to other religions, and indeed missionaries have been in no small measure responsible for the deeper understanding of other religions which has been found in the West during the past hundred years. Moreover, missionaries have contributed not a little to the interest in their own sacred texts which has been found in modern times in other lands. But the plain fact is that even on the basis of the preparation for Christ, the Old Testament is unique, since it belongs to the stream of development that actually led to Christ. He was born a Jew, inheriting the culture and faith of the Jews, and while His message and His salvation are for all men it is in Judaism alone that the spiritual preparation for His work is to be sought, and Judaism alone that can provide the clue to the understanding of His mission and message.

Thus, the Old Testament offers a preparation for the New along a continuous line, whereas between the sacred texts of any other religion and Christianity there is an inevitable hiatus. In some respects, indeed, there is a hiatus between the Old Testament and the New, and the study of the Apocrypha and of other writings that issued from Jewish circles in the last pre-Christian centuries and the century that saw the birth of Christianity may do something to fill the gap. Yet the hiatus here is quite different from that between other sacred texts and the New Testament. For they do not in any sense lead to Christ, whereas the first preachers of the Christian Gospel based themselves firmly on the sure fact that the Old Testament does lead to Christ. It was not merely that in preaching to Jews they took this line. There is no part of the New Testament, for whatever readers it was written, which abandons this attitude. But, as has been said, the Old Testament is more than the preparation for the New. It is integral to the Bible of the Church, for its message belongs to the message of the Church. Old and New Testaments are alike parts of a single whole, as the several acts of a drama belong together. Without the final act it is incomplete, a process that fails to reach its goal; yet the final act by itself alone is robbed of its full meaning for lack of those that should precede it.

Every reader of the New Testament is familiar with the many direct citations from the Old, and verbal reminiscences of the Old, that abound in its pages. But beyond this, and even more significant than this, the New Testament moves in the world of ideas that is found in the Old. It does not always merely repeat them, of course. Often it re-combines and re-interprets them, and of this we shall study some examples later. For it is fatal to ignore the difference between the Old Testament and the New, or to regard the one as merely repeating what is in the other.

There have been some, and alas! there are still some, who regard the whole Bible as on a flat level of inspiration and authority, and who make no differentiation whatever in this respect between the Old and the New Testaments. But if the two Testaments belong together as parts of a single whole, the New Testament is none the less the climax and crown of the whole, in the light of which the meaning of the whole may alone be rightly seen. It gathers up the Old Testament into the unity of the Christian Bible, but to illumine the Old with its own light. For the New Testament must be finally normative for the Christian understanding of the Old.

This means that a truly historical outlook is essential for the understanding of the Old Testament, and the mere reading back of the New into the Old is misleading. Many centuries of religious growth and development are portrayed in the Old Testament, and many of the ideas of one age were outgrown in another, or perceived to be false and inadequate. They have no validity for us. That does not mean that we assume any attitude of superiority, or condemn the men of ancient days because they had less understanding than has been given to us. Often we have reason to be filled with humility and wonder as we perceive the heights they reached. No one speaks with contempt of Newton because science has advanced since his day. All realize the debt of science to Newton for the stage in its advance which he registered, and recognize that if it has gone beyond him in achievement, it has known few who have surpassed him in genius. And similarly, if to-day we have a fuller knowledge of God than many of the Old Testament characters, we can take small credit for it to ourselves, and if we are wise we shall recognize our debt to many whose ideas we should not to-day accept.

For our historical outlook on the Old Testament we are in large measure indebted to the scholars of the nineteenth century, whose work represented a re-discovery of the Old Testament of very great importance. They were filled with a scientific passion to get to the facts, to get behind the traditions which lie on the surface of our present Biblical books, or which have become attached to them, and to discover how and when these books came into being, and what meaning their words had for their authors or first readers. And in their hands the Old Testament became a new book. In the Law they recognized different strands, coming from widely separated ages, and its inner disagreements were thus explained, no less than the apparent ignorance of some strands in ages when they had been supposed to have been known. In the historical books they found various sources, coming from different ages and conflicting in their point of view, gathered together by editors who sometimes sought to impose their own point of view on the collected works. In the prophets they found real men, capable of being set in the circumstances of their own day, whose writings may be re-arranged in something more approximating a chronological order, or at any rate separated from much later material which has become attached to them, to the vast enrichment of their study. The Old Testament was no longer a quarry for proof-texts of Christian doctrine, or for incidents which could be viewed as allegories of Christian truth. It was interesting for its own sake, abounding in literary problems which fascinate the scientific mind.

It is not uncommon to-day to speak with disdain of the work of the school of historical criticism. Their work did not go far enough, indeed, for a merely historical outlook on the Old Testament is insufficient, and however great our success in transporting ourselves to ancient times, and seeing and hearing with the eyes and ears of the men of those days, we are far from the goal of Biblical study. Nevertheless, it is a mistake to belittle the work that has been done. For a historical outlook is of essential, though not of sole, importance. " Patriotism is not enough," said Nurse Edith Cavell, with no desire to depreciate patriotism, and a grateful country that admired the magnificence of her patriotism inscribed those words on the monument it erected to her memory. In the same way it should be possible to say

in the field of Biblical study that historical criticism is not
enough, without any depreciation of historical criticism.
The generation of scholars who laid this foundation rendered a vast service to all succeeding students of the Bible,
and if we are free to turn with more zeal to other sides of
Old Testament study, it is in no small measure due to them.
It is true that many of the conclusions they reached are challenged to-day, and that in the field of literary criticism there
is, perhaps, more variety of opinion than for a very long
time. But the method and fundamental outlook of the critical school remain, and that was the essential contribution
they made to the re-discovery of the Old Testament.

Again, considerable light has been shed on the Old Testament by archaeology, which may be said to have brought a
further re-discovery of this Book. The brilliant achievements of the nineteenth century, more particularly in the
realm of the decipherment of inscriptions in long-forgotten languages, added greatly to our knowledge of the world
in which Israel was set. We know far more of the rise and
fall of empires than the Old Testament itself could have
told us, and we can see how the fortunes of Israel were affected by events that happened far beyond her borders. We
can view her history in perspective, and see how her political and economic life was determined by world events in
that Mediterranean and Mesopotamian world in which she
lived. Nor is the light shed by archaeology merely a matter
of historical texts. The work of the nineteenth century has
been continued in the twentieth, and not alone have further texts of historical interest been found, but a new technique has made unconsidered trifles yield rich secrets, so
that even where no texts are found it is possible to determine and to date some of the outstanding events of the history of excavated sites. Besides this, religious objects and
religious texts have been found, and we have a considerable
knowledge of the cultural and religious background of the

Old Testament. Just as in the historical sphere we no longer depend merely on the statements of the Old Testament, so here we can supplement what the Old Testament tells us from the surviving contemporary material, and can appreciate the cultural and spiritual *milieu* in which Israel lived.

It is perhaps natural that with the vast growth of knowledge of these things, and the clear recognition that neither the history nor the culture of Israel can be understood without relation to those of her neighbours, there should have been an excess of emphasis on these relationships. At the beginning of the present century there was a school which over-emphasized the Babylonian connexions, and the *Babel-und-Bibel* controversy raged fiercely. Everything in the Old Testament was interpreted in terms of things Babylonian, or treated as a borrowing from Babylon, and all spiritual originality was denied to Israel, or at least minimized. More recently, with the fuller knowledge we have of Canaanite life and culture, there is a tendency to read everything in the Old Testament in terms of the primitive origins of Israelite life. While both of these emphases have been mistaken, it should not surprise us that new knowledge should assume a disproportionate importance.

There have been some, on the other hand, who have found in archaeology the basis of a different re-discovery of the Old Testament, and who have used it to attempt to discredit that historical criticism which has been said above to be of essential, though not of sole, importance. They have not always distinguished between archaeological facts, and the views to which they have given rise, and they have hailed everything which seemed to support a Biblical statement as proving the historical reliability of the Bible, while ignoring the many Biblical statements which are in conflict with their views. The outstanding instance of this is the tendency of some writers to seize on anything which appears to support the fifteenth century dating of the Exodus, and to avoid facing the real complexity of the issue, and then to claim that the historical accuracy of 1 Kings vi. 1, which assigns four hundred and eighty years to the period from the Exodus to the building of the Temple of Solomon, is marvellously established.

The dangers of this course are manifest. With the uninstructed or unintelligent reader it may have some success, but even he may one day awake to the fact that many Biblical statements have been jettisoned by these writers, and that so far from establishing the historical reliability of the Old Testament, they have but doubtfully established the reliability of a few texts, on which nothing vital hangs. For the Old Testament is more than a text-book of history, and any writer who offers to his readers a re-discovery of it merely in such terms does a grave disservice to the Old Testament and to his readers alike.

A more balanced view than any of these recognizes that while the Old Testament contains many historical traditions of the highest value, and often of great reliability, it is not a text-book of history. Similarly, while Hebrew religion has its roots in the religion of the ancient Near East, and was continually subject to unprogressive influences that tended to keep it on the level of that out of which it sprang, there was something quite unique in the religious development of Israel. With Moses something new in the history of religion happened, and under the dynamic of his personality — of his inspired personality, we need not hesitate to believe — Israelite religion was lifted to a new and higher level. Often it fell below the level of Moses, but in her history Israel was blessed with a succession of great spiritual leaders, and especially with the prophets, who not alone recalled her to the heights of Mosaic religion, but interpreted the meaning of her faith in terms of the needs of the hour, brought out the implications of her faith, became the channels of new and larger revelation of the nature and will of God, and so became the agents of a great spiritual growth. Rarely were they heeded in their own day, yet their influence is seen in the later religion of the Old Testament. For when, in post-exilic days, the religion we call Judaism took its shape, its founders aimed to embody the message of the higher prophetic religion. The stately ritual they established, many of whose uses were not themselves new, indeed, was intended to be the organ of the prophetic faith, and to preserve that faith from fresh contamination of the kind that had called forth the prophetic denunciation. The fixity of priestly religion, that became a barrier to progress, and that has become in our thought the antithesis of prophetic religion, was created with no hostility to prophetic religion, to prevent regress, and not to check progress.

From the crude origins to the nobler heights of Old Testament faith we may recognize a great development, and we may also recognize the unique quality that belongs to that development, differentiating it from all the things to which it is related. We may recognize the hand of God in that development, and may study the interplay of divine and human factors. We may perceive that the men who were the agents of the development spoke as they were moved by God, and that they were moved by God because they were men who were willing to respond to His moving power. We may find the story to be less the record of man's groping after God than the record of God's progressive revelation of Himself to man. As such it is without equal in the world's religious literature. Yet, as has been said, it is more than this. For if it were no more, we might ask whether it were not better to concentrate on the goal of the development, rather than study the history of the development, however fascinating it might be. The history of science may be a very entrancing story, but to be abreast of

present-day scientific knowledge is a more urgent task of
the scientist than any mere retrospect as an idle luxury.
And if we have no more than the academic interest of the
scholar in the development of Old Testament religion, it
would seem superfluous to ask that the Old Testament
should remain in the Bible of the Church. The historical
outlook on the Old Testament, therefore, and the recognition of the religious development it records, must be related to some higher purpose. It must, indeed, be related to
a fundamentally religious purpose. For the Old Testament
is essentially a religious book, and it has its place in the Bible of the Church solely as a religious book.

Many students of the Bible are far too inclined to forget
this. It is studied merely as a record of the past, and men
try to recapture ancient situations, ancient political, social
and religious conditions, and they imagine that if they can
somehow hear the accents of the prophets' voices as their
first hearers heard them, or understand their words as those
hearers understood them, they have reached the goal of
Old Testament study. Nothing could be farther from the
truth. For there is nothing essentially religious in that. Religion is more than the study of religion, and unless the
study of the Bible is a religious exercise, it misses its deepest purpose. This is not to say, of course, that all Bible
study should be made the organ of worship, for worship is
by no means the whole of religion. But it is to say that in all
Bible study the religious quality of the story should be realized, and the religious teaching and message emphasized.
For all Bible study should minister to the spirit as well as
to the mind, and should bring richer apprehension of divine truth.

This is more than the apprehension of words as their first
hearers or readers apprehended them. For the first hearers
or readers may have very imperfectly understood the significance of the words. In the Gospels we are told that the dis-

ciples failed to understand the meaning of many of the Master's words, which they nevertheless cherished in their memory, and it was only afterwards, when they considered them again in the light of what had happened since their utterance, that they perceived their real significance. It was the same with utterances of the prophets. The hearers of Jeremiah did not perceive the significance of his proclamation of a religion which could subsist without the Temple, whose Covenant should be inscribed on men's hearts. It is very improbable that Jeremiah himself perceived the full significance of his message. Often the significance of an utterance lies in what it shall come to mean, even more than in what it first means. Words are seeds, whose full fruition may take long to mature, and like seeds they can only be understood in the light of what they become. No one would dream of interpreting the acorn without relation to the oak of which it is the promise. To describe its size, shape, colour, weight, texture, and chemical composition, would be recognized to be ludicrously inadequate. And words are as dynamic as the acorn, especially when they are divine words, expressing vital truth. Hence, beyond the understanding of Old Testament teaching as its first hearers or readers understood it, we need to understand the meaning it has come to have in its developing life, the unfolding meaning it has yielded down the years, and oft-times the fuller meaning it may have for us in the light of Christ.

Some years ago the present writer quoted a word from a forgotten source, which has lain for many years in his memory. It was: " Old Testament prophecies run to Christ, as tidal rivers to the sea, only to feel His reflex influence upon them." That is true of more than prophecies. It is when we read the Old Testament in the light of the New that we perceive its real significance. We must, of course, beware of attributing to those who wrote the Old Testament the understanding which we have gained in the light of the New.

That is why a historical sense and outlook are essential for the understanding of the Old Testament. Without it we merely reach confusion, reading back the New Testament into the Old at some points, and being then bewildered by those elements in the Old Testament which cannot be squared with the teaching of the New. We need both a historical and a teleological understanding, appreciating everything in relation to its contemporary situation as a moment in the process of the development, and appreciating it too in relation to the goal of the process.

In some quarters there is to-day a reaction from the attitudes to the Old Testament which have been described above, and an emphasis on its religious quality no less strong than that of the present writer. But sometimes men who are familiar with the work of scholarship tend to slight the fruits of scholarly work on the Old Testament, and to give the impression that the religious re-discovery of this Book renders all else obsolete. Father Hebert speaks of this disposition to return to a " fundamentalist " attitude by some who are seeking for a more adequate theological view of the Bible as the word of God, and wisely adds: " Yet it will be a disaster if in making this re-discovery the gains of the Liberal period are lost; for there is a scientific truth of fact, and the scientific-historical methods of our day are far in advance of the crude methods of the Anglican Divines, the Scholastics, or the Fathers." [2] Anything which savours of a new obscurantism is fraught with peril, and the recognition of the religious quality and message of the Old Testament does not mean that everything in it must be accepted without discrimination as a word of authority for us. Phythian-Adams objects to those who welcome the message of Jeremiah as congenial, and depreciate the message of Ezekiel. The present writer would agree that Ezekiel often gets far less than justice, but he finds danger in Phythian-Adams'

[2] *The Throne of David*, 1941, p. 32.

observation in this connexion that " the Bible is a vehicle of Revelation, and it is not open to a believer to select from it only such passages as suit his personal taste." [3] The reader is likely to suppose that what is meant is that whatever is in the Bible must be accepted because it is there. That Phythian-Adams does not really mean this, however, is clear, since on another page he depreciates ideas of the Epistle to the Hebrews, as merely reflecting the writer's mistaken thoughts.[4] It is not easy to see what canon of judgement, other than the test of congeniality to his theme, discriminates in favour of Ezekiel and against the Epistle to the Hebrews, but the present writer finds danger alike in the suggestion that whatever is in the Bible must be accepted in unquestioning faith and the idea that the subjective fancy of the reader is an adequate standard.

No true re-discovery of the Bible can go back on all the work that has been done, or, in its eagerness to penetrate the religious message of this Book, abandon a truly historical outlook. Both must be held firmly together as parts of a single whole view. It is true that the historical understanding and the spiritual appreciation are distinguishable activities, and it is sometimes thought that they must be kept quite distinct. For the one the Bible must be treated as a purely human document, and examined with unfettered freedom, while for the other it may be treated as the vehicle of revelation. But the complete separation of these two activities must lead to greater confusion than their combination, since it can only imply that they are unrelated activities and that the fruits of the one are without concern to him who pursues the other. But a historical outlook prepares us to recognize that many things were outgrown in the course of the story. Primitive ideas of God were followed by higher ideas, and therefore the primitive ideas are

3 *The People and the Presence*, 1942, pp. 87 f.
4 *Ibid.*, p. 108.

no longer valid for us. We may therefore expect to find a great deal in the Old Testament which is in no sense normative for our faith or practice, since it belongs to the transcended past. Yet equally we may expect to find some things carried forward from that past into the present. There is a continuing thread through all the Old Testament, which binds it all together and gives meaning to it all.

Life is essentially a leaving behind and a carrying forward. The self of any moment is not identical with the self of the moment that preceded it, yet with equal firmness we may proclaim the identity of the continuing self. We may view human consciousness analytically, and affirm that it is never the same for two consecutive moments, or we may view it dynamically, and recognize the unity of the consciousness of the two moments. From the moment that has passed away a deposit is carried forward. The self of to-day is not wholly other than the self of yesterday. It carries the marks of yesterday's experience upon it. For life is a stream, ever changing yet ever the same.

And because history is the record of a living process, it reveals the same phenomenon. Its concern is not with a series of unrelated tableaux, but with an unfolding development. Something is ever carried forward, and it is the significant something that conveys the life of one moment into the next. Sometimes its significance is carried far forward through many ages, for it possesses an enduring vitality. Of this Magna Carta and the Declaration of Independence are familiar examples. Born of particular situations out of the conditions of the immediately preceding years, their vitality is still not exhausted. And in Israel's life we continually find the same thing. Amid all that is of passing significance in the Old Testament there is much that is of enduring significance, and that has a meaning for our age as real as for the age in which it first appeared. But just because the Old Testament is a fundamentally religious book, the vital things here are not political developments and civil liberties, but religious messages.

It should, perhaps, be made clear that the unfolding development which is here referred to is quite other than the evolutionary process which has been widely supposed to provide the clue to everything. It is not for a moment suggested that the time process of itself ensures advance, or that advance is in any way continuous. There is a dynamic power in events and ideas which may influence the subsequent course of the life of men and of communities, but it is never the sole influence. The history of to-day is born of the situation of yesterday, yet it is never wholly determined by that situation. Man is confronted with an ever-renewed demand for choice, and though the choice of yesterday may limit the freedom of to-day's it can never wholly destroy that freedom. There is never anything inevitable in the course of the development, as though it is only a continual bringing into the light of what was already latent and implicit.

Into the making of the Old Testament there went human and divine factors. Few to-day regard it as a purely superhuman book, whose words bear none of the marks of the spirit of its human authors, but perfectly and exactly reflect the *ipsissima verba* of the inspiring God. Yet are we unwise if we regard it as a merely human document, reflecting man's search for God and progressive discovery of One who passively concealed Himself behind His works. Divine and human factors here intertwine and interpenetrate one another. For God was actively revealing Himself to men, in so far as they were spiritually able to apprehend Him, and through men, in so far as they were able to transmit the revelation through the opaqueness of their personality. The revelation came through the organ of their personality, and it took something of the character of that through which it came. Just as light that passes through coloured glass is wholly modified by the glass through which it passes, yet does not derive from the glass itself, so God's revelation of Himself, while it has its source wholly in Him, is obscured to a greater or lesser degree by the medium through which it reaches us. The imperfections and false ideas of the men through whom God revealed Himself were a limitation upon God, yet through their imperfections and false ideas some light shone from Him. And all light that came from Him is enduring light, and all truth that is from Him is unfading in its significance. All that belongs merely to the medium, obscuring the light and hiding the truth, is but of passing significance, while all that is of God marks with its abiding worth the record of the Old Testament. Yet even the passing may have some enduring message. It brings no word of authority to us, but it may have a different message. It may remind us that God can use even imperfect men to serve His purpose, and to reveal His will, and can in some measure clothe His spirit with their personalities. Simple, fallible, but sincere and consecrated men may be extensions of the divine personality, charged with the word of God. That is a message of profound importance in all ages to men who, while deeply conscious of their fallibility, may yet be the channels of a divine word to their fellows.

The message of the Old Testament is essentially religious. And it has already been said that religion is more than worship. Ought we not then to define what we mean by religion? Yet who can define it? Innumerable attempts have been made, yet few definitions can satisfy more than their creators. For it is vain to attempt to imprison in a formula the living reality that is religion. When Olivia satirically proposed to give the inventory of her beauty, she proceeded: " Item, two lips, indifferent red; item, two grey eyes, with lids to them; item, one neck, one chin, and so forth." [5] Beauty is not so defined; and religion is not defined in the analysis of some of its elements. For the indefinable quality which gives vitality to the elements is lost in the process of analysis. Hence, if we recall some of the chief elements of religion, we must not be supposed to be attempting to define it. For religion is more than the sum total of all its elements.

Many of the definitions of religion that have been proposed express it solely in terms of belief, and some in terms of such belief as would leave no place in religion for so fundamentally atheistic a faith as early Buddhism. It seems wiser to recognize that religion is a much richer complex of elements, which exist to a varying degree and in varying combinations in particular religions. Some elements may be found in only negligible degree in some religions, but whereas the whole essence of religion cannot be expressed in terms of a single element which is wholly lacking in any religion, it is quite a different matter when it is expressed in terms of several elements, of which one may not be found in a particular religion. Man is correctly described as a biped, even though some men have but a single leg, or none at all. But if we were to say that the entire essence of manhood lay in the possession of two legs, we should deny the title to manhood of all who were not two-legged.

Religion affects belief, worship and conduct. It involves belief in some power, or principle, behind or in the universe, whether embodied in a personal Being or Beings or not. It involves some expression of itself in contact with the object of the belief, whereby the power or principle which constitutes the object of the belief becomes the active helper of the worshipper, or becomes identified with him. And it affects the conduct in ordinary life. It may impose arbitrary taboos on its devotees, or it may make ethical demands, or it may go far beyond ethical demands in the call for the self-

[5] *Twelfth Night*, I, iv, 205 ff.

sacrificing spiritual service of men. In each of these elements the Old Testament has contributions of enduring
worth to make.

It unfolds its revelation of the personal God who stands
both behind and in the universe, and it not alone insists
that He is, but it declares what manner of Being He is.
More significant than the fact of God is the character of
God, and the Old Testament has much to say on that character which is as true for us as it was for ancient Israel. The
Old Testament also carries us deeply into the spirit of worship. That profound awe which marks all true worship, for
which Otto has coined the word Numinous, the *mysterium
tremendum et fascinosum,* filling the worshipper with mingled elation and dread, is seen again and again in its narratives. " What is man that thou art mindful of him? And
the son of man, that thou visitest him? " asks the Psalmist,
shrinking before God in the sense of his nothingness. " For
thou hast made him but little lower than God, And crownest him with glory and honour," he continues in his elation.[6] " Woe is me! for I am undone," cries Isaiah in the
presence of God, humbled to the dust at the sense of his
unworthiness; " for mine eyes have seen the King, Yahweh
of hosts," he continues, in wonder at the greatness of his
privilege.[7] But beyond this sense of awe, which belongs to
the spirit of all true worship, the Old Testament gives rich
expression to that spirit in thanksgiving, in confession, in
petition, in noble words that are still able to provide the
vehicle of our worship to-day. It knows the experience of
profound fellowship with God and of joy in that fellowship,
while in its sacrificial ritual it expresses a complex of elements to which we shall have occasion to return. To every
side of worship the Old Testament has much to contribute,
and even though its sacrificial ritual is one of the things we
have left behind, that ritual has made an enduring contri-

[6] Ps. viii. 4 f. (Heb. 5 f.).   [7] Isa. vi. 5.

bution to our religion. On human conduct the Old Testament has very much of enduring value to say. So much so, indeed, that the worth of the Old Testament is sometimes assessed rather in ethical than in religious terms. No religion lays stronger emphasis on the inter-relation of religion and life. Many of its requirements are on the sub-ethical plane of taboo, but its more characteristic demands are for a high ethical quality of life arising from its religious insight, and directed by a religious motive. Beyond this, the springs of Christian teaching, making those supra-ethical demands, to which reference has been made above, are found in the Old Testament, whose noble and penetrating words will ever have meaning for those who will listen.

Put in a different way, we may observe that religion touches man's whole personality. It concerns his intellect, his emotions, and his will. Nowhere is this more clearly seen than in the Old Testament, and it will be remembered that when our Lord was asked which commandment is the first of all, He replied in words taken from the Old Testament: " Thou shalt love the Lord thy God with all thy heart, and with all thy soul, and with all thy mind, and with all thy strength." [8] Love for God, not dread of God, or mere obedience to His commands, is thus enjoined in the Old Testament, but its love is no mere emotional luxury or empty sentiment. It is a love into which our whole manhood and all its powers must go; it is a love which must express itself in every side of our life. And this is proclaimed not in a single verse alone. It lies at the heart of a great deal of the teaching of this Book, making it enduringly valuable to men. Moreover, when our Lord added a corollary to this love of God, He did so in terms which were once more taken from the Old Testament: " Thou shalt love thy neighbour as thyself." And again that is a text on which much in the prophetic books provides an illuminating

8 Mark xii. 30.

commentary. This means that from the Old Testament there has been carried into Christianity the recognition that man is not merely an individual, owing allegiance and love to God, and obedience to His will, but a member of society, with a duty to his fellow-man, and a duty that cannot be expressed in formal acts alone, but one that springs out of an inner attitude of spirit towards him. He is called to serve his fellow-man, not simply because God enjoins it, and his not to reason why, but because he loves his fellow-man, and because he and his fellow-man are parts one of another.

At all these sides of the message of this great Book we shall have to look in closer detail. For the moment it suffices to indicate thus briefly the essential standpoint of our study, and the nature of the re-discovery of the Old Testament which it hails and shares. It is a return to religious values, but without depreciation of all the literary, historical, and archaeological work of the past century and more. It is rather to values which have become clearer in the light of all that study. For upon that study it bases itself. The building is ever more than the foundation, but the superstructure has no call to despise that whereon it rests. A recent writer, who reviews with approval the present-day movement towards Old Testament theology, refers with evident disapproval to the period in which scholars studied the history of Old Testament religion, rather than Old Testament theology. Speaking of a standard English work of this kind he says: " Is it without reason that one rises from the reading of this book with the idea that, if no more than this can be said, then, as far as Christians of to-day are concerned, the Old Testament may safely be ignored? " [9] But the authors of the work in question would be the last to claim that no more than this can be said. They would, however, claim, and rightly claim, that until the spiritual pilgrimage

[9] *The Journal of Religion,* xxiii, 1943, p. 128.

of Israel is grasped in its historical development, it is idle to attempt to assess the theological significance of the Old Testament. It is possible to disagree with them at this point or at that in their account of the development, but it is not possible to write an adequate study of the theology of the Old Testament if a historical outlook is abandoned. The books on the theology of the Old Testament that are appearing, and that will doubtless continue to appear, are and will be better books because of the histories of Old Testament religion that have been written. Humble and grateful recognition of the work that has been done, insufficient though it may be recognized to be, is an indispensable part of the equipment of those who would carry the work forward. We may rejoice that their labours have made possible a more satisfying study of the religious meaning and message of the Old Testament, resting on sound learning and a power of discrimination that only a true historical outlook can give. To build the tombs of the prophets of a former generation while stoning the prophets of one's own day is admittedly a poor performance. To depreciate those who laboured before us while entering into the inheritance of their labours is no better.

In the following chapters no attempt is made to write either a history of Israelite religion or a handbook of Old Testament theology, but rather to illustrate the spiritual treasures that men to-day are discovering afresh in the Bible. Religion is wider than theology, as has been above indicated, and a mere history of the past, whether in the realm of action or of thought, has been declared insufficient. Our purpose is not to see what men's religion has been, but what religious meaning men are finding in the Old Testament to-day. They are approaching it equipped with all the knowledge that has been so patiently gathered, but to ask what it has to say to us across the ages, and what is the enduring word of God that sounds through its message in our ears. Our studies may enable us to realize how this Book may be not alone the object of our study, but the living oracles of God to us and the organ of our religious growth. Only if it is such a Book can it really fulfil its mission as a part of the Scriptures of our faith.

II. ARCHAEOLOGY AND
THE OLD TESTAMENT

IN THE PRECEDING chapter reference has been made to the
new light in which the Old Testament was set by literary
criticism and by archaeology. Of literary criticism nothing
more will be said here, since the final establishment of its
method belongs to a past generation. Many of the results
attained by earlier scholars are to-day being challenged,
but the challengers all recognize that their work can be
successful only if it is as scientific in its method as that
against which it is directed. No reliance on dogma or tradition can suffice to establish the date, authorship and composition of the books of the Old Testament. These are questions that can be settled only by patient and untrammelled
study, no more inconsistent with deep reverence for the Bible than blind and unthinking acceptance of tradition.
Minds can be consecrated to God as well as hands and
hearts, and the consecrated mind functions as a mind, but
in humble recognition that the God to whose service it is
consecrated can quicken it and illuminate it and aid it in
its working.

Of archaeology more must be said, since it commands
widespread interest to-day, and many extravagant claims
are made in its name. It has made, and in our day is continuing to make, great contribution to the re-discovery and
understanding of the Old Testament. Yet it is desirable to
make a just assessment of its contribution, and neither to
ignore it as of no relevance to the religious study of the
Old Testament nor to attach undue importance to its
achievements.[1]

[1] Of the many books devoted to the study of archaeology and the Old
Testament, mention may be made of Millar Burrows' *What Mean These*

The last hundred years have been fruitful above all others in bringing to light an abundance of material which has transformed the study of the Old Testament, and it is hard for us to realize how much knowledge is open to us that was not available a century ago. In the interval between the two world wars there has been very great archaeological activity, and material has been brought to light faster than it could be fully studied and assimilated. Not a few people imagine that the chief value of archaeology is to confirm the historical statements of the Bible, and it is sometimes supposed that it has proved the Bible true. Rarely, indeed, does it prove a Biblical statement true. It does, however, shed a wealth of light on the Biblical narratives in a great variety of ways.

The contribution of archaeology to the philology and exegesis of the Old Testament will be left wholly out of account here. The new texts brought to light in long-forgotten languages have given to lexicographers and grammarians an ever-growing stock of material, and have shed light on many an obscure passage of the Old Testament. But of that more technical side of Old Testament study nothing will here be said. Rather is it proposed to select a few of the more notable discoveries, to illustrate the light thrown on the historical, cultural and religious background of the Old Testament.

That the monuments of Egypt and Assyria and Babylonia have shed much light on the historical background of the Old Testament scarcely needs to be said. For no modern text-book of Israelite history ignores this light, and no

Stones? 1941, to which the reader who would pursue the subject is particularly recommended. Professor W. F. Albright, whose scholarship is phenomenal, and who is a distinguished archaeologist with a profoundly religious interest, has written two recent books which bring out the meaning of archaeology for the student of the religion of the Old Testament, which may also be strongly recommended to the serious student. They are *From the Stone Age to Christianity*, 1940, and *Archaeology and the Religion of Israel*, 1942.

one would to-day dream of studying the history of the Hebrews except in the setting of the larger history of the ancient Near East. It is not only from texts, however, that light is shed. Explorations and excavations that yield no scrap of written material may yet bring help to the historian.

An illustration of this is provided by the Danish excavations at Shiloh. In the early chapters of the first book of Samuel, we find an important sanctuary at Shiloh, kept by Eli, and treasuring the Ark. Then we read that the Ark was captured by the Philistines, and held by them for a short time, after which it was returned to Israel. But it did not return to Shiloh. For some years it was at Kirjath-jearim, and from there it was taken by David to Jerusalem. Moreover, when the family of Eli next appears, it is found not at Shiloh, but at Nob. What had happened to Shiloh and its Temple? Nowhere in the Bible are we told. But we read in the book of Jeremiah references to some great disaster which had befallen Shiloh at some unspecified period of history.[2] There is nothing in Jeremiah's references to suggest that this disaster long antedated his day, but in view of the other considerations noted above it has long been supposed that Shiloh was destroyed by the Philistines, when they defeated Israel and captured the Ark. In recent years a Danish expedition has excavated Shiloh, and by the evidence of the pottery it has established that there was a break in its history from the middle of the eleventh century B.C. until the sixth century B.C. The middle of the eleventh century is precisely the period of the Philistine defeat of Israel and capture of the Ark.

In modern archaeological work, pottery is of the greatest possible importance. Its value lies in its worthlessness and indestructibility, for it is broken pottery which is so useful. Nothing is easer to break than pottery; but few things are

2 Jer. vii. 12 ff.; xxvi. 6, 9.

harder to destroy. It is cast out, to become buried in the dust and to preserve its story. It was cheap and plentiful, and once broken was useless, save sometimes to serve as writing material for ephemeral purposes as ostraka. Its life was normally short, and hence in most cases the broken fragments lie in the deposits dating from the age when they were used. But types of pottery are continually changing. The very shape of vessels varied from age to age, and still more the ornamentation. In one locality pottery of a certain type may be found side by side with material that can be dated within close limits, and so the approximate date when that type of pottery was used can be determined, to be confirmed, perhaps, in another district by independent evidence of the age of a deposit. And then, by the careful study of the types of pottery found in places where there is no other evidence for the age of the deposit, the comparison with the datable types becomes important. It was the late Sir Flinders Petrie who first perceived the significance of this evidence, and while his sense of its importance was received at first with some derision, its value is to-day universally recognized and the scientific care with which it has been studied and classified enables it to be used with reasonable confidence.

Again, Bethshean has been excavated, and it shows that Egyptian influence continued down to the beginning of the twelfth century B.C., when it was followed by Philistine influence. In the age of Saul we know that the Philistines had spread their influence into the Central Highlands, from which Saul succeeded in dislodging them. But he failed to dislodge them from the coastal plains. When they marched against him to defeat him at the fatal field of Gilboa, it was by the circuitous lowland route, leading to the Vale of Esdraelon, that they came to attack him from the north. From the fact that the bodies of Saul and Jonathan were afterwards displayed on the walls of Bethshean, it is clear that this city was allied with, or dependent upon, the Philistines. That it long maintained its independence of Israel is recognized in the Biblical statement that at the time of the Conquest the Israelites were unable to take it.[3] But we are not told in the Bible when it was taken, or what became of it. But the excavation of the site has shown that it was unoccupied from the tenth to the fourth century B.C. It is therefore probable that David captured and destroyed it about 1000 B.C. We are told of his capture of the Jebusite fortress of Jerusalem, and now it appears that Bethshean was also taken. But whereas Jerusalem became his capital, Bethshean was left in ruins.

Turning to Jerusalem, we may note how archaeology has shed light on its capture in the time of David. The account given in 2 Sam. v is rather obscure. Jerusalem in those days was a small city on a single one of the hills on which it stood later. Its position was one of great natural strength. So strong was it, indeed, that when David came to the attack, the Jebusites hurled their taunts at him across the valley, and boastfully declared that if there were only the blind and the lame to defend the city they would be sufficient. But though the city was strong, its water supply was very poor. Within the city there was no natural supply, for its only spring was outside, below the city. But a channel had been cut, known to-day as Warren's Shaft, with the aim of simplifying the problem. It was roughly in the shape of a Z, but with the down stroke vertical. The water ran from the spring along the channel corresponding to the bottom horizontal, while the people in the city walked along the passage corresponding to the top horizontal, until they were vertically over the water. A rough shaft had then been cut through the rock, so that they could draw water from the top. The watercourse provided David his entrance into the city. He promised to make the first man who should enter the city through the shaft his commander-in-chief.[4] And Joab, already commander-in-chief, and not meaning to lose the post, himself led the attack. Apparently the Israelites went through the water along the bottom, and then clambered up the rough sides of the rock up the shaft, and were in the city before any of the besieged had any idea that so bold a plan had been conceived.

The age of David and Solomon stands out as unique in the history of Israel for the extent of its dominion and the wealth which is credited to its king. That this was the only period in which the Israelite tribes were fully united under a single administration is but one of the causes of this, though a very important one. For the external conditions in that age were favourable. Babylon had declined, and the Assyrian power was only in its beginnings. It had not yet spread to the west, and was only concerned to establish itself in the Euphrates valley. In the north the Hittite power had declined, and the state of Mitanni was too much occupied in watching Assyria to entertain any ambitions for the control of Palestine. Egypt had passed through a long period of weakness, and though in the time of Solomon it was beginning to awake once more, Solomon allied himself with the Pharaoh, whose daughter he married, with the result that the Pharaoh sent an army and reduced the Canaanite fortress of Gezer, which had apparently never yet been conquered by the Israelites. Apart from this incident, Palestine and Syria seem to have been free from outside interference during this period, so that the strongest power within that little world was able to reduce its neighbours to subjection. At a later period, under similar conditions, the kingdom which had its centre at Damascus was the strongest individual power, and almost succeeded in establishing its empire in the region. But now, owing to the union of the Israelite tribes for the first time on so large a

4 1 Chron. xi. 6.

scale, and owing to the vigorous military leadership of David and Joab, Israel established a dominion of which it never ceased to dream.

Solomon, who inherited the kingdom, and did not have to waste its resources on war, was able to undertake great building works. He is said in the Bible to have possessed almost fabulous wealth, but to have maintained so costly a court and to have spent so much on his enterprises that he had to cede territory to Tyre in payment of his debts. For in addition to the building of the Temple he carried on much building activity elsewhere. He is said to have built chariot cities, in which to keep his fourteen hundred chariots and their horses.[5] One of the places named in this connexion is Megiddo. Megiddo has been excavated, and in a stratum which is dated archaeologically in the period of the early monarchy, stables for some four hundred and fifty horses, and accommodation for about one hundred and fifty chariots have been unearthed. As to the sources of Solomon's wealth, archaeology is able to add something to our knowledge. Some of the sources are clear enough. The heavy taxation of his own people, the tribute exacted from the subject peoples, and the customs levied on the transit trade need little mention. In times of peace a considerable trade passed through Palestine between Egypt and Asia Minor and the Mesopotamian countries. During this period only did these dues fall entirely into the Israelite exchequer. There were other periods of unified control, of course, but they were never periods of Israelite control. Then, too, Solomon engaged in state trading enterprises from the Red Sea port of Ezion-geber. This site was excavated by Nelson Glueck in the years 1938–1940, and he found that the first buildings were erected on virgin soil in the tenth century B.C., i.e., in the period of Solomon. The location of the settlement was at first surprising, because it

5 1 Kings ix. 19; x. 26.

was in an exposed position where the strong north winds
would sweep it, whereas more sheltered sites lay close at
hand. However, the reason appeared when a copper smelt-
ing furnace was found, with the backs of the fires on the
north side, where the winds would do the fanning of the
fires. The refinery covers an acre and a half, and it was sur-
rounded by a brick wall. Nothing like it is known anywhere
else in the ancient Near East, yet, as Albright observes, it
was so relatively insignificant that it is not mentioned in the
Biblical sources.[6]

From Samaria a number of ostraka have come. These
were found in a palace which was believed to be Ahab's, but
which is to-day regarded as that of a later king, while an
older palace is thought to be that of Omri and Ahab. The
ostraka proved to be but consignment notes, recording the
quantities of wine despatched from different districts, presumably to the royal steward. From Megiddo a jasper seal,
valued at £2,000, and bearing the name of Shema', the servant of Jeroboam — doubtless Jeroboam II — comes. In a
site which is identified by some with the ancient Mizpah, a
seal of Jezaniah has been found, and it is possible that he is
the person of that name mentioned in 2 Kings xxv. 23 and
Jer. xl. 8. In Lachish and in Mizpah seal impressions bearing the name of Shebna have been found, and again it is
possible that it is a person named in the Bible, in Isa. xxii.
15 ff. From the fact that one of the impressions was found in
the Ashtarte temple in Mizpah, if the site is correctly so
identified, it has been inferred that Shebna was perhaps a
devotee of that goddess, in which case this might have accounted for the prophet's hostility. From Judah a large
number of inscribed jar-handles, bearing the words " belonging to the king," followed by one of the four place-
names, Hebron, Socoh, Ziph, and Mamshath, come, and

---

[6] *From the Stone Age to Christianity*, p. 223.

also a few jar-handles inscribed "belonging to Eliakim, steward of Yokin."

Each of these finds, trivial as they seem, has some value. The Samaria ostraka throw light on the administration of the kingdom. The lines of the taxation districts, as revealed by their place-names, ignored the old divisions of the tribes. Apparently taxes were paid in oil and wine. So, too, in Judah, where the jar-handles suggest that the royal wine tax was collected in standard jars, and that the land was divided into four administrative districts for the purpose. The jar-handles of Eliakim, steward of Yokin, would seem to indicate that the estate of the unfortunate Jehoiachin — with whose name Yokin is perhaps to be equated — was maintained in his name after he was carried into captivity. The seal of Shema' offers its silent testimony to the wealth and luxury of the reign of Jeroboam II, when Amos and Hosea were attacking the social inequalities. If the owner of the seal of Jezaniah is rightly identified, the finding of the seal at Mizpah might seem to indicate that he was not one of those who carried Jeremiah down to Egypt, but that he remained in Mizpah, since he would almost certainly have carried his seal with him wherever he went.

Few texts have been found in Palestine. It has been surmised that the reason for this may be that the piety of a later age insisted on destroying ancient monuments because religious ideas represented on them were no longer acceptable. But this does not explain the very surprising fact that even in buried cities that were left unoccupied for long periods no historical monuments have been found. In Moab, the Moabite stone, dating from the age of Ahab's sons, has been found, and it might be supposed that similar monuments must have been prepared on the west of the Jordan, and that some, overwhelmed in the ruin of cities, might have been buried far from the hand of any supposed pious destroyer, and might have been brought to light by the excavator's pick and shovel. Yet no Israelite monument, comparable with the Moabite stone, has been found, and until very recent years the written finds that Palestine has yielded have been of the most meagre character.

At Gezer a small Hebrew or Canaanite scrap, older than the Moabite stone, has been found. But it records merely the succession of the months, according to the agricultural operations proper to them. In the Siloam tunnel a brief inscription is cut on the face of the living rock, but it records merely the manner in which the tunnel was cut, the workmen starting from the two ends, but without modern instruments of precision to ensure their meeting in the middle, and therefore being guided as they approached one another by the sound of their hammering on the rock.

The recently discovered Lachish letters are therefore the more welcome, as they bring us documents written in Hebrew of greater volume than anything we possessed before from archaeological sources, though still meagre compared with the texts which come from non-Palestinian sites in other languages. These letters are written on scraps of pottery, and they contain military correspondence dating from the closing days of the Hebrew monarchy. Altogether about a score of letters have been found, but some are very brief or fragmentary. Unfortunately, precarious theories have been erected on the documents. In one of the texts there is a reference to a prophet, but only the last two letters of the prophet's name survive. Torczyner identifies him with Uriah, who is mentioned in the book of Jeremiah as a prophet who was extradited from Egypt and put to death by Jehoiakim. Since the correspondence belongs to the reign of Zedekiah, Torczyner is then compelled to maintain that we should read Zedekiah instead of Jehoiakim in Jer. xxvi. J. W. Jack identifies the prophet of these letters with Jeremiah, and on this erects a very different interpretation of the texts from Torczyner's. In fact, both of these identifications are highly precarious, and few scholars are ready to accept either of them. Most are cautious of committing themselves to any interpretation until the text has been more surely established. For it is never an easy matter to read such texts. Chance marks are apt to mislead decipherers, and similarities between letters bring further pitfalls. Moreover, it is often possible to divide groups of letters into words in various ways, or to read the same group of consonants in several different ways. But already enough is known with security to show us that the language of these texts is very similar to that of Jeremiah, and a number of idioms found in the Old Testament are also found here.

The texts were found in a military guard-room, and they date from two years before Jerusalem was taken. They show that communication was by fire-signal, and use the same word for fire-signal as is found in Jer. vi. 1. We learn from Jer. xxxiv that Jerusalem, Lachish and Azekah were the only three places that held out against the forces of Nebuchadrezzar. In these letters we find that the signals from Azekah were interrupted, and grave apprehension was felt. A military mission on its way to Egypt to beg for help had stopped at a small garrison to secure provisions for the journey. We are brought into an atmosphere of tension and crisis. The officer of the outpost who sends in his reports to Lachish defends himself against charges of remissness made against him by his superior officer. None of this adds to our knowledge of history in any material way, but it lights up the situation by giving us a glimpse through strictly contemporary sources into the interior of that guard-room, where were men who were fighting against heavy odds in a forlorn cause.

Of more material aid to the historian was a Babylonian tablet which was deciphered in 1923, which showed that the fall of Nineveh did not take place in 606 B.C., as the

older text-books had surmised, but in 612 B.C. This has
found its way into recent text-books of history, but as our
commentaries have not yet been replaced by new ones, the
necessary corrections have not been made there. Our Bible
tells us that when Josiah went to Megiddo to meet his end
he confronted Pharaoh Necho, who was marching *against*
Assyria.[7] Hence it had been supposed that Josiah was loyal
to his Assyrian overlord, though how he could have carried
through his religious reform in that case no one troubled to
inquire. It is now known that Assyria was helped by Egypt,
who sent forces to her aid in 616 B.C., so that Josiah was
clearly anti-Assyrian. His reform, therefore, was doubtless
associated with his bid for independence at a time when Assyria was tottering to her fall, and in our Bible the ambigu-
ous Hebrew preposition has been mistranslated, and we
should read that Pharaoh Necho was marching *to the help
of* Assyria.

For the post-exilic period archaeological materials are
more scarce, and it unfortunately happens that our materials from other sources are not plentiful for this period.
Hence every ray of light is to be welcomed. Here we may
single out the Elephantine papyri found in Egypt in the
early years of the present century. These papyri are written in Aramaic, and some of them are in a very good state
of preservation. They bring us the information that on the
little island of Elephantine in the Nile, near Assuan, there
was a Jewish colony, of a military character, and that they
had a temple there. We learn that they were there prior to
the year 525 B.C., when Cambyses conquered Egypt. The
texts date from the fifth century B.C., and many of them are
exactly dated by a double system, giving the date by the
Egyptian calendar and also by the Babylonian calendar. A
number of the texts deal with transfers of property, and
they give us much insight into the social conditions of the

[7] 2 Kings xxiii. 29.

colony. There is a list of donations to the shrine, and we find with some surprise that Yahweh has more than one consort in this shrine.[8] Clearly conditions which no longer obtained in Palestine still held here, and the elements in the religion of Palestine against which the prophets had declaimed were still found. One of the papyri is commonly referred to as the Passover papyrus. Actually it is broken, and the word Passover does not occur in it, though references to the associated feast of Unleavened Bread seem still to survive. The papyrus is an order in the name of the Persian authorities to observe the feast. This is of importance as showing that there is nothing inherently impossible in the Biblical account of the missions of Ezra and Nehemiah being furnished with State authority. In the year 410 B.C. the Temple of Yahweh at Elephantine was destroyed in a riot, and two years later the little colony sought the help of the mother community in Palestine, and begged that its good offices might be used with the Persian authorities, to secure permission for the rebuilding of the Temple. The surprising thing is that appeal is made both to Jerusalem and to Samaria.

In the books of Ezra and Nehemiah we read of the two men whose names these books bear, both of whom lived and worked in Jerusalem during the reign of Artaxerxes. Three kings of that name ruled, and the usual identification has been with the first. It would appear that Ezra and Nehemiah were contemporaries, yet in the account of each the other seems to be ignored, and where they do figure in the same narrative, one is a mere passenger. It is now more than fifty years since the Belgian scholar Van Hoonacker suggested that they were not really contemporaries, but that whereas Nehemiah belonged to the reign of Artaxerxes I, Ezra belonged to that of Artaxerxes II. Various considerations seemed to point to this. For whereas Ezra ostensibly

8 That some dispute the interpretation is noted below.

arrived in Jerusalem before Nehemiah, he apparently found the walls already rebuilt, while Nehemiah rebuilt the walls. Moreover, Nehemiah was a contemporary of the high priest Eliashib, whereas Ezra is represented as the contemporary of Johanan, the grandson of Eliashib. Van Hoonacker's view finds some support in the Elephantine papyri, and it is to-day adopted by a large number of scholars, though there are still some who do not follow it.[9] In these papyri we find that the letter sent to Jerusalem in 408 b.c. refers to Johanan as high priest at that time. As this was towards the end of the reign of Darius II, who preceded Artaxerxes II, the latter would seem to be the Artaxerxes to whose reign Johanan's high priesthood belonged.

The same papyrus tells us that the Elephantine Jews had also sent to Delaiah and Shelemaiah, the sons of Sanballat, the governor of Samaria, to ask for their aid. It is interesting to find here the name of Nehemiah's adversary, and to find that he had the official position of governor of Samaria, a detail we do not learn from the Bible. But in 408 b.c., though Sanballat was still alive and in office, he would seem to have been an aged man, no longer personally administering the province, since the Elephantine Jews, though they communicated with the Persian governor in Jerusalem, and with the high priest there, communicated with the sons of the governor of Samaria. The period of Sanballat's active opposition to Nehemiah must therefore be placed before 408 b.c., and therefore in the reign of Artaxerxes I. This evidence from Elephantine, therefore, slight as it is, goes to support the view that Nehemiah was earlier than Ezra.

This evidence comes from outside Palestine, and consists of a copy of a letter — or, to be more precise, of two drafts

---

[9] Professor Albright, who followed the above view in 1940 (*From the Stone Age to Christianity*, p. 248), now tells me in a private letter that he has reverted to his earlier view that Ezra belongs to the later years of Artaxerxes I (*The Archaeology of Palestine and the Bible*, 1932, p. 219).

or copies of a letter — which was sent from Egypt to Palestine. Many years ago there were found in Egypt at Tel-el-Amarna a number of cuneiform tablets, written in the Babylonian language, many of which consisted of letters sent from Palestine to Egypt in the fourteenth century B.C. They formed part of the State archives of Egypt, and many of the tablets were letters from Palestinian princes to the administration. The fact that these princes used Accadian in writing to the Pharaoh was the first great surprise of the discovery. It used to be supposed that the Canaanite language had not been reduced to writing at this time, but a few years ago an ostrakon was found at Beth-shemesh, inscribed in the old Canaanite or Hebrew characters, and dating from the fourteenth century B.C. — though Dussaud brings the date down much later — and in 1923 the sarcophagus of Aḥiram was discovered at Byblos, bearing an inscription in the same archaic script, and dating from the thirteenth century B.C. One would have expected the Palestinian princes, in writing to their overlord, to have used either Egyptian or their own language. Yet they used neither, but Accadian. This fact carried its testimony to the range of the influence of Babylonian culture in that age, and subsequent discoveries elsewhere have confirmed this testimony. For many of the tablets found at Boghaz Keui and at Ras Shamra, to which we shall come later, are in Babylonian cuneiform, and at the Hittite capital, Boghaz Keui, a copy of a treaty between the Hittite king and the Pharaoh was found in that language. A copy of the same treaty in Egyptian hieroglyphic had long been known.

Reverting to the Amarna tablets, they give us a vivid picture of conditions in Palestine in the fourteenth century B.C. In that age some people who are called Ḥabiru in the texts that come from the king of Jerusalem, but SA-GAZ in other texts, were gaining possession of the land, and many appeals for help were sent to Pharaoh. The Pharaoh to whom many of them were sent was Ikhnaton, who was a religious reformer. He elevated the sun, hitherto worshipped at Heliopolis, to be the sole deity, and proscribed all other worship. He broke with the Theban priesthood of Amen, that had normally provided the ministers of State, and moved his capital to the place now known as Tel-el-Amarna. He did not reign for long, however, and after a few years there was a reaction, and the old worship was restored and the new capital abandoned, to lie forgotten until 1887, when it was excavated and the famous tablets discovered. In recent years some further tablets belonging to the same archives have been found on the site.

The Tel-el-Amarna letters were written in Accadian. But they contain a number of Canaanite glosses, written, of course, in the cuneiform character. From these we learn that the language of Canaan in the fourteenth century B.C. was practically the same as Hebrew. It was not, therefore, the Israelites who brought this language to Canaan, but they found it there. The Moabite stone displays only the slightest dialectic differences from Hebrew, and the same is to be said of the Phoenician inscriptions. The tongue of the Israelites in the historical period, therefore, was almost indistinguishable from that of their immediate neighbours. What they spoke before the immigration into Canaan can only be conjectured. Many have supposed it was some dialect of Aramaic. For in a familiar text in Deuteronomy [10] Jacob is referred to as " a wandering Aramaean," and his kindred, to whom he goes in search of a wife, are represented as Aramaeans. That the speech of Jacob and that of Laban are sharply distinguished from one another in the story of the final interview between them, when one calls the heap of witness by the Hebrew name, Gal-'ed, and the

[10] Deut. xxvi. 5. The English R. V. renders, " a Syrian ready to perish," but the American Jewish Version, Moffatt and the American Bible of Powis-Smith and Goodspeed all have the more probable rendering, " a wandering (or nomad) Aramaean."

other by the Aramaic name, Yegar-sahadutha, is not really evidence against this view, if that story, as is commonly supposed, is a reflexion into the past of the conditions that prevailed in a later age. For Israel was bounded on the north by the Aramaean kingdom of Damascus, and while we have no inscriptions to witness to the dialect of Damascus, it was doubtless indistinguishable from those of her more northerly Aramaean neighbours, whose inscriptions we possess.

Turning now to some sites outside Palestine, whose finds cannot be directly linked with Palestine, like those of Elephantine and Tel-el-Amarna, apart from the great and familiar finds in Egypt and Assyria and Babylonia, we may look first at the Hittite texts. At Carchemish and many other places old inscriptions have been found in a hieroglyphic script quite different from Egyptian. These had long been suspected of being Hittite, but the question is now settled beyond doubt. For early in this century the excavation of Boghaz Keui, in Asia Minor, brought to light vast quantities of tablets, of which some twenty thousand bear inscriptions in cuneiform script. Some were written in Accadian, and could therefore be read at once, and they proved that Boghaz Keui was the Hittite capital. And since at Boghaz Keui there are also many sculptures with hieroglyphic inscriptions similar to those at Carchemish and elsewhere, it is certain that these are Hittite. They are still undeciphered, though a beginning has been made with the task. While cuneiform writing is from left to right, and the other Semitic scripts known to us are from right to left, the writing on these Hittite monuments is boustrophedon, i.e., one line reads from right to left, and the next from left to right. In addition to these two kinds of material from Hittite sources — in Accadian cuneiform and Hittite hieroglyphic — there is a third kind. Many of the tablets are in a cuneiform script, but in the Hittite language. These are now happily able to be read, and it is to be hoped that the hieroglyphic texts will ere long be equally accessible.

We may be encouraged in this hope when we remember the brilliant achievement with the Ras Shamra texts. In 1928 a French expedition excavated Minet-el-Beida, on the Syrian coast, opposite Cyprus, and also Ras Shamra, in the immediate neighbourhood. Here they found a large number of tablets, and evidence of an important settlement that was destroyed by fire. The period when Ugarit — the ancient name of Ras Shamra — flourished was the fourteenth century b.c. Some of the tablets found here were in Accadian cuneiform again, but others, while they were in a cuneiform script, were in an unknown character. Accadian is a syllabic script, with a vast number of signs, each representing a syllable; but these tablets appeared to employ no more than twenty-seven signs — twenty-nine, with a few minor variants, they proved ultimately to be. It was at once apparent that they were in an alphabetic script, and not a syllabic. Three scholars, working quite independently, at once set to work on them, and almost simultaneously they published their first results. Virolleaud, to whom the texts had been officially entrusted, reported to the French *Académie des Inscriptions et Belles Lettres* the progress he had made in determining some of the signs, and Hans Bauer and P. (now E.) Dhorme in the same month published their claims to have identified all the signs. It was found that they agreed in some of their results, and three months later, Dhorme, having corrected his earlier work with the help of Bauer's, published the first translation of the 1929 texts in January, 1931. Meanwhile, more inscriptions were being found in the same locality, and for ten years a steady stream of them was published. The latest ones to be published are still not available in this country owing to the war. It should be added that the 1929 texts are particularly difficult, and their translation is still far from sure. But the identification of the signs, as published by Dhorme in 1931, was almost perfect, and subsequent work has only varied his results in the slightest degree.

Returning to the Hittite texts, we find they do not bear very directly on Israelite history, though they contribute to the background of the early history of Palestine, and when the hieroglyphic texts can be read they may well contribute more richly. There is, however, a Hittite Code of Laws which is of some interest. About the beginning of the present century the Babylonian Code of Hammurabi attracted great attention, and the similarity of many of its provisions to those of the Pentateuch gave rise to the belief that the one was directly based on the other. This extreme view was much disputed, however. For the differences are as noteworthy as the similarities. It is to be remembered that the Tel-el-Amarna letters show the persistence of Babylonian cultural influence in the West, after Babylonian rule had been withdrawn, and it would not be surprising for Babylonian legal influence still to have continued in the West, and many of the provisions of Babylonian common law still to have been observed. Moreover, the traditions of the Hebrews said that their ultimate roots were in Babylonia, from which Abraham is said to have sprung. To-day, however, we see the law of Israel in a much wider setting. We now know that the Code of Hammurabi did not wholly originate with that king. A Sumerian Code of Laws, antedating that of Hammurabi by at least seven hundred years, is now known, and the Code of Hammurabi is apparently a re-codifying of the older law. Twenty years ago Hrozny published a translation of the Hittite Code of Laws, and that too bears much similarity to the Babylonian. It dates from about the fourteenth century B.C. Finally, an Assyrian Code is also known now. None of these codes is strictly a code, but rather a collection of case law. Neither is any arranged in a strictly logical order. There are differences between them all, which are as important as the area of similarity. But they show that the common law of all this area rests on a common basis. We are therefore able to study Hebrew law to-day, just as we have been able for many years to study Hebrew history, in the setting of a wider context, instead of dealing with it by itself alone.

The Ras Shamra texts, to which reference has been made above, are almost wholly religious and mythological, and so far no historical texts have come to light. Historical theories have been based upon them, however. There are references to Kadesh, which has been identified by one school with Kadesh Barnea, where the Israelites are represented as having spent so large a part of the period of the wanderings. Further references to Edom have been found. Also the name of Sharuḥen, which is unknown in North Syria, but which is known in the Negeb, or southern steppe-land,[11] has been found in these texts, and the familiar Ashdod. Dussaud and Virolleaud have therefore propounded the theory that the Ras Shamra community had connexions with the district of the Negeb, and that Israel spent much of the period of the wandering in the environment from which the Ras Shamra community sprang. This theory has been followed by some English writers, and appears in a number of English works. It has been firmly rejected by most of the scholars who have independently tested the theory, however, including Albright, de Vaux and Pedersen. In many cases the texts on which the theory is based have proved susceptible of a different reading, or the places have been found to be quite differently located.[12] Just as in the case of the Lachish letters, therefore, we have to beware of a too hasty theorizing.

One of the Ras Shamra poems is consecrated to an eponymous hero, Keret. It is possible that this name is connected

---

[11] Josh. xix. 6. Cf. *Cambridge Ancient History,* i, p. 315, ii, p. 67.
[12] Engnell rejects all the geographical interpretations of these texts.

with that Negeb-ha-Kerethi mentioned in 1 Sam. xxx. 14, and since the name occurs in a Ras Shamra text which antedates the settlement of the Philistines in Palestine, it probably has nothing to do with the Philistine people. It cannot therefore be used to connect the Philistines with Crete, as was done in many of the older books, and the Cherethites of the Old Testament may be connected rather with these early Phoenician inhabitants, but may be a clan that was incorporated with the Philistines after their settlement, just as Canaanite elements were incorporated with Israel. That the Philistines early became " Canaanized " is evident from a number of considerations, and such a process implies the intermixture with pre-Philistine elements that survived amongst them. Among the indications of the Canaanizing of Philistine culture, we may note that a number of the names ascribed to Philistines in the Old Testament, or on the Assyrian inscriptions, are definitely Semitic. Indeed, Macalister says that of the twenty-six Philistine personal names recorded " at the outside not more than eight can be considered native Philistine." [13] Their gods seem to have been taken over from the pre-Philistine inhabitants. Their principal god was Dagon, who used to be thought to be a fish god, but who was certainly a corn god. That he was older than the Philistine immigration had been held to be probable on the ground that Dagon appears as an element in personal names in Babylonia as far back as the third millennium B.C., while in the Tel-el-Amarna letters, which antedate the Philistine settlement, the same element is found in a personal name. But it could not be proved that this element consisted of a divine name. Now, however, the name is found in the Ras Shamra texts, where it is certainly that of a god. In the same way another Philistine god is given a Semitic name in the Old

13 *The Philistines: Their History and Civilization* (Schweich Lectures for 1911), 1913, p. 82.

Testament. He is called Baalzebub, or lord of flies. In the New Testament the Greek has Beelzeboul. It is now clear that this is the truer form of the name, and the form found in the Hebrew is doubtless a contemptuous alteration of the kind that is quite familiar. For in the Ras Shamra texts we find frequent mention of Zebul, lord of the earth. He was therefore a pre-Philistine god. It is probable that this divine name is connected with the name of the tribe of Zebulun. This tribal name, and also that of Asher, have been found by some scholars in the Ras Shamra texts, though again Albright disputes the interpretation.

Some of the tablets found at Ras Shamra, written in alphabetic cuneiform, are in the Hurrian language, which is attracting much attention to-day by reason of a large number of texts found in other places.[14] In 1925 an American expedition began to work at Kirkuk, which was the site of the ancient city of Arrapha, an important Hurrian city. Their most important finds were made close by, at Nuzi, where they found many thousands of tablets during the years 1925–1931. These tablets date from the fifteenth and fourteenth centuries B.C., and are written in Accadian, but with many Hurrian words and constructions. Since 1935 Mari, the ancient Amorite capital on the Euphrates, has been excavated, and it has yielded further Hurrian material. The Hurrians are the Biblical Horites, most probably, who should no longer be regarded as cave-dwellers, and their language is different from Semitic, Sumerian and Indo-European. Considerable progress has been made in work on the language, and Professor E. A. Speiser, one of the pioneer workers in this field, has now published an important study of it.[15] Meanwhile, in the Nuzi Accadian texts we have a picture of an ancient Hurrian community more

[14] R. de Vaux (*Revue Biblique*, xlviii, 1939, p. 621 n.) speaks of the "Hurrian invasion" with which the Bible is threatened.

[15] *Introduction to Hurrian* (Annual of the American Schools of Oriental Research, xx), 1941.

intimate than any we have from elsewhere in the ancient world. The texts are not historical, but family records, business transactions, court proceedings, and so forth. There is little that is of direct importance to the Biblical student, though everything that helps us to understand the life and conditions of the world in which Israel was set is of value.

The Nuzi texts bring before us references to Ḥabiru, and these have been used as a contribution to the problem of the Israelite settlement of Canaan. For the Ḥabiru of the Nuzi texts are a social class, a class of voluntary slaves. It is therefore argued that the Ḥabiru of the Amarna letters are revolting slaves, rather than the invading Hebrews that others have found in them, and that the word Hebrew originally had nothing of an ethnic meaning. This question cannot be appropriately discussed here, but it is mentioned to show that something in the finds at almost every site in the ancient Near East proves to have relevance to something in the field of Old Testament study.

Brief mention may be made of a few of the papyrus finds which have a more direct bearing on the study of the Old Testament, but this time finds of material of much later date, with a bearing on the study of the text of the Old Testament, rather than of its historical or cultural background. In 1902 a small fragment of papyrus was presented by Mr. W. L. Nash to the Cambridge University Library, inscribed with the ten commandments in Hebrew, followed by the Shema'.[16] This was held to date from the second century A.D., but Albright has recently argued that it belongs to the second century B.C. When we remember that our oldest Hebrew manuscripts are a thousand years later than this, the interest of the find is obvious. In this fragment the sixth and seventh commandments are reversed, as in Luke xviii. 20, and as in the Vatican manuscript of the Greek text in Deut. v and Exod. xx. There are also some additional pref-

16 I.e., the passage beginning " Hear, O Israel " in Deut. vi. 4 ff.

atory words which do not stand in the Hebrew manuscripts, but which are represented in the Septuagint.

Some years ago a large collection of papyri found in Egypt became known, of which the greater part was purchased by Mr. Chester Beatty, and deposited by him in the British Museum. Mr. John H. Scheide bought part, however, and deposited it at Princeton University, and smaller parts are now in other places. The texts on these papyri are mainly Greek texts of the Old and New Testaments, though there are also parts of the book of Enoch and some other texts. The Old Testament texts include parts of Genesis, Numbers, Deuteronomy, Isaiah, Jeremiah, Ezekiel, Daniel and Esther. Part of the Ezekiel text is in the Chester Beatty collection, and part in the John H. Scheide collection. The dates of the fragments vary, but some belong to the first half of the second century A.D. They are thus much older than any of the codices we possess. There are, of course, a number of variants from the texts found in our chief manuscripts. The most interesting of the texts is that of Daniel. The Septuagint text of Daniel early fell into disuse, and the translation of Theodotion was substituted for it in the Septuagint manuscripts. Only one manuscript of the true Septuagint text was known. This was the Chigi manuscript, from which the text is printed side by side with Theodotion's in Swete's edition of the Septuagint. The text of the Chester Beatty papyri, however, proves to be the Septuagint. Unfortunately we have not the whole of the book, but only the section ii. 20–viii. 6.

One other papyrus fragment may be mentioned. This is the Rylands Library fragment of Deuteronomy. Twenty-five years ago some pieces of papyrus that had formed mummy cartonnage were acquired by Dr. Rendel Harris. For this purpose any odd scraps of unwanted papyrus would serve. In this case the fragments contained scraps of text from the *Iliad,* and some demotic Egyptian texts. The latter are dated by experts on palaeographic grounds from the second or early first century B.C. A few years ago amongst these pieces of papyrus some fragments of the Greek text of Deuteronomy were discovered. On palaeographical grounds these too are dated in the second century B.C., so that they form the oldest copies of the Greek text of the Bible that we possess. Since the Greek Pentateuch was only prepared in the third century B.C., these fragments date from little more than a century, at the most, after its first appearance. Unhappily, they are but very small fragments, and altogether they give us but some fifteen verses. The text agrees closely with the Chester Beatty text of Deuteronomy, and is nearer to the Alexandrine manuscript than to the Vatican manuscript, which has usually been treated as the standard manuscript for the Septuagint.

This brief survey of the material archaeology has provided is, of course, merely selective. It has sought to indicate the variety of locality and of material, and the variety of the uses to which the student of the Old Testament can put it. That it is all full of interest to the Biblical student is clear, but its relevance to the unfolding of the religious message of the Old Testament is less clear. It has seemed worth while to give some attention to it because of the claims put forward that it has " proved " the truth of the Bible. How far it is able to " prove " the historical truth of individual statements will become clearer in the next chapter, but it may already be manifest that it in no sense proves the spiritual truth of the Bible. And it is its spiritual truth which is of supreme importance to all generations of men. Nevertheless, archaeology should not be ignored by the serious student of the Bible. Its research has been financed by men and women who have known a deep devotion to the Bible, and their instinct has been a sound one. That it has a value for the spiritual penetration of the significance of the Old Testament may become clearer as we proceed, even though that value is less direct than might be desired. But any idea that this is all unnecessary for the student of the Bible, who needs no more than a pious heart to extract the spiritual treasures it contains, does little honour to the Bible. No modern text-books on any side of Old Testament study could be written by men who ignored this material, and the serious student will feel that this great Book is worthy of his best efforts to master it. Mental sloth will not yield the highest spiritual returns, even though mental activity alone is insufficient. True religion commands all our powers, and the bringing of these fields of knowledge into the service of our study of the Bible can enrich that study, and contribute to our fuller discovery of its meaning and message.

III. ARCHAEOLOGY AND
THE OLD TESTAMENT (continued)

THE PREVIOUS CHAPTER essayed a brief survey of the field of Biblical archaeology, with special reference to the more important finds of the present century. The present chapter has a rather different aim. It will seek rather to illustrate how material from various sources can be brought together to deal with a single problem, and to show how complex the question of the synthesis of the material may be. It will also seek to give some idea of the light shed by archaeology on the cultural and religious background of the Old Testament.

In 1 Kings vi. 1 we read that the Exodus took place four hundred and eighty years before the founding of the Temple, in the fourth year of King Solomon. This would place the Exodus about 1445 B.C. If the wandering in the wilderness occupied forty years, the attack on Jericho would fall about 1405 B.C. Some years ago Professor Garstang excavated Jericho, and in particular some tombs there, and since the latest scarabs he found in them were of the Pharaoh Amenhotep III, who was reigning about 1400 B.C., he dated the fall of Jericho at about that time, and found this date to be supported by the evidence of the pottery. He also found evidence that part of the wall collapsed, and that the city was utterly burned. This has been hailed triumphantly as a proof of the accuracy of the Old Testament. It certainly seems to accord well with the chronology of 1 Kings vi. 1, but, as we shall see below, it does not accord with a whole series of other Biblical statements.

If the attack on Canaan began with the capture of Jericho about 1400 B.C., and occupied roughly a generation, as the Bible seems to indicate, then it took place in the Amarna age. In that age, it will be remembered, the Palestinian kings were appealing for help to the Pharaoh against the Ḥabiru or SA-GAZ, as they are variously called. What is more simple than to equate the Ḥabiru with the Hebrews, and to find in the Amarna tablets contemporary evidence of the settlement of the Israelites under the leadership of Joshua? In the time of Seti I, who reigned at the end of the fourteenth century B.C., we find a reference to Asher, apparently as the name of a people occupying the very district that Asher later occupied. Moreover, as was said in the previous chapter, there are thought to be references to Asher and Zebulun in the Ras Shamra texts of the fourteenth century B.C. Further, in an inscription of Merneptah, who began to reign in 1235 B.C., the name Israel is mentioned, apparently as the name of a people in Palestine, whom the Pharaoh harried in an expedition against Palestine. All of this well fits the chronology of 1 Kings vi. 1.

Again, in Exod. xii. 40 it is said that the Israelites were in Egypt for four hundred and thirty years. Reckoning back from 1445 B.C., we are brought into the period of the Hyksos. What period could better fit the Biblical narrative of the descent into Egypt? For the Hyksos were Asiatic conquerors of Egypt, who made their headquarters in the Delta region. They were of Semitic or Hurrian stock, and so they would be just the people to welcome Semites, and to entrust a Semite like Joseph with high office.

Thus, by selecting a few Biblical and archaeological items and ignoring the rest, a most attractive theory can be easily built up. It is presented in a number of English works, and, as has been said, it is somewhat vigorously claimed that this is an excellent illustration of the proof of the Bible by archaeology. Unfortunately a great deal has to be ignored in the interests of this theory. To take first the Biblical statements, we find that scattered through the Old

Testament there are a number of genealogical statements. For the period of the sojourn in Egypt they usually run to four generations. The longest list runs to seven generations, and the shortest to three. We are told that Moses' mother was the sister of one of those who went down with Jacob into Egypt. This is unpromising for a period of four hundred and thirty years. Again, from the Exodus to the founding of the Temple is given as a matter of six generations. This again is too few for a period of four hundred and eighty years.

The Biblical account places the wandering in the wilderness after the Philistine settlement. But the Philistines did not come to Palestine until the beginning of the twelfth century B.C. Hence this is in conflict with the dating of the Exodus in the fifteenth century B.C. Further, there are half a dozen references in the Bible to the fact that the Settlement in Canaan took place in the Iron Age. But the Amarna age fell before the Iron Age in the Bronze Age.[1]

Again, the Pharaoh of the Oppression is said to have employed the Israelites on his building enterprises. Since they continued to dwell in the land of Goshen, these enterprises must have been in this region.[2] The exact location of Goshen is uncertain, but it is generally agreed that it must have been in the Nile Delta region. Moreover, it is clearly implied in the narratives that the Pharaoh had his royal residence in the neighbourhood of Goshen at the time of the Exodus. The Pharaoh's daughter was liable to find herself close to the Israelite settlements when she went down for a bathe. The theory under examination identifies the Pharaoh of the Oppression with Thothmes III. But all of his building enterprises were in Upper Egypt, and there is no trace of any building or residence of his in the Delta

---

[1] Little weight can be attached to this, however, for there are a few references to iron in the Amarna texts.

[2] Exod. viii. 22 (Heb. 18), ix. 26.

region. The Biblical account says that the cities the Israelites laboured on were named Pithom and Raamses. The latter looks as though it were named after Rameses, and Rameses II, who reigned for nearly seventy years from the beginning of the thirteenth century B.C., rebuilt the old Delta city which had been the capital of the Hyksos, and renamed it Pi-Ramesse, and made it his second capital. It is not uncommon for those who adopt the fifteenth century date for the Exodus to dismiss Exod. i. 11 as unreliable, or at least to eliminate the names Pithom and Raamses from the text. The theory that proves 1 Kings vi. 1 to be true has less use for Exod. i. 11.

Again, there is no reference to Egyptian activity in Palestine from the period of Joshua to the time of Solomon. Yet Rameses II was a great warrior, who held Palestine strongly and fought against the Hittites in the north. It is surprising to find no reference to his hold of Palestine in the book of Judges if his reign fell after the period of Joshua. Professor Garstang, indeed, holds that Egypt is referred to in the book of Judges, under the metaphor of the Hornet, and that the deliverances from oppression recorded in the book of Judges were really effected by Egypt. This would not seem to uphold the reliability of the Biblical statements, however, since they attribute the deliverances to Israelite Judges, who were raised up by God for the purpose.

Turning now to the archaeological side, the equation of the Ḥabiru with the Hebrews is vigorously attacked in some quarters. The Nuzi evidence that Ḥabiru had a social connotation, and that the Ḥabiru there do not seem to have been an ethnic group, has led to the view that in Palestine they were just rebel slaves, and not immigrant invaders. The equation of the terms Ḥabiru and Hebrews is not quite so easy as the English spellings suggest. Moreover, the latest evidence from Ras Shamra shows that we should probably write Ḥapiru. and not Ḥabiru. Then again, there are Egyptian references to 'Aperu, who were foreign slaves engaged on taskwork, to whom there are references long after the time of Thothmes III, and even after Rameses II. It will be seen that this is a complex philological, as well as archaeological, problem. On the whole it seems probable that the names Ḥabiru, Hebrews and 'Aperu are to be equated, but the area of meaning is not necessarily the same in all the texts where they appear. The present writer believes the Ḥabiru of the Amarna letters were Hebrews, but not those led by Joshua.

For the account of the conquest of Joshua bears no resemblance to that of the Amarna letters. It is sometimes said that Joshua and Benjamin figure in the Amarna letters as Yashuia and Benenima. The equations are quite unscientific, and belong to the same class as the schoolboy's supposition that the Derbe and Lystra visited by Paul were the English towns of Derby and Leicester. As Garstang has said: " No historical connexion can be traced between the Ḥabiru revolution and the original invasion of Canaan by the Israelites under Joshua. The two movements were essentially distinct." [3] The Ḥabiru were pressing up from the south towards Jerusalem, and some of them got as far north as Shechem, while others, called SA-GAZ, but certainly kindred groups, were pressing down from the north. The movement Joshua led, on the other hand, is represented as having come from across the Jordan at Jericho, whence it spread from the Central Highlands. The only place in the Central Highlands mentioned in the Amarna letters is Shechem. We are told that Labaya and Shechem had given all to the Ḥabiru. There is another text which mentions Labaya, but the name of the city concerned has not survived. If it was also Shechem, the text would have great interest. For it says: " The city was conquered by treachery. As with one who had made peace, and as with one who had

[3] *Joshua-Judges*, 1931, p. 255.

taken an oath, was the chief with me. Hence the city was conquered." This is curiously reminiscent of Gen. xxxiv, where we read of a treaty made with Shechem, followed by a treacherous attack on the city. But this was not in the age of Joshua. It was in the days of Jacob, prior to the descent into Egypt. The treachery was perpetrated by Simeon and Levi, and it brought on them the rebuke of their father, and also their curse in the Blessing of Jacob, where it is said that they should be scattered in Israel.[4] This would seem to be the closest link between the Amarna letters and any Biblical incident, and it is in conflict with the theory of the Exodus that we are considering.

Again, according to the Biblical account the Israelites made a circuit round Edom and Moab, because these peoples were unwilling to let them pass through their territories. There is archaeological evidence from these districts, which must be considered as much as that from Jericho. Nelson Glueck has established that for about half a millennium there were no settled occupants of these districts. Their settlements had been occupied, but then fell into ruin until the thirteenth century, when they were re-occupied. In the fifteenth century no more than scattered nomad groups could have been found there to dispute the passage of Israel.

Coming to Jericho, we may note that Garstang has now slightly modified his date, and brought it down to about twenty years later. Albright for some time strongly resisted Garstang's date, and placed the fall of Jericho about 1360 B.C. He is now prepared to push it back somewhat, so that there is little difference between these two archaeologists on this point to-day. It should be added, however, that Albright does not associate the fall of Jericho with Joshua, or with the Israelites who had come out of Egypt, but places it long before the Exodus. On the other hand Vincent, the

4 Gen. xlix. 7.

eminent French archaeologist, puts the fall of Jericho more than a century later, in the second half of the thirteenth century B.C.[5]

Further, Lachish is said to have been captured and destroyed by Joshua within a few years of the destruction of Jericho. Yet the destruction of Lachish is archaeologically dated at the end of the thirteenth century B.C. Similarly the evidence from other sites cannot be harmonized with the Biblical accounts on the fifteenth century dating of the Exodus.

It is clear that the question is not quite so simple as at first appeared. So long as we concentrate on Jericho and ignore all other sites, and so long as we confine ourselves to one view on Jericho, and the single Biblical text 1 Kings vi. 1, it looks very easy. But actually we have a very difficult complex of Biblical and archaeological material to deal with, and no simple or easy solution is possible. It is not proposed here to offer any solution of the problem, but rather to illustrate how archaeology, despite the welcome light it sheds on our problems, can also complicate them. Within the sphere of this inquiry scientific method, unembarrassed by any prejudice, must be left to do its work. Nor are its results without importance for other questions. Millar Burrows, whose fine work on Biblical archaeology has been referred to above, in a moment of undue pessimism allowed himself to suggest that the date of the Exodus is a matter of no moment, and that it is doubtful if Moses ever knew it.[6] That Moses was unaware of the particular Pharaoh in whose reign he led Israel out of Egypt is an idea that will commend itself to few. Nor would archaeology be

---

[5] G. E. Wright (*Bulletin of the American Schools of Oriental Research*, 86, April, 1942, p. 34) says: " Absolutely all that we can now say with any certainty is that the city fell to the Hebrews some time between cir. 1475 and 1300 B.C."

[6] *Bulletin of the American Schools of Oriental Research*, 86, April, 1942, p. 36.

worth while if it were useless to attempt to piece together its materials and to use the data it produces. Actually it is possible to synthesize a very large proportion of the Biblical and the archaeological evidence in a view which neither places the Exodus in the fifteenth century, nor merely attempts to rehabilitate the thirteenth century date and to ignore the evidence of the Amarna letters. We have in the Bible a whole variety of traditions fused together, traditions which contain sound historical material, but upon which a unity that does not belong to their orginal form has been imposed. This is characteristic of the Hebrew spirit. The whole of its sacred law it ascribed to Moses, though it really belongs to widely separated ages; the Conquest of Canaan it ascribed to Joshua, though again it seems really to have been the fruit of several separate movements in different ages; almost the whole of its sacred poetry it ascribed to David, though once more its real authorship is more varied; and most of its Wisdom literature it ascribed to Solomon, though few would to-day venture to defend the ascription. When, with the aid of the archaeological material, we sort out the traditions of the Exodus and Conquest, the result is not without bearing on the religious development of Israel, and it helps us to understand the difference of the traditions preserved in Judah and in Northern Israel, and the uniqueness of the work that Moses did. Of this something must be said in a later chapter.

Meanwhile, we may observe the way in which archaeology has supplemented our knowledge of the cultural and religious background of the Old Testament. Just as Israel did not live her political life to herself, but was set amidst empires greater than her own, into the stream of whose affairs she was again and again swept, so she was not culturally isolated. She shared the same inheritance of culture as the peoples around her, and while there were periods when her progress lagged far behind theirs artistically and culturally, yet through her intercourse with them she came constantly under their influence. On the other hand, while her spiritual progress was far in advance of theirs, she had to reckon both with the rooted conservatism of her people, and also with the influence of the neighbours with whom she had intercourse, and the different directions in which they had developed from the common inheritance.

We have already seen that Babylonian culture was widely spread at an early date. In Palestine, North Syria and Asia Minor the Babylonian language was used for a variety of purposes, and it is but to be expected that Babylonian cultural and religious ideas had also reached these distant regions, to colour the inheritance of the peoples who should live there. In addition to this, we have the Biblical tradition that the first father of the Hebrews came out from Ur of the Chaldees, bringing with him inevitably something of the culture of the region he left. Of the antiquity of that culture and of its attainments, excavations in recent years have sufficiently convinced us. The city of Ur was the great centre of the worship of the moon god, Sin. Similarly, the Mesopotamian city of Ḥarran, to which Abram's family is said to have migrated, had an important Temple to the same god. There may therefore have been some ancient connexion between the two cities, so that if a clan or family were forced for any reason to leave Ur, there were good reasons for going to Ḥarran. In this tradition, therefore, we may find one of the many links between Israel and moon worship.

Israel therefore had a Babylonian strain in her inheritance, and she found in Canaan and around her peoples who also had something of Babylonian culture in their inheritance. It is not, then, surprising that lying behind the Old Testament we should be able to recover connexions with legends and myths that are found in Babylon. The Pan-Babylonian school, that flourished a generation ago, overstressed these connexions, and represented much in the Old Testament as mere borrowing from the Babylonians, while minimizing the significant differences that appear. To-day we can appreciate the links between the two peoples, while appreciating also the yet more important differences.

It is well known that Babylonian sources provide us with a great epic of Creation, telling how Marduk fought with the primeval dragon Tiamat, and splitting her body in twain made of it the heaven and the earth, whereupon all living creatures were made. We have also the great Gilgamesh epic, part of which tells of the destruction of men by a flood, and recounts how Ut-napishtim was forewarned and prepared a boat, which he covered within and without with pitch, and in which he was saved. That there is some connexion between these ancient stories and what we read in the early chapters of Genesis is quite clear. But the idea that the Hebrew author just borrowed the accounts from Babylon is no longer seriously maintained. For the differences are as striking as the similarities, and it is clear that the old stories have been entirely re-created in the hand of the Biblical author. The Babylonian accounts are full of polytheism, while the Biblical narrative is purified of it all, and though the name of the dragon Tiamat remains in Genesis in the form Tehom, it does not stand as the name of a goddess, but as a common noun, indicating the formless chaos of the primeval deep. The Biblical name of Noah is so different from Ut-napishtim that it has often attracted attention. The name Noah now appears to be found as the name of a god in Mari and other Hurrian texts, and it is possible that the Flood story reached Israel through a Hurrian *milieu*. In all these stories the simplicity and dignity of the Biblical accounts contrast with the Babylonian, and it is clear that while the Biblical and the Babylonian accounts have a common ancestry, in Israel the traditions had been refashioned by her purer religious faith. It is true that the older Biblical accounts, both of the Creation and of the Flood, are marked by a naïve anthropomorphism, but it is also true that the later account of the Creation, which is the more closely linked to the Babylonian Creation epic, is immeasurably its superior spiritually, presenting us with the conception of a God before whom we are constrained to bow in reverence and awe.

The Ras Shamra finds should do something to check still further any danger of overemphasizing Israel's cultural debt to Babylon. For the Ras Shamra texts in alphabetic cuneiform are almost wholly religious and mythological. Amongst them there is a long text recording the conflict of Aleyin and Mot. But this is quite dissimilar to the Babylonian epics, and seems to preserve a distinctively Syrian mythology, intimately related to the fertility cults and the Adonis myth. The deep influence of the fertility cults in Syria and Palestine was already well known, but here we find them rooted in a mythology, and that in a literary form, at this very early date.[7]

These texts provide us not merely with a number of gods and goddesses, but with a pantheon, in which they stand in definite relations to one another. There are two chief groups. One consists of Asherat of the Sea, with her son Baal or Hadad, Asherat the consort of Hadad, and Aleyin and Anat the son and daughter of Hadad; the other consists of El, with Elat as his consort, Ashtarte and Mot, their daughter and son. In the epic Aleyin and Mot engage in conflict. Mot, whose name connects with the word for death, but who is in reality a corn spirit, slays Aleyin, whereupon his

[7] Engnell (*Studies in Divine Kingship in the Ancient Near East*, 1943) has argued that the Ras Shamra texts are cultic and ritual. The ritual acts were accompanied by the recitation of the texts, in which their significance was expressed, and the " myth " was not merely a story of the past, but an expression of what the ritual of the present effected. The " myth " both interpreted the ritual and was integral to it. Cf. S. H. Hooke, *Myth and Ritual*, 1933, and *The Origins of Early Semitic Ritual*, 1938.

father Hadad and his grandmother Asherat are overcome with grief. We may note in passing that this may explain Zech. xii. 11. There we read: " In that day there shall be a great mourning in Jerusalem, as the mourning of Hadad-rimmon in the valley of Megiddo." The verse had been connected with the Adonis rites, but the mention of Hadad-rimmon was unexplained. But here in the Ras Shamra text we find the myth that lies behind the Zechariah passage, though preceding it by many centuries. After the death of Aleyin, his sister Anat takes up the conflict with Mot, and succeeds in slaying him. Both Aleyin and Mot are later resurrected. In the course of the epic we are told of the seven operations of Anat in connexion with agriculture at harvest time, during which operations leaven is forbidden. This would appear to connect with the Israelite feast of Mazzoth, or Unleavened Bread. It is probable that each of the operations occupied one day, and that this is the origin of the seven days of the feast, which is therefore of pre-Israelite origin.

Before the discovery of the Ras Shamra texts it had been conjectured that Terah, the father of Abraham, reflected a divinity. Virolleaud and Dussaud claim to have found this god in the Ras Shamra texts. Dussaud connects the name with the Hebrew word for " moon," and finds here additional evidence to connect Israel with the moon cult. He interprets the Keret legend as the account of a conflict between the moon cult and the sun cult, with the triumph of the latter, and finds here the explanation of the account of Terah's departure from Ur. Again, however, this theory has been too readily accepted by some writers, and Albright disputes the ground on which it rests. For he interprets the word in the text as a common noun, meaning *bridal gift,* and eliminates all mention of Terah from these texts. Hence we should be cautious before we identify Terah with a moon god. Similarly we should be cautious before accepting the statements that Yahweh, the God of Israel, is found in these texts. Virolleaud believed he had found a god Yw here. In the Moabite stone and in the Lachish letters the name is quadriliteral, Yhwh, as in the Old Testament, while in the Elephantine papyri it is triliteral, Yhw. In this biliteral form, Yw, it is found as an initial element in many Old Testament proper names. But again Albright interprets the Ras Shamra evidence wholly differently, and finds no trace of a divine name in the text.

For evidences of fertility rites in Palestine we are not dependent on the Ras Shamra texts alone. The frequent polemic against practices connected with such rites standing in the Old Testament, and the allusions to the Adonis myth found there, would sufficiently demonstrate that these things had entered into the texture of the life of the people. The Queen of Heaven, who figures in the book of Jeremiah as an object of popular worship, is probably to be identified either with the Ashtarte or with the Anat of the Ras Shamra texts, and in either case is to be connected with this cycle of myths, and the rites that belonged to them. The goddess Anat has left her name in some place-names, including Anathoth, Jeremiah's birthplace, and a Beth Anath in Judah and another in Galilee. She appears in Bethshean, where she is connected with Resheph, the Syrian god of the Underworld, who figures not only in Ras Shamra texts, but also in Aramaic inscriptions from North Syria. More surprising still, we find this goddess mentioned in the Elephantine papyri, as having a place beside Yahweh in the Temple there.[8]

Archaeology has frequently reinforced this evidence of the hold of the fertility cults on the people by turning up large numbers of figurines of a nude goddess, with exaggerated emphasis on sex. It is not difficult to see why grave moral evils and impurities were associated with this wor-

8 But see below.

ship, or why the Israelite prophets should so vigorously op-
pose it. The feast of Mazzoth could be assimilated and made
innocuous, but with this there could be no compromise.

Many other elements of Canaanite origin secured some
place in Israel, and around these the inner religious con-
flicts raged. Albright refers to " the extremely low level of
Canaanite religion, which inherited a relatively primitive
mythology and had adopted some of the most demoralizing
cultic practices then existing in the Near East. Among these
practices were human sacrifice, long given up by the Egyptians and the Babylonians, sacred prostitution of both sexes,
apparently not known in native Egyptian religion, though
widely disseminated through Mesopotamia and Asia Minor, the vogue of eunuch priests, who were much less popular in Mesopotamia and were not found in Egypt, serpent
worship to an extent unknown in other lands of antiquity.
The brutality of Canaanite mythology passes belief." [9]

The Canaanite Hadad was worshipped under the figure
of a bull, and the golden calves of the northern kingdom
probably owed their form to this worship. Dussaud has argued that one of the Ras Shamra texts, in which there are
references to a divine bull, refers to the district in which the
sources of the Jordan lie. On this ground he connects the
Dan sanctuary with this pre-Israelite cult of the district,
running back to the fourteenth century B.C. The later conscience of Israel condemned the golden calves, but it must
be remembered that for long no voice was raised in protest
against them. Neither Elijah nor Elisha seems to have ob-
jected to their worship. Bulls figure in the furnishing of
the Jerusalem Temple. The brazen sea, which probably
represented the cosmic ocean, was supported by bulls,
which probably owe their origin to the bulls of Hadad. For
the Temple was erected with the aid of Tyrian artificers,
who doubtless introduced into its ornamentation many mo-

[9] *Studies in the History of Culture,* 1942, pp. 28 f.

tifs which were connected with Canaanite religious ideas, that would have been condemned by a later conscience, but that were readily acceptable in that age.

It has been thought by some that Nehushtan, the brazen serpent which Hezekiah destroyed, was really made by the artificers from Tyre that were employed in the building of the Temple. That it really dated back to the time of Moses, as narrated in the book of Numbers, is most improbable. For had it really had associations with that great leader, we might have expected to have some hint as to when it was brought into Jerusalem, and where it had been from his day to the time of its removal thither. All that we can learn is that it was an ancient symbol in Jerusalem in the days of Hezekiah. But the archaeologist has found many traces of serpent worship in ancient Palestine. At Bethshean there are evidences of a serpent cult; at Beth-shemesh jugs with serpent ornamentation have been found; elsewhere figurines of a nude mother-goddess, with a serpent in various positions on her body, have been found. Even more interesting is a seal with Hittite signs, representing a cult object surmounted by a crescent, with a priest standing before a pole, on which is coiled a serpent. Naturally this has brought Nehushtan to mind. When we remember that outside Jerusalem there was a serpent-stone beside the spring En-rogel, we may perhaps suppose that this pre-Israelite serpent worship was already found in Jerusalem in the Jebusite shrine that existed there before the capture of the city by David. It is probable that Zadok, who suddenly appears on the scene after David's removal of the capital to Jerusalem, but who is unmentioned earlier, and who, though he is fitted with Aaronite genealogy by the Chronicler, had no genealogy in the original form of the text of Samuel, was really the priest of the Jebusite shrine in Jerusalem. Later, he succeeded in ousting Abiathar from Jerusalem, and when Solomon's Temple was built, he became installed as the priest. The old Jebusite shrine may well have disappeared at that time, and its serpent symbol as well as its priest may have been transferred to the new and more splendid Temple. This would account for the lack of record of the bringing of this ancient symbol into Jerusalem.[10]

It is becoming more and more clear in the light of archaeology that Israel dwelt in a world in which polytheism prevailed, a world in which myths were current, to which definite ritual acts were attached. And just because her peoples were mixed, these ideas and practices had root in her life. It is true that the group of immigrants whom Moses led regarded Yahweh as their God, but they were by no means the whole population of the land. The mixed peoples who were already there remained there, and they and Israel, through intermarriage and the pressure of common troubles, and especially the Philistine oppression, became welded together to form a single people. The common acceptance of Yahwism became the great unifying bond between them, but of necessity the religious and cultural ideas cherished by the various elements of the population contributed to the common stock, until gradually, and especially under the influence of the prophets, the more ignoble of these ideas and the practices that went with them were attacked and discredited, while others were assimilated, and either divested of meaning, or related to the higher religion.

That the battle was not won so early as we might suppose is suggested by the Elephantine papyri. For, as has been observed, in the Temple there Yahweh was not the sole deity worshipped. In a subscription list we find the gifts allocated as follows: 126 shekels for Yahweh, 70 shekels for Ishum-bethel, 120 shekels for Anath-bethel. In another text one Menahem swears by the God Yahweh, by the Temple and by Anath-yahu. In another text one is challenged to swear by Herem-bethel, the god. Apparently Anath was the consort of Yahweh. For the god Ishum-bethel we may compare a late Syrian-Greek bilingual inscription, in which the divine name Sumbetulos figures. The tradition that the Samaritans worshipped a deity named Ashima has also been recalled, and it may be that Amos viii. 14 refers to this. There the Revised Version renders " that swear by the sin of Samaria," though we might equally well render " that swear by Ashimah of Samaria," and the name of the divinity would well suit the context. On the other hand, however, it may be noted that Albright again interprets the evidence differently, and finds in Ishum-bethel, Herem-bethel and Anath-bethel hypostatized aspects of Yahweh.[11]

When we turn to the realm of literature we again find evidence that Israel belonged to the world of her environment. From both Egypt and Babylon come literary remains which may be compared with some of the literature of the Old Testament, and in particular with the Wisdom literature and the psalms.

The technique of Hebrew poetry is still by no means perfectly understood, but some things at any rate seem to be clear. Of these the first is the principle of parallelism, an exceedingly common, though not universal, characteristic; and the second is a rhythm that depends on accented syllables, rather than on the total number of the syllables. Babylonian poetry presents the same phenomena. Moreover, it was similarly used for religious and liturgical purposes. Amongst our surviving texts there are psalms and hymns to accompany sacrifices, thanksgivings, lamentations, peti-

---

[11] A Jewish scholar, Cassuto, has recently maintained that they were foreign gods, worshipped by the Gentile colonists, but not by the Jews. This, however, is a very improbable view.

tions, litanies for both public and private use. Both the form and the variety of the Hebrew Psalter, therefore, are paralleled in Babylonian literature.

It is not therefore surprising that some scholars have noted verbal similarities between Hebrew and Babylonian psalms, and have argued for the direct dependence of the Hebrew on the Babylonian. Here, as always, we must beware of letting our conclusions overstep the evidence. There are differences between the Babylonian psalms and the Hebrew even more notable than the similarities, and it is improbable that anyone would wish to embody the Babylonian freely in modern worship. For spiritually the two literatures are on different planes, and despite the superficial links of form and diction, there is a deeper contrast in spirit and thought. All that we are justified in finding here is evidence that the religious poetry of the Babylonians and of the Hebrews grew from a common stock. But just as Hebrew religion, though it grew from a root common to it and to the other religions of the world in which the early Hebrew lived, became something far richer than Babylonian or Egyptian or Canaanite religion, so the psalmody in which it expressed itself became a nobler growth.

The same fact comes out when we turn from the Psalms to the book of Job. In recent years a Babylonian text containing what is often referred to as the " Babylonian Job " has come to light, and some have found in it the source of the Biblical book of Job. That there is a difference in the names in the Babylonian story and the Hebrew provides little difficulty when we remember the Ut-napishtim of the Babylonian Flood story. The so-called " Babylonian Job," however, is very different in spirit and content from the Biblical book. It is a fragmentary account of a hero or king, who was reduced by disease to groaning, and who reflects on the mysterious ways of the gods, which are beyond human comprehension. In the description of his malady there are parts which recall the description of Job's. But the differences from Job are considerable. For apart from differences of form, we find that the Babylonian sufferer, while he is not conscious of anything that can explain his sufferings, is far from certain that he has not committed some sin, perhaps unconsciously, which has brought it all upon him. This is in marked contrast with the rectitude of Job, announced in the Prologue, and confirmed by his own conscience. The two works are therefore divided far by their purpose and outlook. The one is still dominated by the idea that sin and suffering are inevitably linked, while the other is a fine protest against such a view. The book of Job does not, indeed, solve the problem of innocent suffering, nor did it set out to do so. What it did set out to do, and how far it did it, will be considered below. Here all that we need to note is that if the Babylonian poem and the Hebrew could be proved to go back to a common tradition, we should once more have to recognize a whole world of difference between them.

Similarly with Egyptian literature, in which also parallels have been found. Once more models of some of the psalms have been found, and in particular, Ps. civ has been connected with an Egyptian hymn. The heretic king, Ikhnaton, who suppressed the old religion of Egypt and exalted the sun god to be the sole god, composed a great hymn in praise of the sun god, and this has been held to be the origin of Ps. civ. Some have held the borrowing to be indirect, and some direct and conscious. There are, indeed, in the poem passages which bear a striking resemblance to passages in the psalm, but rather in the thought than in the diction. Moreover, some verses of the psalm have been compared with another Egyptian poem, of an even earlier date, known as the Cairo Hymn to Amen. But again there are important differences, and though the Egyptian poems, as one would expect of the composition of Ikhnaton at least, manifest deep feeling and religious insight, they have not the simple directness and the vibrant passion of the Hebrew. Sellin well observes: " The literatures of Ancient Egypt and of Babylon show us that in respect of religious lyric, as of prophecy, the people of the Revelation reached a height absolutely unique among the nations of the Ancient East. In spite of all the formal affinities of style, imagery, etc., it is here alone that the ethical is set free from the bondage of the natural; it is here alone that a consciousness of salvation is attained which in places already bears an almost New Testament character; it is here alone that the keynote is the hope of a kingdom of God which is to embrace all nations, along with the heavens and the earth, a kingdom where ' mercy and truth are met together, and righteousness and peace have kissed one another.' " [12]

Again, it may be noted that for some sections of the book of Proverbs Egypt provides some interesting parallels. These are mostly short fragments, of which the oldest is the Teaching of Ptaḥ-ḥotep, which goes back to the third millennium B.C. We may also mention that amongst the Aramaic texts from Elephantine there were found some fragments of the Aḥiḳar story. This story was already known in several languages, and it contains a number of sayings comparable with those collected in the book of Proverbs, but embodied in a story. The story achieved a wide popularity, as its rendering into several languages shows. The Elephantine fragments are older than any other surviving versions.

Of more importance is the Egyptian text known as the Teaching of Amen-em-ope. This is thought to date from the middle of the eighth century B.C. Here striking parallels can be found between this work and the little section of the book of Proverbs contained in xxii. 17–xxiii. 14, where readings that have always been obscure in the Hebrew are

[12] *Introduction to the Old Testament*, E. Tr. by W. Montgomery, 1923, pp. 205 f.

now cleared up in the light of this text. That Egyptian Wisdom was not unknown in Israel may be readily credited. There was a good deal of intercourse between the two lands at many periods, and proverbs that pithily crystallize the experience and the observation of men would readily cross the frontiers on the lips of travellers, to produce the many little parallels between sayings in the book of Proverbs and sayings in Egyptian texts. So far as the Amen-em-ope text is concerned, however, the evidence does seem to point to something more than this, and to suggest direct borrowing.

Yet another literary problem of the Old Testament has had light shed on it by the Ras Shamra texts. There are references in the book of Ezekiel to Daniel, who is classed with Noah and Job, and who is referred to as conspicuous for wisdom and righteousness, and who would appear to be known to the Tyrians. It has always been difficult to suppose that these references were to the hero of the book of Daniel, who is represented as having been a young man in Babylon at that time. The modern view of the book of Daniel is that it was composed in the second century B.C., and that its stories are not properly historical. But even if it were a strictly historical work, coming from the sixth century B.C., the problem would still remain. For it would be surprising for Ezekiel to mention a young contemporary along with Noah and Job. Hence it has long been thought that Ezekiel's Daniel was a legendary hero of antiquity. We now have an epic poem from Ras Shamra about a Daniel. The name is spelt as in the book of Ezekiel, slightly differently from the spelling of the book of Daniel. This Daniel appears to have been an ancient king, going back beyond the fourteenth century B.C., and Virolleaud believes that he was a king of Tyre. It is in this text that the doubtful references to Zebulun and Asher have been found by some scholars, and it has been suggested that the legend may be connected in some way with these tribes.[13] The Daniel of this text is nowhere called righteous or wise, as in the book of Ezekiel, but he is said to have dispensed judgement in the gate, and to have protected the widow and the orphan.

There is little in the content of this epic to throw light on the Old Testament, save the fact that it is about a Daniel, who is almost certainly the figure to whom Ezekiel alludes. The story of the epic moves in a different world from the literature of the Old Testament. For it belongs to the cycle of myths associated with the fertility cult. Hence once again we find that this literaure can only help us to understand the background of the Old Testament, and it provides us with a foil by which we can appreciate the better the greatness of the Old Testament. Writers sometimes speak of the two religions of Israel, because it is clear from the Old Testament itself that there was a popular religion, with which the religion of Yahweh was often mingled and fused, but which was fundamentally different from it, and against which the prophets with increasing clearness protested. These texts enable us to understand more clearly against what the prophets declaimed. From the start there was the consciousness that Yahweh was the God of Israel, and that the indigenous fertility cult was not Israel's true faith. While there were periods when this consciousness receded into the background, in all times of national revival it awoke anew and came to the fore.

In this rapid survey a vast field of knowledge has been but most inadequately touched on, and the debt of the Biblical student to the archaeologist but illustrated in a fragmentary way. It may perhaps have become clear, however, that beyond its very considerable help in the field of philology, archaeology has helped to make some Old Testament narra-

[13] The text is again more probably to be treated as a ritual text than as a legend, and Engnell holds that Daniel was a divine king with whom the reigning king was identified by the ritual, which belonged to the annual enthronement festival.

tives live afresh, and has placed Israel in her contemporary world; it has shown us the stock from whence she came, the cultural inheritance she began with, and the world into which she came; it has shown the nature of the constant struggle Israel had with the ideas and practices that prevailed around her, and helped us to realize that by her very geographical position she was exposed to influences that were hard to resist. It has not diminished our regard for the Bible, nor our respect for Israel. For in the light of her origin and her environment we are the better able to appreciate the heights she attained. We see the finger of God more clearly in her story, and wonder at the way He led her from such a beginning, and through such an environment, to such heights. And our regard for the succession of men we call the prophets, who served as the mouthpiece of God to Israel, is deepened. The uniqueness of the religious quality of the Old Testament, its profound insight and spiritual penetration, are more manifest than ever in the light of all that Israel had to discard, both within and around her.

For the vital things, the things that gave to Israel her undying meaning for the world, were not the things she shared with others, but the things that were hers alone, the things that were communicated to her through her experience by God. We need not shrink in any way from recognizing the reality of her debt to others. She enjoyed intercourse with the great empires to the east and to the west of her, and both contributed to her cultural inheritance. She also entered into the stock of ideas and practices that prevailed in Canaan. From some things she divested herself in the course of her development, but others she carried with her, assimilating them and making them the vehicle of her own spirit. From Egypt she caught something of the Egyptian love of Nature, and from Babylon she inherited [14] the form of her poetry, many traditions, and perhaps many a turn of phrase.

[14] Either mediately, or directly. Cf. above, p. 67.

But with all this she brought a contribution of her own, vital to the flavour and character of her literature, and vital to the character of her religion. She brought a deeper consciousness of sin than Egypt knew, and a higher concept of God than Babylon attained. Her debt to her Semitic inheritance, and to her environment may be readily acknowledged. But deeper than both, because infusing her literature and her life with that spirit which has made it endure, and which makes it still of living worth to men, was her debt to her own experience. The most enduring things that Israel attained were not the things she had in common with others, but the *differentiae,* that were progressively born out of her growing experience of God. For the appreciation of the religious significance of the Old Testament, then, the study of Biblical archaeology is not without value. It brings into crystal clarity the recognition that nothing it can unfold can really explain the Old Testament in its deepest meaning, and beyond gratitude for the measure of light it brings, it induces a profound sense that the only satisfying clue to all it leaves unillumined must be found in the perception of the hand of God in Israel's life and in her Scriptures.

IV. THE MEANING OF HISTORY

THE PRECEDING CHAPTERS will have shown that archaeology, no more than literary criticism, is sufficient to unlock the richest treasures of the Old Testament. It can contribute very much to the study of the Old Testament, but it can in no sense offer an explanation of its enduring quality. It was not in virtue of its common origin, and points of contact with religions that have passed away, that Israel's faith survived, but in virtue of something which it did not share with them. So, too, in the field of history. The Old Testament contains a good deal of historical narrative. Some of it is of high value as history, and much is finely written. But none of it was written from a scientific motive, in an effort to discover and to preserve the facts for their own sake. Greater than the facts is the significance of the facts, and the Old Testament historians were interested primarily in their significance. The books that we commonly refer to as the " historical books " of the Old Testament belong in the Hebrew Canon to the " prophets." And this was by a sound instinct. For they were intended to set forth and to illustrate spiritual principles, which were dearer to the men who compiled them than the material they used for their purpose. Hence we cannot fully apprehend them until we go beyond the facts to their underlying principles.

The Old Testament writers believed that religion and history were not unrelated. Indeed, religion to them was something that belonged to the whole of life and experience, both individual and corporate. There is, in their view, no aspect of our life from which God is excluded, or in which He is uninterested. Nor is He merely the spectator, watching to approve or to disapprove, to confer or to withhold His favour. He is a participator in the drama of all our life, and especially in the drama of history. It is this that gives meaning to history in the eyes of these writers. They find God's hand in it all, and seek to penetrate His purpose and to understand what He is saying through it to men. Some of the profoundest and most fruitful theological ideas were born of Israel's history.

One great and ever-memorable fact of Israel's history was the great Exodus. It is stamped deeply on all her traditions, and the memory of it is kept fresh in the annual feast of the Passover. The origin of the Passover is lost in the mists of the past. It is commonly believed that it goes back far beyond the time of Moses, and that it was associated in its origin with the pastoral pursuits of Israel, and probably with moon worship. We have already noted connexions with moon worship in the traditions that associate the ancestors of Israel with Ur and with Ḥarran. The Passover was observed at the spring full moon, and we may observe too that when the Israelites left Egypt they went to a sacred mountain called in some of the sources Sinai, where the name recalls the name of the moon god, Sin, worshipped in Ur and Ḥarran. The sprinkling of the blood in the original ritual is thought to have had a prophylactic purpose, and to be designed in some way to preserve flocks and homes from evil. But however far that may or may not be true is of no more than academic moment. For from the time of the Exodus the feast was associated with the memory of that great event in Israel's history, and kept that memory alive. Nor was its aim merely to say to Israel, " Let us remember that we came forth from Egypt." It was to remember what God had done for Israel. " It shall be when thy son asketh thee in time to come, saying, What is this? that thou shalt say unto him, By strength of hand Yahweh brought us out from Egypt." [1]

[1] Exod. xiii. 14.

We are told in Exod. vi. 2 f. that " God spake unto Moses, and said unto him, I am Yahweh; and I appeared unto Abraham, unto Isaac, and unto Jacob, as El Shaddai, but by My name Yahweh was I not known to them." That there are a number of passages in the Bible in direct contradiction of this, where the name Yahweh appears on the lips of the patriarchs, is well known, as is also the analysis of the Pentateuch into different sources, reflecting variant traditions on this matter. Literary criticism cannot shed light on the origin of these diverse traditions, however, but can merely recognize their existence. An attempt will be made below to offer some explanation of that diversity, but here it may suffice to say that there is reason to believe that Exod. vi. 2 f. correctly signifies that Moses first introduced the name Yahweh, as the name of their God, to the Israelites whom he led out of Egypt. In the light of this we can see how the great ideas of the divine grace, of the divine election of Israel, and of the saving character of God were born in Israel of the historical experience of the Exodus.

The doctrine of election has been frequently and hotly discussed amongst theologians, and the speculative arguments for and against the idea marshalled in formidable array. Israel was never troubled by such speculations. She was sure of her election, not because some daring thinker hit on the idea and taught it to his disciples, until it spread through the nation, but because she passed through a concrete experience that had no meaning apart from such an explanation. The experience was an undeniable fact, and her election was not a mere deduction from the experience but announced to her beforehand, to be the basis of the experience. It was because she trusted the announcement that she knew the experience.

A fugitive from Egypt, far away in the desert, had a great spiritual experience one day, as the result of which he was deeply convinced that Yahweh was calling him to go into

Egypt, and to bring thence a company of slaves, who may or may not have heard of the name of Yahweh, but who did not know Him as their God. He shrank from the mission, both on account of its difficulty and apparent hopelessness, and on account of his sense of his own unfitness for it, and the mission was in itself of an astonishingly unusual character. Yet the constraint laid upon him was imperative. Either he was completely deluded, or Yahweh was not alone choosing him for His service, but also choosing this weak and enslaved people to be His people. Either Moses was deluded, then, or the divine election of Israel was a fact, not a theory. On the other hand, if Moses was deluded, whence did this strange idea arise? Did it arise merely in the disordered brain of this exile? Such an explanation could only lead to fresh questions still harder to answer than any raised by the problems of the divine election of Israel. If he had culled out of his own spirit the hazardous enterprise of challenging the might of Egypt, he might have been expected to act in the name of the God familiar to the slaves as the name of their God. They might be expected to understand their own God stirring Himself on their behalf, but could only be filled with astonishment at any other God interesting Himself in their plight. It is true that Moses declared to them that this God Yahweh was really the same as their fathers' God, but none the less the introduction of this new name could only raise questions which might have been avoided by the use of the old and familiar name. This identification of Yahweh with the God of their fathers was syncretism, and however effective syncretism may be in the long run it is never immediately effective. We know that after Israel came to Canaan a new syncretism took place, and Yahweh was identified in the popular mind with Baal. Yet there was always an underlying consciousness that Yahweh and Baal were not really the same. And Moses could scarcely expect that immediately and without misgiving these slaves in Egypt would achieve the full and complete equation of Yahweh and the God of their fathers. Moreover, we know that long afterwards Israel cherished the thought that in the time of the Exodus Yahweh had chosen her to be His people, and that she had not therefore really been His people before. " Thus saith the Lord Yahweh: In the day when I chose Israel, and lifted up Mine hand unto the seed of the house of Jacob, and made Myself known to them in the land of Egypt, when I lifted up Mine hand unto them, saying, I am Yahweh your God, in that day I lifted up Mine hand unto them, to bring them forth out of the land of Egypt." [2] Further, if Moses drew from no deeper source than his own spirit this idea of Yahweh's choice of Israel, its supreme audacity is still to understand. To have produced the idea of a God choosing a people who already worshipped another God, and adopting them to be His people, would have been surprising enough if the people had been a strong people, worthy of the power of the deity concerned. But to have produced out of his delusion the idea that a God who was powerful enough to perform this surprising feat of deliverance was adopting a people of negligible importance would have been still more astonishing. Unless it really was borne in on him from beyond himself, it would seem so unnecessary, and so much simpler to have gone in the name of the God of the fathers to attempt his daring enterprise.

But, *mirabile dictu,* the deliverance Moses announced was experienced. The Pharaoh did not immediately yield and release the Israelites, but he did ultimately allow them to depart. But it was not due to the persuasive tongue of Moses that he yielded. It was due to events wrought by no human hand, to disasters which fell upon Egypt, in accordance with the word of Moses, but which Moses himself neither claimed to control, nor could be presumed to control.

[2] Ezek. xx. 5 f.

He maintained that he was speaking in the name of this God Yahweh, and that the might of Yahweh was being displayed. If he was deluded, we have still to explain what was the power that moved the Pharaoh to give way, and by what strange accident the desert dream of Moses became a reality. And not only so. The Pharaoh repented of his weakness and pursued the Israelites and overtook them by the Red Sea. And again Israel was saved by a signal act of deliverance in which no human hand played a part. The critical examination of the narrative may show that the miracle has been heightened in the tradition, and the numbers of the Israelites concerned greatly swollen. But no critical examination can discredit the story that Israel had an amazing deliverance, a deliverance that could never be forgotten in all her history, and a deliverance that never ceased to call forth wonder and thanksgiving. If Yahweh really did call Moses to this task and choose Israel in her weakness to be His people, and if He did break the Pharaoh's proud spirit and snatch His people from destruction by His unperturbed control of the winds, we do have a single and self-consistent explanation of the whole story. But if He did not, then we must assume that Moses was deluded, and his delusion cannot of itself account for its justification by such means. Nor can any one of the chain of fortuitous accidents which brought about the deliverance explain any other, and still less the faith of Moses that it would happen, nor again can they severally or jointly offer any explanation of the idea of the divine choice of Israel with which Moses came to the slaves in Egypt. At any rate, Israel believed that Yahweh had chosen her to be His people because when Moses announced it to her, and she followed him in trust, she found the announcement justified by the event. A scientist who puts his hypothesis to the test of experiment and finds it justified is honoured by a scientific age for the propriety of his method. It was by that scientific method, in an age that was far from scientific, that Israel tested her election, and the faith or hypothesis that inspired the test offers the simplest explanation of its success.

It is sometimes supposed that the doctrine of election is inherently unworthy of God, and that it implies an arbitrariness of spirit that is incompatible with His love of all men, or even with common fairness. Israel did not at first realize all the meaning or all the purpose of her election, but if, as she came in the person of her greatest teachers to see, God chose her that He might teach her, and that she might in turn teach the world and be a light to the Gentiles, there is nothing arbitrary, unfair or unworthy. Israel's election was not ultimately for her own blessing alone, but for service, and for the service of the world. It is true that so far as we can perceive across the ages there was little in Israel herself to account for God's choice of her, and Israel was conscious of the same fact. She was not notably better or worse than other peoples at the time of her election. But God saw that she was serviceable for His purpose, and therefore He chose her. There is nothing in this to justify the harsh perversion of the doctrine of election into the arbitrary selection of some individuals for salvation and of others for damnation. Election is fundamentally for service, though it also and necessarily brings privilege. It is because we isolate the privilege in our thought, and think of election solely in terms of some great boon conferred on the elect, that it provides problems for us.

In countless ways the principle of election enters into our common life, without arousing in us any sense of its unworthiness. When a Prime Minister is faced with the task of appointing an Archbishop, there may be before him the names of several men, between whom there is little to choose for the post. But he is bound to select one. The one chosen will enjoy the high privilege and honour, and all the influence of the appointment, but it is not primarily for this that he is appointed. It is for service that he is appointed, and if the Prime Minister in making the appointment is moved solely by his judgement of fitness for that service, he will not feel that there is any unfairness to the other possible candidates. The same thing is true when a headmaster is chosen for a school, or a business appointment is made, or a child is selected to present a bouquet of flowers to the Queen when she attends some local ceremony. In each case some measure of honour and privilege attends the choice, but it can be condemned as unfair only if some ignoble motive determines the choice, and not simply the measure of fitness for the task. For the specific service a specific individual must be chosen. And when God wants a specific task performed, He chooses an instrument appropriate to the task. He could choose Jeremiah, or Paul, for certain tasks, and He could equally choose Israel for another service. Of course election carried with it high privilege, but that high privilege was not something in which to boast, but something to fill the heart with trembling by the constraint it laid upon the elect.

That God elects to salvation is undoubtedly true if the story of the Exodus has meaning. He elected Israel to salvation from the bondage of Egypt. But the corollary is not that others are elected to neglect, or to damnation. It is that the purpose of the salvation, and the ultimate purpose of the election, is service. And unless the service is rendered the election fails of its purpose, and the salvation is thrown away. That is the message of the prophets on more than one occasion. Yahweh is not bound to Israel by anything that is inherently in Israel. He chose her for His service, and if she ceases to serve Him, He can cast her away. The prophets do not believe, indeed, that the election can wholly fail of its purpose, but betray a faith in a surviving Remnant that shall be serviceable and that shall justify the election. The corollary of this doctrine is not that whoso is not chosen for salvation is arbitrarily rejected by God, but that whoso is not saved is not serviceable.

For a specific task one only may be chosen. But God has many tasks, and His service is infinitely varied, so that He can choose for some task, and therefore for the privilege and honour of His election, all who will respond to His choice. Whoever is chosen is conscious of the wonder of his privilege and of the greatness of the honour conferred upon him, and is profoundly aware that there is no worth in him to correspond to the privilege and honour, but that he is chosen because he is willing to respond to the choice and to be used by God, and that there is laid on him the sacred responsibility of fulfilling the purpose of his election. Israel was chosen for a unique mission, to be the religious teacher of mankind. She did not at first know the full meaning of her mission, but her religious leaders, who were ever deeply conscious of the privilege of her election, were always sure that it had a purpose, and that it laid great obligations on her. And this sprang out of the vivid and dramatic experience of the Exodus, and not out of a cloistered study.

Intermingled with what has been said on election is much that bears on the other two great theological ideas which have been mentioned as born of the Exodus. Other profoundly significant ideas which took their rise in Israel from the historical complex of circumstances that attended the Exodus and the resort to Sinai will be mentioned in other connexions. For few events of history have been more deeply significant for the whole world than the apparently insignificant departure from Egypt of a little company of slaves, and the figure of Moses towers as the greatest, because the most serviceable to God, in all the spiritual history of mankind before the Incarnation. But here the ideas of the divine grace and of the character of God as a saving God will alone be mentioned, because both are intimately associated with the idea of election.

God could have chosen some great and powerful nation to be the medium of His supreme self-revelation, but He could not at the same time have revealed His grace and His saving character. His choice would have appeared to be dictated by the worth and strength of the elect people, and they would hardly have recognized their need of salvation, save such as they could achieve for themselves. But to Israel it could be said, " Yahweh did not set His love upon you, nor choose you, because ye were more in number than any people; for ye were the fewest of all peoples: but because Yahweh loveth you." [3] Their very impotence made it clear that His choice of them was not dictated by their worth, but by His grace. And grace is the unmerited love of God. It cannot be explained, for its explanation is hidden in the heart of God. He set His love upon Israel because He loved her, and beyond that tautologous explanation we cannot go, save in so far as we have already gone in saying that God chose Israel because He saw that she could serve His purpose, and that she could serve His purpose partly because she was so helpless and so worthless.

Israel's religion is not the only religion of salvation. To cite no others, Indian religions are religions of salvation. But the salvation for which they yearn is from life itself, from the ceaseless round of rebirth to suffering, whereas in Israel's thought life is supremely good. Salvation is from all that hampers life's freedom and limits its fullness. Yet it did not begin on any high spiritual level in its thought of salvation. It began with the glad experience of deliverance from the Egyptian taskmaster's lash, and for long the deliverance for which men looked to God was from oppressors without or within the nation who crushed men under their yoke. Later there developed a deepened consciousness of sin, and the realization that it held men in a more tyrannous grip, and a more degrading slavery, than any physical or eco-

[3] Deut. vii. 7 f.

nomic oppressor. But from the start it was recognized that
salvation carried obligations with it. It was not merely salvation from something, but salvation to something. The
salvation of the Exodus led to the Covenant of Sinai, and a
deeper sense of the nature of the need for salvation led to
the thought of the New Covenant in Jeremiah. These corollaries of salvation will fall to be considered later. What has
here to be emphasized is that just as Israel believed in her
election because of a historical experience, so she believed
in the divine grace because she had experienced that grace,
and believed in the divine salvation because she was actually and undeniably saved, yet saved by no human hand.
Her faith was firmly rooted in history, where she found the
hand of God because no other interpretation of the facts
presented so satisfying a view.

It is possible that some scientific reader will wish to protest that whereas it has been said above that Israel's test of
her divine election, which Moses announced, was in full accord with scientific method, no scientist would rest such far-
reaching conclusions on a single experiment, or series of
experiments. Obviously, if the hypothesis were susceptible
of repeated experiment, experiment would be repeated.
But if, by the very nature of the case, it were not so susceptible, and if his hypothesis provided the sole reasonable
explanation of the facts of a single experiment, there would
be nothing unscientific in it. If, for instance, his experiment, by its very nature, required planetary and stellar conditions which could not recur within his lifetime, there
would be nothing unscientific in dispensing with a second
experiment. Hence, since all the circumstances of Israel's
test of her election were such as could not be artificially produced to repeat the test, and since, as has been said, no other
single explanation could account for all the phenomena,
whereas God's election of Israel, accepted as a fact by Moses
at the very beginning of the test, does supply a single and

sufficient explanation of all, the belief in that election is fully scientific.

It is not the case, however, that Israel's consciousness of her election knew no other foundation than that single, unique experience of the period of the Exodus. The towering figure of Moses was followed by a whole succession of men, who felt no less than he that they were the messengers of God to Israel, and through whom religion in Israel rose to heights it attained nowhere else. They believed that God who had chosen Israel to be His own peculiar people was through them leading His people into the secrets of His heart, and that they were marked out for their mission, not by their own desires, but by the election of God. That they were the media of an immensely fruitful spiritual advance cannot be gainsaid, and if the constraint under which they acted was a mere delusion, then delusion could claim to be the most potent and beneficent instrument of human advance, and there would be as strong a claim on science to further the large-scale production of such delusion, and to study its uses, as there is to further the production of electrical power, and the study of its uses. But again a theory of delusion is not really satisfying. It might claim to explain how it was that men supposed themselves to be the instruments of God when they were following the impulses of their own hearts, but it could not explain why external events responded to their delusions. For it was not alone in the experience of the Exodus that Israel was saved from disaster by forces beyond all human control, and it was in that response of the powers of Nature to her need, no less than in the leading of men who believed they were acting under divine constraint, that Israel found the justification of her faith in her election. Moreover, not once nor twice in her history her spiritual leaders, acting precisely as Moses did, called her in the name of her God to adventure herself in an apparently hopeless enterprise, feeling sure that while she had no sufficiency in herself she had sufficiency in God, and circumstances responded to that faith. No hypothesis that the spiritual leaders were the victims of delusion could explain the issue of their experience, and the response of Nature to the need of Israel in so many crises of her history can find no more rational explanation than Israel's faith that the God who had chosen her to be His people, and in whose hand Nature and all its forces lay, was coming to her aid.

When Joshua had made a treaty with the Gibeonites, a number of the neighbouring city states together attacked Gibeon. In their need the people of Gibeon sent an urgent appeal for help to Joshua, who was encamped at Gilgal. By a forced march through the night Joshua was nearing Gibeon at dawn and was greatly helped by a timely storm which was brewing, and by the lowering sky which enabled him to fall unseen on the unsuspecting foe, and then by the storm which broke over the battleground and filled his foes with terror. A gathering storm and a dark morning are not in themselves uncommon, but Israel was in no danger of regarding them as merely accidental. Their timely help in their hour of need convinced them that " Yahweh fought for Israel." [4] The victory appears to have been celebrated in an ancient song, of which a fragment is preserved in the Old Testament. That fragment is followed by a comment, which misunderstands it, and to which the attention of readers has commonly been riveted, because it enhances the miracle, and turns it into something wholly alien to the normal happenings of Nature. It declares that " the sun stayed in the midst of the heaven, and hasted not to go down about a whole day," so that " there was no day like that before it or after it." [5] There is no need to enhance the wonder. But on the other hand it is vain to suppose that by ignoring the prose comment, the miracle is got rid of, and the hand of

[4] Josh. x. 14.　　　　　[5] Josh. x. 13 f.

God is dismissed from the incident. For God's hand in history is seen in the shaping of events, in the control of men and of Nature, and not merely in that which reverses Nature's way. And the older poetic fragment knows nothing of such a reversal. It represents Joshua as crying, " Sun, be thou silent upon Gibeon, And Moon, in the valley of Aijalon. And the sun was silent, and the moon stayed, Until the nation had avenged themselves of their enemies." [6] The sun is not silent when it blazes forth from the heavens, but when it does not shine. Moreover, it is common for the sun to represent the day and the moon the night, and in the poetic statement that the moon remained it is natural to see a reference to the prolongation of the night. The location of the speaker is between Gibeon and Aijalon, apparently, with the sun over Gibeon to the east, and the moon over Aijalon to the west. It is therefore the morning hour, and the fragment means: " Sun, do not shine in the east, nor Moon break through cloud in the west. And the sun was veiled and darkness reigned until Israel fell on her foes." That this is a sound interpretation of the poem is borne out by the reference to the portentous storm which broke over the battleground. It was the darkness of the morning which favoured Israel, and screened their attack, and its response to their need persuaded Israel that Yahweh had come to their aid.

When the Canaanites of the Vale of Esdraelon, with Sisera at their head, were getting the upper hand of the Israelites who lay to the north and the south of that belt, the prophetess Deborah called on Barak to assemble the Israelites on the slopes of Mount Tabor. It is to be observed that this action was initiated by a prophetess, acting not in her own name, but in the name of Yahweh, and moved, as she declared, by Him to this action. That common human wisdom might well dictate the policy of getting all the tribes

[6] Josh. x. 12 f.

that were being reduced to submission to unite in a larger
Israelite coalition than had hitherto been known to function
is doubtless true. Yet it would be quite out of the question to
suggest that Deborah was displaying human prudence, and
reinforcing it with a religious motive by invoking the name
of Yahweh. For the contest to which she summoned men
was a very unequal one. Sisera and his hosts were equipped
with chariots, whereas the Israelites were ill-equipped and
untrained, a rabble that gathered in little groups to make
the company assembled on the hillside. Their chances
seemed about as good as we to-day should think the chances
of a cavalry unit against a panzer division. Yet the Israelites
won a great and notable victory, and the power of the Canaanites was broken, and Sisera fled as a fugitive to die by a
woman's hand. And the Song of Deborah, which has preserved the memory of that victory, ascribes it to God and to
divine aid. Nor was this a pious fiction. The vital factor in
the winning of the victory was not anything within the control of human wisdom. " The stars in their courses fought
against Sisera," sang Deborah.[7] For once more at the vital
moment a storm burst over the assembled hosts, and in a
few moments the chariots were immobilized in the morass,
to become an embarrassment instead of a strength to the
Canaanites. The lightly equipped Israelites enjoyed a freedom of movement denied to their foes, and swiftly ex-
ploited an advantage they had done nothing to secure. No
human prudence could tell Deborah that an opportune
storm would respond to their need, and no supposition that
the storm by a mere coincidence happened at that moment
can even pretend to offer any explanation of Deborah's confidence that Yahweh would come to their aid. Frequently
have meteorological conditions played a decisive part in
events, and men of every race have called on their gods for
help in battle, so that whichever side was the winner could

[7] Judg. v. 20.

claim that their god had come to their aid. But this is not quite on all fours with such things. Deborah was a prophetess, and this means that she was not so much one who called on Yahweh to help as one who responded to a constraint which she believed to have its origin in Yahweh, and found events beyond human control respond to that constraint.

To take another example, in the reign of Hezekiah Israel joined in a rebellion against Assyria, behind which stood Egypt. The prophet Isaiah consistently opposed that rebellion, and pronounced woes to those who relied on Egypt for help, and humiliation for Jerusalem. His words were unheeded, and plans for the rebellion went forward. Pressure was put on the Philistine towns to join in, and Padi, the king of Ekron, was dethroned and taken to Jerusalem, because he did not favour the project. Then Sennacherib marched to the west, and soon all Judah lay in his power. He boasts that he besieged and took forty-six walled cities and over two hundred thousand people, and that he shut up Hezekiah in Jerusalem like a bird in a cage, until he was overcome by the terrifying power of Assyria. In substance the Old Testament agrees with this, for it tells us that Hezekiah asked for terms, and paid a considerable indemnity to Sennacherib. From Assyrian sources we learn that Padi was handed over, to be restored to his throne, and also some of the princesses and some ladies from the king's harem. Clearly Jerusalem had tasted the humiliation that Isaiah had predicted. Yet equally clearly amongst the terms imposed by the conqueror there was no demand for the military occupation of Jerusalem. Isaiah appears to have declared from the start that though there would be humiliation for Jerusalem, the city itself would be spared. But then Sennacherib sent a small force to occupy Jerusalem. Hezekiah's concern at their approach, and his uncertainty as to what course he should pursue would suggest that this represented a new demand, beyond the terms of the armistice granted to him. And in his uncertainty he appealed to Isaiah for guidance. The prophet, who had in advance condemned the rebellion, now without hesitation counsels resistance to the demand. The city that had so lately been terrified by the majesty of the Assyrian, and had ceded its treasures, was scarcely in a position to offer any effective resistance now. Hence the prophet could not have based his counsel on any estimate of material factors. But he was certain that the Assyrian king who was going back on the terms of his own armistice, and whose messenger gibed at the power of Yahweh to defend the city, was now powerless. Isaiah did not base this certainty on his own deductions, or on his own intuition, however. He claimed that he was speaking not his own word but Yahweh's when he promised complete protection and deliverance for the city, without effort on its part beyond quiet confidence in Yahweh's word. And again deliverance came by no human hand. The Biblical account says the angel of Yahweh went forth and smote great numbers of the Assyrian soldiers. This is the Hebrew way of describing an epidemic. In describing the pestilence that fell upon Israel in the days of David, the Bible says, " So Yahweh sent a pestilence upon Israel. . . . And when the angel stretched out his hand toward Jerusalem to destroy it, Yahweh repented him." [8] As there, so here the angel symbolizes pestilence. For it was by the outbreak of disease in his army that Sennacherib was forced to withdraw. Here, once more, it might be possible to regard the outbreak as fortuitous, but a fortuitous outbreak of plague could not explain Isaiah's confident assurance of deliverance; on the other hand no mere wishful thinking on Isaiah's part could explain the outbreak of the plague. It is this response of circumstances beyond human control to the needs of Israel, and also to the promises of

[8] 2 Sam. xxiv. 15 f.

those who believed they were speaking not their own promises but God's, which disposed Israel to believe in the divine control of history and the divine choice of Israel to be
His people.

Yet it has to be recognized that Yahweh did not always
save, and there were many occasions when circumstances
did not respond to Israel's need of assistance against her
foes. Sometimes when the prophets of Yahweh promised deliverance with as much assurance as Isaiah displayed, the
deliverance did not come. In the days of Ahab a large assembly of prophets announced the coming victory and
urged the king to go up to Ramoth-gilead. Yet Ramoth-
gilead spelt disaster for Israel and death for the king. On
that occasion we find that opposed to the prophets who
urged the king to go up was the lone figure of Micaiah, who
knew full well that the king would go up, and who announced that it was the will of Yahweh that he should go
up, but to his death and not to victory. The problem of
false prophets will concern us below. Here we may observe
that there is no charge of insincerity against them. They
are actually said to be doing the will of Yahweh in persuading Ahab to go up to his doom. For disaster from the hand
of Yahweh, not deliverance, was here purposed. According
to Micaiah they imperfectly apprehended the will of Yahweh, yet not wholly misapprehended it. Their prophecy
was false prophecy to the extent that it promised a false
outcome of events. Yet Yahweh could use their false hopes
to serve His purposes.

That there were many occasions when Israel was not delivered by any timely help of circumstances is freely recorded in the Old Testament. There were times when Israel suffered from the oppression of her foes for long years,
times when she was crushed and lay helpless in the power
of her enemies. If Israel was the elect of Yahweh, why did
He allow this? Was it that His power was lacking, or was

His love the love of a moody friend? Both ideas are firmly rejected in the teaching of the Old Testament. Here it is held that the reason was that Israel had forgotten the corollaries of her election, and had been faithless to Yahweh. It was not that Yahweh had cut the bonds that bound Him to His people, but that they had cut the bonds and deserted Him. Israel did not always understand how she had offended Yahweh, or what it was necessary to do to be restored to His favour. At the battle of Aphek she thought her discomfiture at the hand of the Philistines was capable of being changed to victory by the act of bringing the Ark to the battlefield. But she was sure that when she was right with God she need have no fear of her foes. For Yahweh was in control of history.

This was ever the faith of the prophets. But what they sought to do was to help Israel to realize what getting right with God meant. They perceived that it meant understanding the true nature of God, and reflecting that nature in all the relationships of life, that it meant so living with God that He might live in His people. It involved something deeper than an outward act. It involved the inner spirit of men. And so, because the prophets saw the absence of those conditions which they perceived to belong to the true well-being of men, they were sure that there could be no well-being. The prophets again and again promised disaster, and not deliverance. So much so, indeed, that some modern writers have written as though the prediction of woe is of the essence of true prophecy, while the prediction of weal is the hall-mark of false prophecy. But Isaiah was as true a prophet when he promised the deliverance of Jerusalem as when he warned against the perils of rebellion, and the characteristic note of the great Deutero-Isaiah is struck in his opening words, " Comfort ye, comfort ye My people." [9]
Nevertheless, the prediction of woe is more characteristic of

9 Isa. xl. 1.

most of the prophets than the prediction of weal. " You only have I known of all the families of the earth," said Amos; "therefore will I visit upon you all your iniquities."[10] Disaster is here declared to be the consequence of election, because the true corollaries of that election have been neglected. When the prophets declared that Assyria or Babylon should afflict Israel, it was not because they measured the might of armies, and saw that Israel was no match for the mighty hosts of these great powers. Had that been the case Isaiah would not have promised deliverance for a helpless Jerusalem that had already but recently capitulated to her powerful adversary. No, the prophets were sure that material resources were not the final determining factor of history. They were equally sure that history was not at the mercy of blind chance. To them Assyria could appear as the rod of Yahweh's anger, and Babylon as raised up by Him to execute His will upon His own people. He could save His people when His purpose required their salvation; but He could equally chastise them when His love required their chastisement. For Yahweh was the supreme and undisputed controller of history.

This does not, of course, mean that the Old Testament teaches that God is the author of all that happens, and that He is responsible for the entire course of history. It does not mean that nothing can happen of which He does not approve. For nowhere does the Old Testament treat men as the mere puppets of God. They are conceived as living out the purposes of their own hearts, and as creatures to be morally judged by the good or evil of those purposes. If Israel's desertion of Yahweh were merely the fulfilment of His will, it could scarcely call down divine punishment upon her. The very essence of the message of the prophets was that men were contravening the will of God, and that much was happening on earth which was the antithesis of

[10] Amos iii. 2.

His will. Nevertheless, history lies in the hollow of God's hand, and He is able to make men's acts serve His purposes. This does not make them any the less their acts, and does not in any way involve the divine approval of the acts He uses. For God does not have to infringe human freedom to make men serve His purposes any more than He has to vary the laws of Nature to make winds and storms serve His purposes. The New Testament teaches that the Cross of Christ is the source of infinite blessing to men, and that in the purpose of God Christ crucified is the Redeemer of the world. Yet it nowhere blesses those who crucified Him, or exalts Judas Iscariot for his share in bringing God's great purpose to fruition. And even so the Old Testament can condemn Assyria and Babylon for the harsh cruelty of their way, even when it declares that God is using that cruelty to fulfil His purpose, and to bring home to Israel the folly of her way.

" Ho Assyrian, the rod of mine anger, the staff in whose hand is mine indignation! " Isaiah could cry,[11] as though Assyria is the helpless tool in God's hands. Yet he could continue, " Howbeit he meaneth not so, neither doth his heart think so." [12] Assyria is all unaware that she is serving God's purpose, in which she has not the slightest interest. She is following the bent of her own heart, and executing the cruel purpose that she there cherishes. Hence, even though Yahweh is using her cruel will to serve His own purposes in relation to His people, He does not approve of those purposes, and when they have served His purpose He will punish Assyria for their iniquity. " Wherefore it shall come to pass, that when the Lord hath performed His whole work upon mount Zion, and on Jerusalem, I will punish the fruit of the stout heart of the king of Assyria, and the glory of his high looks." [13] Clearly there is no thought of the divine approval of all that happens.

[11] Isa. x. 5.   [12] Isa. x. 7.   [13] Isa. x. 12.

Neither does the Old Testament teach that outer fortune and inner worth are invariably matched. It is true that the book of Deuteronomy does declare that when Israel is faithful to God she will know the fullest economic prosperity and material welfare. When in some circles this was individualized to yield the view that a man's circumstances reflected his desert, the book of Job was written to protest against it and to teach a deeper truth. And the real message of the prophets is not that obedience to God is the golden way to prosperity. It is that obedience to God is itself the truest well-being. From the death of Abel on we find that the righteous often suffer. Yet there is no suggestion that righteousness is ever a mistake, or that it is to be deplored even when it does not lead to outer blessing. And Deutero-Isaiah reaches the heights of the doctrine of vicarious suffering, where the outer experience is the antithesis of the inner worth, and the spirit in which it is faced converts it into a spring of blessing for others.

It is not necessary therefore to suppose that the Old Testament teaches that righteousness always triumphs. For if might is not right, neither is right always might. When the prophets foretell doom at the hands of Assyria or Babylon, they nowhere suggest that Assyria or Babylon is righteous in the eyes of God, or that conditions in those lands reflect His will any more closely than the conditions they condemn in Israel. It is not because Assyria is in the right and Israel in the wrong that Assyria is given freedom by God to wreak her will on Israel. The recognition of the hand of God in history no more involves the thesis that right always prevails than the recognition of His hand in individual experience involves the thesis that the good always prosper. It leads to the view that the process of history is linked to a moral purpose. But just as in warfare strategy is to be distinguished from tactics, and tactics when viewed in isolation will often fail to reveal their purpose, though they

have a relation to the strategic purpose in the mind of the
general, so there is a strategy of history which can reveal
the moral purpose of the God who controls its course, even
though the tactics of the process may not individually reveal that purpose with equal clarity. Nevertheless, the tactics are not unrelated to the strategy.

The Old Testament is not interested in the history of the
world at large, or in the universal process of history. It is
interested in the purpose of God for Israel, and it believes
that nothing in the process of history can interfere with
that purpose. In its broad strategy that purpose was to
choose Israel to be His people, that He might reveal Himself unto her and lead her into the secrets of His nature and
will, and that she might mediate unto the world the treasures into which she was led. But Israel was not a passive instrument in His hand. She had a will and a purpose often
out of harmony with His, and therefore the stern discipline
of events had a place in the divine tactics as well as the gracious blessing of deliverance. Whether at every point in her
history relative righteousness triumphed was of lesser moment than whether Israel was learning the things that God
was seeking to teach her through her experience. That is
the real meaning of history as it appears from the Old Testament. It goes beyond a moral purpose, indeed, and declares that history can be rightly understood only in the
spiritual sphere. Since God is active in the field of history,
it must be so. For He is not alone interested in righteous
dealing as between man and man, and nation and nation,
but in the revelation of Himself unto men, and the sharing with men of the riches of His fellowship and will.

That this view of the meaning of Israel's history was
sound may be confidently accepted. For the course of events
responded to it. Israel was indeed led through her experiences and through her spiritual leaders into a deeper knowledge of God, and to a religious level unique in the ancient

world. She was not led to material power and political influence, but all her history reveals its true significance only
in the sphere of religion. And through the Christian
Church, which was born out of the womb of Judaism, the
spiritual treasures which Israel came to possess have been
mediated to men of every race.

We may still ask, however, how far this throws light on
the wider meaning of history. To survey the whole course
of history and to establish its meaning would carry us much
too far from the theme of the Old Testament, to which the
present study is devoted, and would claim more than a few
lines at the end of a chapter. Yet the reader is entitled to ask
how far the writer believes the principles he finds in the
Old Testament to have a wider relevancy. If God is active
in human history, He can hardly be supposed to confine
His activity or His interest to the things which directly
concern Israel. That He is not responsible for all that happens, and does not approve of all that He nevertheless inte-
grates into His purpose, may be as readily believed in the
wider setting as in relation to Israel. But that He has some
purpose, and that that purpose is fundamentally spiritual
may be expected to be as true generally as of Israel. The
process of history cannot be left to the mere interplay of
human passions and schemes if God is active in that process. For He cannot be thought of merely as one of the innumerable actors in that field, but only as the Supreme
One, whose will is finally operative.

The purpose of history may be expected to be educative
for peoples other than Israel, as well as for Israel, and to be
directed to a spiritual goal. For though God chose Israel to
be His peculiar people, to be entrusted with the revelation
of Himself, because He saw that she was serviceable to Him
for this purpose, He could also choose other peoples for
other tasks, and could ensure that the discipline of events
should minister to their education for those tasks. For the

service of God is infinitely varied, and He can issue His call
for such tasks as will evoke a response. The uniqueness of
Israel was in the nature of the purpose for which she was
chosen, and the richness of the fellowship with God to
which her election led. Moreover, just as the revelation entrusted to Israel was not for herself alone, but to be shared
with the world, so the inheritance of other peoples is to be
shared. Yet, since the vocation of Israel was unique in its
glory, greater are the things to be learned from her than
those that any other people has to teach.

By the discipline of events God can teach some things.
But the deepest things are not so taught. It was by men in
whose spirit He lived that events were interpreted and
made to minister to Israel's spiritual growth. And it can
only be when men have entered into the treasures of Israel's inheritance, and known an intimacy with God which
lifts them into His will and purpose, that the meaning of
history will truly appear. For God has a will for nations and
for individuals, and it is only as they consciously and will-
ingly reflect His will in all their life that they can apprehend the deepest treasures of experience. Until they do so
reflect His will they will stumble along, but not always forward, and will often find that by the discipline of circumstance a beneficent God is telling them that they are going
astray, since they are too obtuse or too unwilling to receive
His message in any other way. His richest messages were
given to Israel not through events, but through men who
knew the intimacy of His counsel. And when the nations
will enter into the inheritance of Israel, and seek a like intimacy and follow men who have it, they will be led into
the things that belong to their true well-being, and all their
experience will enrich their spirit.

V. THE GROWTH OF MONOTHEISM

THE LITERAL READING of the early Biblical narratives gave rise in former times to the general view that at the outset of human history man was monotheistic. In modern times there is a school of serious students which seeks to maintain this view with all the support of comparative anthropology, and which argues that the lower we get in the scale of civilization, and the nearer we get to primitive culture, the more clearly monotheism emerges. That spiritual maturity belonged to the cultural and intellectual infancy of mankind is a surprising proposition, and its advocacy might be expected to lead to the abandonment of all the arts of civilization — including the service of the printing press, whereby the proposition is made known. In ancient Israel the Rechabites believed that in the nomadic life of their fathers lay greater spiritual purity than in the fuller cultural life of the towns, and in settled agricultural pursuits. But the Rechabites were sufficiently serious in their belief to accept its corollaries, and to eschew dwelling in houses with all the fruits of civilized life, and to continue themselves to live in the old simple ways. The modern exponents of the lofty heights of primitive life are less eager to return to it.

The examination of the anthropological evidence they assemble may be left to the anthropologists, who are in general quite unconvinced. Here it may be noted that the Biblical evidence, on which the view formerly rested, has little validity for the purpose. For if in one of the documents of the Pentateuch Yahweh is represented as having associated freely with the first man, and Eve to have had His name on her lips, while in another place it is said that in the days of Enosh "men began to call upon the name of Yahweh," [1] and if Yahweh is represented as having visited the patriarchs and made Himself known to them, there is a Biblical passage in another of the documents, to which reference has already been made, which declares that Yahweh first became known to Israel in the days of Moses. A whole series of considerations, some of which have already been noted, favour the probability that the latter statement is correct, so far as the group led by Moses is concerned. The other statements, preserved in the traditions of the group that was not with Moses, but that took over its worship of Yahweh by gradual penetration,[2] reflect the inability of this group to say when the worship of Yahweh began, and their sense of the great antiquity of His worship. While these traditions enshrine an important measure of truth, and are not just to be dismissed as inconsistent with the other, they cannot be regarded as sober history. The Biblical evidence cannot be relied on, therefore, to support the theory of primitive monotheism.

Another view, which commands the support of some of the most distinguished of living scholars, is that Moses established monotheism in Israel. Most scholars would contest this view, and maintain that the emergence of monotheism must be placed much later than this. The difference is not of very great practical moment, however, since even where it is held that Moses attained monotheism it is agreed that in the post-Mosaic age monotheism was abandoned by Israel, and had to be attained afresh in later days. In modern hands the figure of Moses is sometimes presented in greatly shrunken form. That much of the legislation attributed to him took its present shape in later days is certain, and he is sometimes largely dissolved in the mists, and represented as a mere shadow, about whom we can know little

[1] Gen. iv. 26.   [2] See below.

or nothing. To the writer this seems unduly pessimistic. Some things stand out clearly in the searching light of criticism, and so far as Moses is concerned they are the big things. That Moses led the Israelites out of Egypt, and brought them to Yahweh's sacred mountain, where they pledged themselves to Him in a religious bond which lay at the heart of their national consciousness may be confidently accepted. And this is immensely significant, and sufficient to justify that high estimate of the importance of Moses in the religious history of mankind which stands above.

Before we can attempt any estimate of the work of Moses, we must piece together the various items of evidence bearing on the question of the Exodus. Into all the complexities of the issues it is impossible to go here, but it has been already said that the result has far-reaching bearings on many Old Testament questions. This will perhaps become clearer as we proceed.

It has commonly been held that not all the Israelites were ever in Egypt, and that therefore Moses did not lead all the tribes. There is Biblical evidence to suggest that the entry of all the tribes was not simultaneous, and hence the movements represented in the Amarna letters are often treated as the entry of some of the tribes, while the entry of others is placed later. But usually the holders of this view make little attempt to show any connexion between the two groups of immigrant tribes, and still less to explain how the tribe of Levi comes to be so closely associated with both groups.

Further, the variant traditions as to the introduction of the worship of God under the name Yahweh have been referred to. It is common to connect the document which ascribes the beginnings of the worship of Yahweh to the beginnings of time with the tribe of Judah, and the other ancient document which refrains from using the name until the time of Moses with the northern tribes, and particularly with Ephraim, the leading tribe of this group. Both documents are collections of Israelite traditions, and not merely of local traditions, and both date from a time after the bringing of Judah and Northern Israel together in the period of Saul and David. They represent two attempts to incorporate the traditions of north and south in a single corpus, but the one reflects the special standpoint of a southern school and other that of a northern school.

Moreover, it has long been held that Yahweh was the God of the Kenites, before Moses went in His name to lead the Israelites out of Egypt.[3] The father-in-law of Moses is sometimes called Jethro, the priest of Midian, and sometimes Reuel, the priest of Midian. Since it is elsewhere said that Hobab, the son of Reuel, was a Kenite, it is likely that Moses' father-in-law was a Kenite. We are not told the name of the God, whose priest he was, but when Moses led the Israelites out of Egypt, his father-in-law came to meet him, and on hearing of all that Yahweh had done, he cried, " Now I know that Yahweh is greater than all the gods."[4] Thereupon he offered sacrifice unto God, and gave Moses advice, and then departed. The fact that Jethro officiated at the sacrifice for all the elders of Israel makes it clear that it was a sacrifice to this God Yahweh, whose power had been so signally manifested, and probable that this was the God, whose priest Jethro was. His joy at the manifestation of Yahweh's surpassing power would be the more intelligible if Yahweh was the God he served.

We may now essay a synthesis of Biblical and extra-Biblical material bearing on this question, confining ourselves to the major points and ignoring a great many of the

---

[3] J. Lewy (*Revue des études sémitiques*, 1938, pp. 58, 71 f.) conjectures that the doubtful Yw of Ras Shamra was a Hurrian deity, and that the Kenites or Midianites were Hurrians. Equally improbable is the view of E. Littmann (*Archiv für Orientforschung*, xi, 1936, p. 162), which connects the name Yahweh with the Aryan *Dyāu-s, whence come Zeus and Jupiter.
[4] Exod. xviii. 11.

details. In the Amarna age some Israelite tribes pressed into Palestine from north and south. These were the Leah-tribes and the Concubine-tribes, who gained a foothold in some parts of the country, which they gradually extended, and who, with the exception of some Levite elements, did not go down into Egypt. One group of these immigrants consisted of Judah, Simeon, Levi, and some associated Kenite and other elements. This group advanced northwards from Kadesh Barnea, where they had spent some time, and while the Judah group, together with the Kenites, got a foothold in the south, Simeon and Levi pressed farther north to the Shechem district, where they were guilty of an act of treachery which has left echoes both in the Amarna letters and in the Old Testament. In consequence of this treachery they lost their hold on the Shechem district and were scattered.

In the same age Joseph was carried down into Egypt, where in the reign of Ikhnaton he rose to a position of eminence and power. The Pharaoh who broke with the Theban priesthood, which had previously supplied the officers of state, would be likely to look for talent wherever he could find it, and there is evidence that Semites did rise to eminence in his time. Moreover, this Pharaoh exalted the god whose principal seat was at Heliopolis to be the sole god of Egypt. In the Old Testament we are told that the Pharaoh gave the daughter of the priest of Heliopolis to Joseph for a wife, and in no age would this have been so signal an honour as in Ikhnaton's. Further, while the new capital was established at the place now known as Tel-el-Amarna, a second court was maintained at Heliopolis. This would be near enough to the land of Goshen to satisfy the Biblical conditions, and far enough away to ensure that the members of the court would not be offended by the sight of Joseph's kindred. The firmness of the administration of Egypt during Ikhnaton's reign and the lack of help given to the Palestinian princes against the Ḥabiru would alike be explained if the administration of the kingdom were in Joseph's hands.

In the Biblical traditions we are told that Joseph was sent from the Hebron district to Shechem to his brethren, but found they had moved on to Dothan. Hence his journey to Egypt is represented as taking place at a time when the Israelites were in two groups, in Judah and in the Shechem district, and it was from the latter group that he was carried away. When Simeon and Levi failed to maintain themselves in this district, Simeon fell back on Judah, and became gradually absorbed in Judah. Some Levite elements also fell back on Judah, and we can thus account for the many links between Levi and Judah. In particular there were Levites at Bethlehem, and we later find relations of Moses there. But some of the Levites, and perhaps others with them, went down into Egypt in the search for food. From the Shechem district Joseph had been carried down, and these were of the group that had been in that district. Hence there is no improbability in Joseph's recognizing them when he saw them, and a few others being sent for to join them. Only a small group is concerned anyway, for the Bible places the total at seventy.

On this view the kinship of Joseph, the father of the tribes that formed the principal element of the Exodus group, with the Amarna age immigrants into Palestine is recognized, and the connexion of Levite elements with both the Ḥabiru and the group in Egypt.

Shortly after the death of Joseph, Rameses II came to the throne. He is known to have undertaken building operations in the Nile Delta area, where he rebuilt the ancient Avaris-Tanis to be the second capital of his empire, and renamed it Pi-Ramesse. This city was hard by Goshen, and therefore the Israelites were set to task-work to build the city for the Pharaoh. It was sufficiently near for the Pharaoh's daughter, when the court was in residence at Pi-Ramesse, to come into the neighbourhood of Israelite settlements when she went out for a bathe. During this reign Moses was forced to flee from Egypt in consequence of his wrathful action on seeing one of the Israelites being maltreated by an Egyptian, and in the reign of the following Pharaoh, Merneptah, he returned and led the Israelites out of Egypt.

If this reconstruction is correct,[5] the duration of the sojourn in Egypt will have been the four generations of the Biblical genealogies, and it would have been possible for Moses' mother to have been the sister of one of the Levites who had gone down into Egypt. On the other hand, it would be impossible to allow for the four hundred and eighty years of 1 Kings vi. 1 between the Exodus and the building of the Temple. But that figure could be accounted for by the amalgamation of the traditions. The representation of all the tribes as having come in together in a body under Joshua made possible the dating back of the entry of the Joshua group to the time of the entry of the earlier group, and so of the Exodus to the arrival of that earlier group at Kadesh Barnea many years before their advance northwards.

The group that Moses led out of Egypt went to Sinai, and thence after a short interval to the Central Highlands of Palestine, by way of the Jordan. It consisted principally of

[5] I have offered evidence in support of this reconstruction in a number of articles in various Journals: " Israel's Sojourn in Egypt," *Bulletin of the John Rylands Library*, 22, 1938, pp. 243–290; " The Eisodus and the Exodus," *Expository Times*, 50, 1938–1939, pp. 503–508; " The Danite Migration to Laish," *ibid.*, 51, 1939–1940, pp. 466–471; " Ras Shamra and the Habiru Question," *Palestine Exploration Quarterly*, 1940, pp. 90–94; " The Date of the Exodus," *ibid.*, 1941, pp. 152–157; " Habiru and the Hebrews," *ibid.*, 1942, pp. 41–53; " The Exodus and the Settlement in Canaan," *Bulletin of the American Schools of Oriental Research*, 85, February, 1942, pp. 27–31; " Two Observations," *ibid.*, 87, October, 1942, p. 40; " Early Levite History and the Question of the Exodus," *Journal of Near Eastern Studies*, 3, 1944, pp. 73–78.

the Joseph tribes, with some Levite elements. During the last quarter of the thirteenth century B.C. they were spreading themselves over the Central Highlands to the west of the Jordan, but at this stage they were not in contact with the groups to the north and south of them who had come in in the Amarna age. Belts of Canaanite cities separated them for some considerable time.

Early in the twelfth century B.C. the Philistines began to settle on the Palestinian coasts. Gradually they spread their influence along the coastal plain, and perhaps half a century after their arrival the tribe of Dan found it expedient to migrate to the north in search of fresh living-space. In the course of their migration they carried with them a Levite, whom they found in charge of a private shrine. This Levite was the grandson of Moses, and he had come from Bethlehem-Judah. There is no great difficulty in finding the grandson of Moses to be living about a century after the Exodus, whereas the view that places the Exodus in the middle of the fifteenth century B.C. is compelled to make him a more distant relation.

The archaeological evidence fits in general into this scheme of reconstruction better than into any other. The fall of Jericho provides the only serious difficulty. If Vincent's dating of that fall is correct, this difficulty entirely vanishes, while if the dating of Garstang or Albright is correct, it would be necessary to share with Albright the view that the fall of Jericho antedated the age of Moses, and had nothing to do with the group he led out. In the amalgamation of the traditions, incidents in which Joshua almost certainly played no part have been ascribed to him, and it may be that this is one of them. The writer confesses that he is not happy about this suggestion, however, and finds Vincent's dating much easier to accommodate. But the convenience of any scheme of reconstruction cannot determine an archaeological issue, and he therefore must leave the pre-

cise integration of the fall of Jericho in the scheme an open
question, until final agreement is reached by the archaeologists. At the moment the general opinion is against Vincent, and Wright states that the final blow to Vincent's date
has been given.[6]

So far as all other Palestinian sites are concerned, the archaeological dating of their history, as at present known,
accords with the above reconstruction, with the exception
of the date of the fall of Ai, which provides a problem of its
own in no way peculiar to this view. The places whose conquest is dated archaeologically earlier than the time of
Merneptah all lie in the districts occupied by the tribes
whose incursion has been placed in the Amarna age.

With this framework of history, we may now examine
the religious development of Israel. If Yahweh was the God
of the Kenites, but not originally the God of the Israelite
tribes, we may perceive how His worship came into Israel
in two different ways, and may thus account for the two different traditions in the Pentateuch. If Judah, Simeon and
Levi had Kenite elements associated with them, the Kenite
religion could spread by gradual permeation, and in any
case intermarriage between Kenites and the tribes associated with them could take place. That intermarriage is a
common cause of the infiltration of religious ideas and practices does not need to be emphasized. In a later age Nehemiah and Ezra were bitterly opposed to the marriage of
Jews with aliens precisely because such marriages brought
foreign religious influences into the heart of Israel. On the
other hand, not every intermarriage brings effective influence of this kind. It is where there is the cumulative influence of a continual stream of such marriages that the influence may become powerful.

If the Judah group learned its worship of Yahweh by the

---

[6] *Bulletin of the American Schools of Oriental Research*, 86, April, 1942,
p. 33.

gradual penetration of the religious influence of the Kenite elements associated with it, it would be natural for the beginnings of that worship to be ascribed to the beginnings of time. From time immemorial Yahweh had been the God of the Kenites, and there was no memory of any dramatic beginning of His worship. Hence Judah, who also knew no dramatic moment of the adoption of His worship, took over the idea that from ancient times He had been worshipped, and ascribed to their ancestors the worship of this God.

Moreover, quite early in the association of the Kenites with the Israelite tribes, before any spread of the worship of Yahweh was discernible in Israel, a Levite belonging to the group that went down into Egypt could marry a Kenite woman. The mother of Moses has a theophorous name compounded with the name Yahweh. It would thus appear that an ancestor of Moses married a Kenite woman, prior to the migration into Egypt of some of those Levites who fell back from Shechem. This would explain why, when Moses fled from Egypt, he went to a Kenite settlement. He may have gone to some Kenite kinsmen of his mother, just as Jacob, when he fled from Esau, went to his mother's kindred. Not all the Kenites joined the Israelites who pressed into Palestine from the south, any more than all the Levites went into Egypt. It would appear probable that some Levite kinsmen of Moses' father settled in the south with the Judah group, and their families were later found at Bethlehem-Judah. This would explain both the desert sojourn of Moses with Jethro, and the subsequent appearance of his grandson at Bethlehem, where other Levites are known to have been.

The Israelites who had gone down into Egypt had separated from the others before the worship of Yahweh had made any headway in Israelite circles, and had no knowledge of Him as their God. In the little group that went into Egypt there could have been but few with Kenite connexions, and there could be little opportunity for the reinforcement of Kenite influence during the sojourn in Egypt. To this group Moses came with the announcement that Yahweh had chosen them to be His people, and would deliver them from their Egyptian bondage. He led them triumphantly out, and on to the sacred mount of Sinai, where in an ever-memorable experience of consecration these tribes pledged themselves to the God who had delivered them. In their traditions, therefore, the worship of Yahweh began in Israel with Moses and the Exodus.

The significant work of Moses lay therefore in persuading these tribes that Yahweh had chosen them to be His people, and in leading them out of Egypt to Sinai, where they entered into the Covenant, and pledged themselves to Yahweh. In that work there was wrought something new in the history of religion, and something of immeasurable importance to mankind. Many nations have changed their religion, for a variety of reasons. As has been said above, intermarriage and the consequent fusion of two peoples may bring about religious change. Military conquest has sometimes brought the imposition of the conqueror's religion on the conquered. In Egypt for a brief period the fancy of Ikhnaton sufficed to instal the god of his choice as the sole deity of the land, and to banish all other worship. But here in the days of Moses something quite different from all these things was happening. Here Moses declared that God had first chosen Israel and rescued her, and Israel in her gratitude committed herself to the God who had first revealed His love for her. The Covenant is sometimes thought of in terms of a legal instrument, and at other times in terms of a bargain. It is supposed that what it amounted to was an agreement on God's part that so long as Israel was loyal to His worship He would protect her interests, and on Israel's part that so long as God stood by them they would continue to honour Him. This is a complete travesty of the meaning of the Covenant of Sinai. Yahweh had saved Israel. Her salvation was an undeniable fact of history. It was already achieved, and that not as a part of any bargain. And now Israel in her gratitude pledged herself to Yahweh with a pledge as absolute as had been her deliverance. The meaning of the Covenant was not that if God would look after Israel Israel would serve Him, but that because He had manifested His grace to her Israel would give Him her loyalty.

There are many who understand the theory of the Kenite origin of the worship of Yahweh to mean that what Moses did was to get the Israelites to transfer their worship to this Kenite God, and that he just transmitted to Israel the Kenite religion of his father-in-law's people. This is wholly to miss the significance of Moses. It has been said above that whatever the Passover may have meant in the days before the Exodus, its meaning for Israel from that time on was a new one. In the same way whatever the worship of Yahweh may have meant to the Kenites, from the days of Moses it meant something richer and deeper to Israel. He was more than a transmitter from Kenites to Israelites. He was a medium of divine revelation. Kenite worship of Yahweh was not based on any historical experience of His choice of the Kenites, confirmed in a great deliverance achieved before the Kenites had begun to worship Him, or based on the solemn and willing pledge of the Kenites to choose and to serve Him who had first chosen and notably served them. All of this inevitably meant that there was a new quality in the Yahwism of Israel.

Beyond this Moses gave a further new quality to her Yahwism. He who had been sensitive to the message of God to the enslaved Israelites, and who had been the instrument in God's hands for their deliverance, was also sufficiently *en rapport* with the spirit of God to establish Yahwism in Israel on a higher level than it had yet known amongst the Kenites. For from the days of Moses Yahwism in Israel was

an ethical religion. The ethical heights of the religion of
the prophets are universally recognized, but Moses is less
often allowed to have planted the ethical seed which bore
so rich a harvest in their work. The ethical character of the
Decalogue whose establishment in Israel is ascribed to Moses
is allowed, but it is not connected with the work of Moses.
Sometimes the Decalogue is allowed to have been given to
Israel by Moses, but to have represented the general ethical
level of nomad society, and therefore to owe nothing to
Moses. More often it is completely denied that Moses had
anything to do with it, and the Ethical Decalogue is attributed to much later times and to the influence of the prophets. Superficially the argument on which this view rests is a
very strong one. For in Exod. xxxiv we find another series
of commandments, thirteen in number in our present text,
but apparently once ten in number. These commandments
are of a much more primitive character than those of the
familiar Decalogue of Exod. xx, and they are concerned
with things ritual rather than ethical. Hence they are frequently referred to under the name Ritual Decalogue. Yet
this Ritual Decalogue appears to come from an agricultural
community. It is therefore argued that it must date from a
time later than the Settlement in Palestine, and therefore
from a time later than the days of Moses, yet equally clearly
its more primitive character shows that it must be older
than the Ethical Decalogue.

The fallacy of the argument is in its assumption that the
two Decalogues lie in the course of a single development.
Yet even where the integration of the material into a whole
view is different in many points from that which is presented above, it is widely recognized that Yahwism came
into Israel in two different ways, and that not all the Israelite tribes were with Moses at Sinai. If the reconstruction of
the history presented above is correct, there is no problem
whatever in the ascription of the Ethical Decalogue to

Moses, and it excellently fits into the whole picture. For the Ritual Decalogue stands in the southern document, which represents the special point of view of the tribe of Judah, which was not with the tribes that came out of Egypt to Sinai. If Judah took over its worship of Yahweh from the Kenites by gradual permeation, it would take it over at the primitive level, though it would doubtless in course of time modify its practice somewhat in response to changing circumstances. Its Yahwism might therefore continue to be on a much more primitive level than the Yahwism of the group which Moses led. It knew no great personality comparable with the figure of Moses, and it knew no great experience such as the tribes he led had known.

Let it be remembered that the Covenant of Sinai rested on the emotion of gratitude for the deliverance which had been experienced. And gratitude is a fundamentally ethical emotion. Moreover, when we look back over the recorded life of Moses we are not unprepared to find an ethical quality in his work. When Amos saw the oppression of poor peasants in Israel and denounced it in the name of Yahweh, he was giving expression to ethical religion, as every writer perceives. When Moses was in Egypt and saw his brethren suffering under the oppression of the Egyptians, his soul was as deeply stirred as Amos', and with an emotion which was as truly ethical. But at that stage there was nothing religious about his emotion, and it expressed itself in a fruitless murder. In the experience of his call the divine seal was set on the burning sympathy of Moses' heart, and a religious quality was added to it. That Moses must have brooded long and often on the sufferings of his kinsmen may be reasonably presumed, since his exile was due to that sympathy of his heart for them. It was therefore by no accident that Moses was chosen by Yahweh for the task of leading Israel out of Egypt. He was chosen because he was serviceable, and he was serviceable because of that sympathy of his heart, which was now taken up into the purpose of God, reinforced with a power greater than the merely ethical, and made the vehicle of God's will.

A modern European interpreter of Buddhism, whose sympathy with Buddhism is most marked, says of the Buddha: " Nothing lies farther from his mind than the welfare of others. He seeks his own salvation, and that only." [7] Elsewhere the same writer says, " Egoism is indeed the most coldly calculating foundation for morality which this world offers, but it is also the soundest, the most solid." [8] It is true that he recognizes a secondary compassion for suffering fellow-men, but it is clear that this writer regards egoism as both desirable in itself and fundamental to Buddhism. In the work of Moses we see the antithesis of such a spirit. We see compassion for the sufferings of others leading Moses into exile that mere selfishness might have avoided, and we see God setting His seal on that compassion, and declaring by deeds that that spirit was but the reflexion of His own heart, and could only be effectively expressed when linked with His own power. Here is a message fundamentally and profoundly ethical, yet at the same time essentially religious. It is as truly so as the message of Amos, and so far from ethical religion beginning with the great prophets, it began with the father of prophecy in Israel and with the very beginnings of Yahwism in the group that came from Egypt.

Ample are the reasons, therefore, for expecting the religion Moses established in Israel to be something other than the religion of the Kenites. Whatever Yahweh may have meant to the Kenites, He meant something different to Israel. For Israel saw Him through the experience of the Exodus, and His will was interpreted to her through the great and divinely inspired personality of Moses. From the com-

[7] P. Dahlke, *Buddhist Essays*, translated by Sīlācāra, 1908, p. 130.
[8] *Ibid.*, p. 29.

plex of events associated with the Exodus there flowed theological and ethico-religious consequences for Israel that
were of supreme importance for her whole future development. To find in the Ethical Decalogue, in its original un-
expanded form, the hand of Moses is not to find here some
isolated phenomenon, unrelated to all else we know of
Moses, and unrelated to the rest of his work, but to find
something that belongs naturally to it. The transition from
a primitive decalogue of the type of the Ritual Decalogue
to the Ethical Decalogue was not one that would just happen by itself with the lapse of time. It was brought about
by some dynamic personality, and on every ground the tradition that connects the higher Decalogue with Moses is to
be credited.

That Moses attained speculative monotheism, however,
or attempted to establish it in Israel, is very improbable.
Whether Yahweh was the sole God does not seem to have
arisen at all. He was Israel's deliverer, and must now be
Israel's only God, to whom her undivided loyalty must be
given. In the first of its clauses the Decalogue says, " Thou
shalt have no other gods beside Me." [9] There is no denial of
the reality and existence of other gods here, but only of
their legitimacy for Israel. Yet more than this is really involved in the revelation through Moses and through the
events of the Exodus. For the seeds of monotheism are here
from the beginning, even though the full flower did not
bloom for many years. It is probable that Moab believed
that while other gods might be real enough, Chemosh was
the only god that Moab ought to worship, and Ammon similarly believed that Milkom was its only legitimate god, but
not the only god existing. This kind of monolatry is common enough in the history of religion. But before we assume that this represents the work of Moses on this side,
we need to examine the facts.

[9] Exod. xx. 3.

Yahweh adopted a people that already worshipped another God and claimed them for Himself. It is true that this
was facilitated by the identification of their old God with
Yahweh, so that Moses came to the people saying in effect
much as Paul said to the people of Athens: " Whom therefore ye ignorantly worship, him declare I unto you." [10] In
the same way missionaries in China have equated the Shang
Ti of Chinese religion with the Christian God, and have
adopted the name Shang Ti for God, but filled it with a
new and specifically Christian content. Lying behind the
syncretism of Paul and of modern missionaries is full monotheism, and the recognition that the only God recognizes
as offered unto Him all worship that is pure and sincere.
And lying behind all syncretism is an incipient monotheism, though often it does not get beyond the merest incipi-
ence. But here in Israel we observe that beyond this syncretism there is the recognition that Yahweh's power alone
counts. His hand is manifested in Egypt, not alone amongst
the people He had chosen for Himself, but amongst the
Egyptians. This is not represented as a trial of strength between Yahweh and the Egyptian gods. They do not figure
in the story. Egyptian magicians figure, but their gods are
ignored as an irrelevance. Moreover, all the forces of Nature lie in the hollow of Yahweh's hand, and He can use
them for His purposes as He pleases. This is far more than
the demand that though other gods may be real Israel must
worship Him alone. It is the declaration that though other
gods may exist they are completely negligible. That monotheism is implicit in such a view may be agreed, though its
explicit recognition did not come until very much later.

The Settlement in Palestine was followed by a period of
religious declension and of new syncretism. For the new-
comers were now settled amongst people who practised the
primitive fertility religion which has been above described.

[10] Acts xvii. 23.

One of the features of the fertility cult was an annual festival, at which a man and a woman were chosen to represent the god and his consort. They were married, and their union was supposed to bring about by sympathetic magic the union of the god and goddess represented, and so to promote fertility throughout the community. The festival also represented the death of the god and his resurrection. This was not merely a mime, representing the death of Nature in the winter and rebirth in the spring. It was a ritual designed to bring about that which it represented. The festival was celebrated with much wild licence, and much drinking of wine. Moreover, in the shrines associated with this cult there were sacred prostitutes. To the annual festival there are some direct references in the Old Testament, and in recent years a growing number of allusions to it have been found by some scholars. To other aspects of the cult, and in particular to its drinking and sacred prostitution, there are plenty of references in the Bible. It should be remembered that these were part of the very religion, and due to the character of the religion itself. It was an agricultural religion, designed to serve a community engaged in agriculture and viticulture, and it believed that these practices were not alone potent to produce the fertility that was so supremely desired, but necessary to that fertility.

When the Israelites came into the land and settled beside the Canaanites and shared their pursuits, they also shared with them the religious technique associated with them. They found shrines in being, and at these they worshipped along with their Canaanite neighbours. And gradually there was a new syncretism, a fusion of the high religion which Moses had set before them, and the fertility religion of the Canaanites. The Israelites took over the Canaanite term for their god, Baal, or Lord, and followed the rites of their neighbours. Just as Moses had said Yahweh is really the same as El Shaddai, so now men supposed He was really the same as Baal. But whereas the syncretism of Moses had facilitated the raising of religion to a higher level, this syncretism facilitated its debasement to the level of Canaanite religion. If challenged men would have professed that they were really worshipping Yahweh all the time, yet in practice there was commonly little to distinguish their religion from that of their neighbours.

Yet it must not be supposed that this was any simple and uninterrupted process. Israel was always conscious that Yahweh was its national God, and while there were periods in which little emphasis was placed on this, and His distinction from the Baals became blurred, in times of crisis it was always to the national God that they looked, and whenever there was conflict Yahweh was set over against the Baals in sharp antithesis. Thus when Gideon came forth to take the lead against Midian, the first thing he did was to break down the Baal altar at which his own people were worshipping, and to erect a Yahweh altar. When Deborah roused the people against Sisera and hymned their triumph, she sang not of the help the local Baals had given, but of the help Yahweh had given. Behind all the syncretism there was a consciousness that Yahweh was not really Baal.

Moreover, it must not be forgotten that the Yahwism of Judah was more primitive than the Yahwism Moses had established, so that its fusion with the indigenous religion in the south would be still less hampered. Again, the northern tribes whose settlement took place in the Amarna age seem to have had no associated Yahweh-worshipping Kenites with them, nor yet to have shared in the experience of Sinai. Hence there is no reason to suppose that they were Yahweh worshippers at all when they first came into the land. When Deborah gathered together the kindred Israelite tribes from north and south of the Vale of Esdraelon, she did so in the name of Yahweh, whose prophetess she was, and Yahweh, who had once delivered some of these tribes from Egypt, now delivered them all from Sisera and took them all for His people. It may well be that this great occasion, which brought so many tribes into a common action for the first time, extended the recognition of Yahweh as the God of all the confederate tribes. Moreover, we know that the sanctuary of Dan, which became one of the most famous in northern Israel, had for its first Israelite priest a Levite, grandson of Moses, who had been the private priest of a Yahweh-worshipping household in Ephraim.

Further, we know that later a priest of the family of Eli, who presided at the shrine of Yahweh in the Ephraimite city of Shiloh, fled to David and accompanied him in his exile and outlawry, and some years later both this priest and the Shiloh Ark, which had been a notable Ephraimite religious symbol from the days of Moses, were installed in Jerusalem. What impetus of the higher Yahwism of Moses still remained in Ephraim, therefore, was communicated in some degree both to the tribes north of Ephraim and to those in the south.

In such a situation, whatever implicit monotheism there was in the religion of Moses became lost, and Yahweh was not even the only God worshipped within the borders of Israel, either in the narrower sense of the tribes that had been with Moses, or in the wider sense of the kindred tribes that had entered the land in the two waves. Of the reality of the gods of the surrounding peoples there was not the slightest question, and when David was forced to flee abroad from the pursuit of Saul, he reproached the king by saying that this was tantamount to forcing him to serve other gods.

It is true that in the time of Elijah there was staged the great contest between Yahweh and Baal. But here it would seem that it was the Tyrian Baal, whose worship was being promoted in the land under the queen's influence, to threaten the existence of Yahweh as the God of Israel. What Elijah desired to re-establish was that Yahweh was the God for Israel. He was not concerned to eliminate the worship of this Melkart from Tyre. But in order to establish that Yahweh was the God for Israel, he sought to make it clear that the God who had brought Israel out of Egypt was more powerful in Israel than any other god. It was still not monotheism, but it revived incipient monotheism by its demonstration that Yahweh alone counted. His power so greatly exceeded Melkart's that so far as Israel was concerned Melkart was utterly negligible. Elijah's message was not so much that Israel should not worship Melkart because Melkart was not her god, but that Israel should not worship Melkart because Melkart was not worth worshipping. That is a very important step on the way to monotheism.

With the eighth century prophets implicit monotheism becomes increasingly explicit. They emphasize Yahweh's sole control of the natural universe. " For lo, He that formeth the mountains, and createth the wind, and declareth unto man what is His thought, that maketh the morning and darkness, and treadeth upon the high places of the earth; Yahweh, the God of hosts, is His name." [11] " He that maketh the Pleiades and Orion, and turneth deep darkness into the morning, and maketh the day dark with night; that calleth for the waters of the sea, and poureth them out upon the face of the earth; Yahweh is His name." [12] This emphasis on Yahweh's control of universal forces implies the uniqueness of His godhead. There is no categorical denial of the existence of other gods, but there is the clear implication that there can be no other God such as He. He is not merely Israel's God, or *primus inter pares* among the gods, but set in His uniqueness far above all.

This is still further emphasized by the conception of Yahweh's control of history. His interests are not confined to Israel. The migrations of other peoples are equally con-

[11] Amos iv. 13.   [12] Amos v. 8.

trolled by Him. " Have not I brought up Israel out of the land of Egypt, and the Philistines from Caphtor, and the Syrians from Kir? " [13] Moreover, His moral judgements are exercised upon all peoples. He visits punishment upon any nation for offences against humanity, even where Israel is not concerned. None of this implies, however, any weakening of the sense that Israel is Yahweh's special people. " You only have I known of all the families of the earth," declares Amos,[14] where it is clear that " known " means " recognized as my own special people."

Isaiah carried his view of the divine control of history to the length of finding in Assyria the rod of Yahweh's anger, raised up by God to serve His purposes, yet equally serving the purposes of her own heart, and calling down on herself divine judgement because of the self-vaunting spirit with which she carried out her evil purposes. Similarly in the following century the prophets could regard other nations as involuntarily obeying the divine behests when they came against Israel. " I will call all the families of the kingdoms of the north, saith Yahweh; and they shall come, and they shall set every one his throne at the entering of the gates of Jerusalem." [15] " Lo, I will bring a nation upon you from far, O house of Israel, saith Yahweh." [16] " For lo, I raise up the Chaldaeans, that bitter and hasty nation." [17]

Quite clearly in these and in many other passages that could be cited, the prophets of the eighth and seventh centuries B.C. thought of Yahweh as much more than the God of Israel. He has become completely transcendent, far above all principalities and powers, dominant in the world of Nature, dominant in history, and as completely dominant over any other gods that may exist as He is over men everywhere.

---

[13] Amos ix. 7.   [16] Jer. v. 15.
[14] Amos iii. 2.   [17] Hab. i. 6.
[15] Jer. i. 15.

His power is so completely supreme that as against Him all other power can be ignored. While this is not speculative monotheism, it approaches very near to it, and becomes a practical monotheism.

It is not until we come to Deutero-Isaiah that full and explicit monotheism is attained.[18] Here the reality of other gods, and not merely their power, is challenged. " Thus saith Yahweh, the King of Israel, and His redeemer, Yahweh of hosts: I am the first and I am the last; and beside Me there is no God." [19] Familiar is this prophet's ridicule of idols, and his scorn for the man who makes an idol of one part of a tree, and with another part kindles a fire to warm himself. It is frequently said in answer to the critic of idol-worship that no one really worships an idol. The idol is to him but a symbol of the deity he worships, or it is thought of as but housing the spirit he trusts in. This is to miss the whole point of Deutero-Isaiah's polemic. What he says is that there is no reality corresponding to these symbols, since there is no God but Yahweh. Hence there is no spirit inhabiting the piece of wood. It is merely a piece of wood. Deutero-Isaiah does not suppose the worshipper is *ex professo* worshipping the idol. He vainly imagines he is worshipping a god, but the god is non-existent, and his idol therefore mocks him. There is nothing but the idol for him to worship. This is clearly formulated and speculative monotheism. It recognizes Yahweh as not alone the controller of Nature and the Lord of history. It proclaims Him to be the sole God, and therefore the only rightful object of worship

[18] In 1 Kings viii. 60 and 2 Kings xix. 15, 20, explicit monotheism is attributed to Solomon and Hezekiah respectively. The prayer of Solomon bears marks of the influence of Deuteronomy, and is probably to be attributed to the Deuteronomic editor of the books of Kings, who may also be responsible for the form of Hezekiah's prayer. The books of Kings cannot have reached their present form before the age of Deutero-Isaiah, since the last event they record is to be dated in 561 B.C. Both of these passages may therefore reflect the influence of Deutero-Isaiah's teaching.

[19] Isa. xliv. 6.

by all His creatures. It is by no accident that the full corollaries of monotheism appear in Deutero-Isaiah, and at these
corollaries we shall have to look more closely below.

Meanwhile, we may observe that this rapid review of the
growth of monotheism in Israel suffices to indicate the process by which Israel attained it. The quest for unity by the
human mind does not always follow the same path. In
Greece the philosophers, in their attempts to reduce to
unity the welter of gods and goddesses, moved in the direction of an abstract and impersonal monotheism. They did
not move through monarchic theism to the faith in a single
personal God, but from the multiplicity of gods back to the
divine principle operative in them all. Hence they attained
the abstract concept of deity as their goal. In India, on the
other hand, the quest for unity always led in the direction
of pantheism. It took men behind and above all the gods to
the concept of Rita, or Order, of which all the gods were
but manifestations. But it found the same ultimate reality
behind all phenomena, and not alone behind the gods, so
that all that is, whether personal or impersonal, is but the
manifestation of this ultimate reality. Hence it led on to
pantheism. This reality, lying behind all things, is indeed
one, and in it alone all things exist; on the other hand it ex-
ists alone in them, for apart from its self-manifestation it is
not. But in Israel the urge for unity was not speculative,
but practical, and it never threatened the personality of
God. It was not an effort to get behind Yahweh, and Chemosh, and Marduk, to some thing or some One who should
transcend them all. It was the gradual perception that He
who had led Israel out of Egypt, and who unveiled His
character to Israel, was alone the God of all the earth. He
could not be transcended. Israel's monotheism came therefore through the progressive perception of the character
and being of the God she worshipped. Never was He a pale
abstraction, but an intensely personal Being, with a will

and a character. Of the profoundest importance has it been to us that Christian monotheism was reached along this path. For it could never be an arid monotheism. Neither Greek monotheism, as developed by her philosophers, nor Indian pantheism could have led to the worship of the God and Father of our Lord Jesus Christ. But Israelite monotheism was as truly personal as our own.

VI. THE SIGNIFICANCE OF PROPHECY [1]

ONE OF THE chief glories of Israel was her succession of prophets. In New Testament times they appear to have been regarded in Christian circles as primarily men who foretold the advent and the work of Christ. In later times there have been Christian circles which regarded them as primarily men who foretold the details of human history to the end of time. Representatives of these circles are still found, to exercise their skill in reading into the ancient prophecies the happenings of our day, and then to try to pierce the secrets of the future. The study of the history of this kind of interpretation is somewhat discouraging. It discloses the fact that widely different contemporary happenings in many ages have been read back into the same texts, and interpreters have claimed with just as much, or as little, justification that they were specific prophecies of these happenings. Similarly these interpreters have essayed the prediction of the future course of events on the basis of the same texts on which their modern disciples rest, only to have their predictions belied by events with unfailing regularity. There is nothing specifically Christian about this type of study of the prophets, whose only merit is that it provides a hobby for long evenings. It has been so consistently disowned by events that it can lay no claim to respect. When Moses declared that Yahweh had chosen Israel and would deliver her from Egypt, events responded to his word. But here events consistently refuse to respond to a word which can claim no higher source than human curiosity and human ingenuity.

1 Cf. " The Nature of Prophecy in the Light of Recent Study," *Harvard Theological Review*, 38, 1945, pp. 1–38.

The writer recalls that in 1922 a missionary in China wrote to a Shanghai paper to announce the imminence of a great war, in which the Russian armies would march into Palestine, there to be met by British forces at Armageddon, as the prelude to the millennial reign of Christ, which would begin in May, 1923. A few months later he amended his calculations, and pushed the date on a few months to the autumn of that year, only to be mocked still by events. Early in 1940 the writer was assured by an ardent member of the same school of exegesis that the Scriptures showed infallibly that in that year Russia was to enter the war on the German side, together with Turkey. But again, as always, the hard facts of history exposed the folly of the whole method of interpretation.

Against all such schemes of interpretation there has been a widespread reaction in modern times. The prophets have become human figures in human situations, and have been studied in the setting of their times. The predictive element in their work has been denied or minimized, and they have been hailed as preachers of righteousness, social reformers or statesmen. While it is not here pretended that this is by any means a complete representation of their significance, it is undeniable that the lines of study indicated brought a new era in the study of the prophets, and one of great fruitfulness. To see them as historical persons in historical situations is of great value, though something more is needed for their full understanding. That they were preachers of righteousness, social reformers and statesmen, may be in some measure true, but these functions were only incidental to their real mission. On the other hand, prediction seems to have been rather more fundamental to their mission. When the book of Deuteronomy lays down a canon for distinguishing the true prophet from the false, it declares that he whose prediction is fulfilled can alone be accepted. It is true that elsewhere in the same book it is said that the fulfilment of the prediction is not enough, and that it must be reinforced by the test of loyalty to Yahweh. But both passages take it for granted that the prophet is one who predicts. Similarly Deutero-Isaiah points to the fulfilment of prophecy as the basis of trust in the message of hope which he brings.

The prophets first come conspicuously before us at the time of the founding of the monarchy in Israel. The term " prophet," or " prophetess," is used of several individuals of more ancient days, and it is not necessary to suppose that prophecy first began in the days of Samuel. There are passages in which Moses is called a prophet. In some modern studies of prophecy he receives but scanty notice, but Marti's observation that " he is only rightly understood when he is conceived as a prophet " [2] shows more penetration. Balaam is a prophet; Deborah is a prophetess. Moreover we learn from an Egyptian text of Syrian prophets in days roughly contemporary with the prophet Samuel, while in the Bible we learn of prophets of the Tyrian Baal in the time of Elijah. The prophet was not, therefore, an exclusively Israelite figure. He comes out of a wider background, wider, indeed, than has yet been indicated, and it has been conjectured by Jacobi that prophecy of the type that is found in Israel took its rise in Asia Minor, and spread from there to Syria and to Greece. But only Israelite prophecy became of enduring significance to the world. For its true understanding, therefore, we need to look for some quality which belonged to it alone.

Much modern study has emphasized the ecstatic nature of prophecy. The term has been criticized as not very appropriate, but it has become too well established to be eas-

[2] *The Religion of the Old Testament,* translated by Bienemann, 1908, pp. 63 f.

ily dislodged. It has reference to the frenzied abandon which frequently marked the prophets, whether Israelite or non-Israelite, whether of Yahweh or of Baal. When Saul came to Samuel at Ramah, Samuel anointed him and told him that Yahweh willed that he should take the lead in Israel to deliver the people from the Philistines. He gave him various signs, and amongst them was the prediction that he would meet a band of prophets coming down from Gibeah, and that the spirit of Yahweh would come upon him, and he would become another man. When Saul met these prophets, they were playing musical instruments and working themselves up to a state of extreme nervous excitement, which became contagious, and caught up Saul into its abandon. On another occasion we read of Saul being similarly caught up, and rolling on the ground naked all night. It is clear that this kind of behaviour was regarded as characteristic of the prophets, for it prompted the taunting question, " Is Saul also among the prophets? "

In the time of Elijah the Baal prophets who were assembled on Mount Carmel acted in yet stranger ways, and danced about and gashed themselves with knives till the blood flowed freely. Their complete insensitiveness to pain was ascribed to their possession by the divine Spirit.

Within the Old Testament there is a good deal of evidence, which has often been collected, to show that not merely in its origin, but through all its history, there was a strain of abnormality in prophecy, and the prophet seems always to have been a man who was subject to unusual psychological experiences. This has given rise to the view that this kind of ecstatic experience was of the *esse* of prophecy, and that every oracle was accompanied by something in the nature of a fit as its authentication to both speaker and hearer. This seems to be going beyond the evidence. Nevertheless, it is undeniable that the prophet's actions were often not rationally controlled, but were governed by an irresistible constraint laid upon him, and were such as we should unhesitatingly describe as the acts of a madman if we witnessed them to-day.

It is not in the form of these actions, however, that the significance of prophecy is to be sought. Many of these strange actions were themselves prophecies. They were not so much the authentication of uttered oracles as acted oracles. For the Hebrew did not distinguish between word and act so sharply as we do. A common term may be translated *word* or *deed*, and the acted prophecy may convey just as truly the word of God as the spoken oracle. Neither in the form of its acted nor in that of its spoken oracles is the essential significance of prophecy to be sought.

There are, indeed, many varieties of prophets in the Old Testament. Some are called *seers*, and there are two different terms which are translated *seer*. By some it has been supposed that these originally represented men with distinguishable functions, but it seems more probable that the two terms come from the two distinct strands in the Hebrew language, the Aramaic and the Canaanite, and that no difference of function is indicated. It seems more likely that the *seer* was originally distinct from the *nabi'*, whose title is the word ordinarily rendered *prophet* in the Bible. It is sometimes supposed that the *seer* was non-ecstatic and the *nabi'* ecstatic, the *seer* solitary and the *nabi'* gregarious, the *seer* waiting to be consulted and the *nabi'* taking the initiative in delivering his oracles. All of these neat divisions break down. They rest on a contrast between Samuel at the Ramah shrine and the group of prophets whom Saul met on leaving him. Yet in that very narrative we find that while Saul goes to consult Samuel about the lost asses, Samuel takes the initiative in anointing Saul and summoning him to the leadership of Israel. Elijah is a characteristic *nabi'*, yet he is almost invariably a solitary figure. When Ahijah incites Jeroboam to disrupt the kingdom we must declare him, by the above classification, a *nabi'*, yet when Jeroboam sends his wife to inquire if their child shall recover from a sickness, we must declare him a *seer*. Hard and fast lines clearly cannot be drawn, and it seems safer to recognize that within the general concept of prophet the Old Testament presents us with men who engaged in many varieties of activity.

There were individual prophets who were consulted about private matters, either in their own homes, as in the case of Elisha when consulted by Naaman, or at a shrine, as in the case of Samuel at Ramah. The king seems to have maintained at court a royal seer, as David did Gad, or to have consulted about national problems some individual prophet, as Jehoram and Jehoshaphat consulted Elisha. On the other hand the initiative might be taken by an individual prophet, as by Nathan when he waylaid David to rebuke him for his adultery with Bathsheba, and as by the unnamed prophet who waylaid Ahab to rebuke him for his pact with the defeated Syrian king. At other times we find bands of prophets residing at some given spot, such as Jericho, or Bethel, or Gilgal, or maintained at court, as in the case of the Baal prophets whom Jezebel maintained, or the four hundred whom Ahab consulted before the battle of Ramoth-gilead, or roving the countryside, as in the case of the prophets whom Saul met immediately after Samuel had privately anointed him.

In recent years attention has been drawn to the many passages which associate prophets with shrines, and especially to passages which mention prophets and priests in the same breath in connexion with a sanctuary. This would suggest that the prophets had a recognized place in the cultus, and that so far from prophets and priests being opposed types, as is so often supposed, the one being the guardians of the cultus and the other its enemies, they were both cultic officials.[3] Their function was, of course, different, and it is probable that they were recruited quite differently, and were connected with the shrines in quite different ways. The writer is not convinced that the prophets were resident officials attached to particular shrines. The guardianship of the shrine was a specifically priestly function. But the prophet, in virtue of his office, could present himself at a shrine, and his recognized status as a sacred person gave him official standing there. Amos could appear at the royal shrine at Bethel and exercise there his prophetic function. It was not the fact that he was not on the staff of the Bethel sanctuary which got him into trouble, but the character of his prophetic message.

There is much evidence in the Old Testament of an inner cleavage in the ranks of the prophets. Each side declared that the prophets on the other side were false prophets. This cleavage first comes before us in the time of Ahab, when Micaiah alone opposed the battle with the Syrians, while all the other prophets urged the king on to the fatal adventure. It persists through all the period of the pre-exilic prophets. The canonical prophets were opposed by others who supported all the policies they opposed, and who claimed that they were speaking in the name of Yahweh just as much as they themselves did. It is sometimes supposed that the true prophets were non-professional and the false professional, or the true prophets non-ecstatic and the false ecstatic, but no such simple division will suffice. The difference between false and true belongs to the realm of the spirit, and cannot be established by any external or mechanical test. " In externals," says Skinner, " there was nothing to distinguish the one kind of prophet from the other." [4]

3 Cf. A. R. Johnson, *The Cultic Prophet in Ancient Israel*, 1944.
4 *Prophecy and Religion*, 1922, p. 188.

It is not infrequently suggested that the difference is that the false prophets were prophets of weal, while the true prophets were prophets of woe. There is some superficial justification for this, since it frequently happens that the true prophets are the heralds of doom, while their opponents prophesied smooth things. Yet by this test Deutero-Isaiah would have to be set down as a false prophet, and if Moses is correctly reckoned a prophet his promise of deliverance would have to be set down as false. Hence we are once more thrown back to seek some more satisfying distinction.

Mowinckel has argued that the great pre-exilic prophets claimed to have the word of God, and that they despised the spirit as the organ of revelation. The prophets who were opposed to them were possessed by the spirit, and since the Hebrew word for *spirit* means also *wind*, the true prophets regarded this as mere windiness, lacking the intelligible content of the word, which was mediated through them. It is highly doubtful if this represents any sounder a distinction. It is quite improbable that the true prophets would have repudiated the idea that the spirit of God was the source of their inspiration, and equally improbable that the false prophets would have allowed that they had not the word of God. Both sides claimed a like inspiration and a like mission.

Again, it is sometimes supposed that it was a matter of sincerity or fraud. Sometimes, indeed, a charge of insincerity is levelled, and men are said to utter prophecies dictated by the fee they receive, or to steal one another's oracles. But insincerity is not always charged against them, nor is insincerity easily or infallibly detected. That many of the oracles of the false prophets were dictated by wishful thinking may well be true, but wishful thinking may arise more from self-deception than from insincerity. In the case of the prophets who opposed Micaiah, it is agreed by Micaiah that they are utterly sincere. He declares that they are making false promises in the name of Yahweh, because they are not really attuned to His spirit, and that Yahweh is actually using the false hopes they are arousing to serve His own purpose. Yet in spite of their acknowledged sincerity, there is a measure of condemnation implied, and the implication is resented by the false prophets. For it is recognized that they ought to be attuned to the spirit of Yahweh, and ought not to be able to be misled by any lying spirit.

Where, then, is the real essence of prophecy to be sought? It is to be sought in the inner recesses of the spirit, and in the relation of the prophet and his word to God. The mission of the prophet was to be an extension of the divine personality, and the utterer of a word which was not his but God's. Israelite and non-Israelite, true and false, prophets alike claimed to be such extensions of the divine personality, but the truth or falsity of their prophecy depended on the measure of their attunement to the spirit of God. Their word came through the organ of their personality, but in so far as it was true prophecy it did not arise merely from that personality, but from God, while in so far as it was false prophecy it did not really issue from God, but had no deeper source than their own spirit, or some lying spirit that possessed them.

In Exod. vii. 1 we read: " And Yahweh said unto Moses, See, I have made thee a god to Pharaoh: and Aaron thy brother shall be thy prophet." There is another passage, where the actual word *prophet* is not used, but where the same prophetic relationship would seem to be in mind. This is Exod. iv. 15 f., where we read: " Thou shalt speak unto him [Aaron], and put the words in his mouth: and I will be with thy mouth, and with his mouth, and will teach you what ye shall say. And he shall be thy spokesman [lit., he shall speak for thee] unto the people: and it shall come to pass, that he shall be to thee a mouth, and thou shalt

be to him as God." These passages are important evidence
for the conception of the function of the prophet, and they
clearly conceive the prophet as the mouthpiece of God. Similarly, in Jer. xv. 19 we find: " If thou take forth the precious from the vile, thou shalt be as my mouth."

Resort is sometimes had to the etymological argument to
establish the essence of prophecy. Here it is sometimes
claimed that the word *nabi'*, or prophet, means *an ecstatic*.
It is very improbable that this is true. That the associated
verbal root denotes wild and uncontrolled behaviour is undeniable, for it is used of Saul, when he hurled a javelin at
David. But this meaning appears to be secondary. The
verbal form is a denominative from the noun *nabi'*, and it
means *to behave like a prophet;* and since ecstatic behaviour was admittedly a common characteristic of prophets, it
came to have this secondary meaning. Moreover, if *nabi'*
did have the etymological meaning of *ecstatic*, it could not
help us to understand the essence of prophecy, since it
would belong merely to its outward expression, and not to
its inner quality, or would direct us rather to the psychol-
ogy than the metaphysic of prophecy. It is more likely,
however, that the word *nabi'* comes from a root meaning
to call, to announce. By some it is then taken to be active
in form, and to mean *speaker,* while others, and amongst
them Albright, take it to be passive, and to mean *called.*
The passive sense is the more usual for words of this form,
and in any case it must mean something more than *speaker.*
We should have to supply the further idea of *one who speaks
another's message,* and that seems to depend on a reading
back of the function of the *nabi'* into the etymology. The
etymological argument does not therefore get us very far,
and is not really conclusive.

That the prophet is fundamentally one who speaks a
message not his own, but God's, has been already said. That
Albright is right in finding the necessity of a call in true

prophecy is also certain. For beyond any evidence that etymology may provide, there is ample evidence in the Old
Testament. The prophet is not one who elects to prophesy,
but one who is inescapably constrained to prophesy. Or at
least, the true prophet is. How non-Israelite prophets were
recruited we do not know; nor are we informed how the
members of the prophetic guilds mentioned in the Old
Testament were recruited. But we are given an account of
the call of so many of the prophets who are unmistakably
set forth as true prophets that we are justified in finding the
call to be an essential of true prophecy. And that implies
that the prophet's relation to God is all-important. In his
call the prophet knew God in the immediacy of experience,
and felt an imperious constraint laid upon him. From that
experience he came forth with the consciousness that he
was an extension of the divine personality. Sometimes he
could use the third person when speaking of Yahweh, but
at other times he could pass over to the first person. His
word was so directly God's word that God could be thought
of as uttering the words through his mouth.

" By a prophet Yahweh brought Israel up out of Egypt,"
said Hosea,[5] thus clearly hailing Moses as a prophet. And if
the true prophet was one who was called by God to be the
extension of His personality and the mouthpiece of His
word, there is no Old Testament character who can more
appropriately be called a prophet. For the work of Moses
was utterly and altogether prophetic. Of his call we have a
familiar account, and it shows that he tried to resist the call,
and to evade its constraint by the plea of his unfitness for
his mission.

It has been already said that in some passages Samuel is
called a seer. In his childhood he is said to have been dedicated to the service of the shrine by his parents, though it is
not clear for what category of service he was to be trained.

[5] Hos. xii. 13 (Heb. 14).

We have, however, in one of the narratives dealing with his childhood an account of a numinous experience Samuel had as he lay in the shrine beside the Ark one night. It is clear that this is regarded as having relevance not alone to an *ad hoc* message to Eli, but to the prophetic career of Samuel. The story is prefaced with the remark that " the word of Yahweh was rare in those days; there was no open vision," [6] and it closes with the observation that " all Israel from Dan even unto Beer-sheba knew that Samuel was established to be a prophet of Yahweh." [7] What marked him out to be a prophet was that Yahweh's word came to him by the divine initiative, and that in his childhood the gentle constraint of God, that continued until it found its response, claimed him for the office.

Of the call of Amos we have no detailed account, but he makes it very clear that he had such an experience, and that it laid an utterly irresistible constraint upon him. " The lion hath roared, who will not fear? The Lord Yahweh hath spoken, who can but prophesy? " he said.[8] And again, " I was no prophet, neither was i a prophet's son; but I was an herdman, and a dresser of sycamore trees: and Yahweh took me from following the flock, and Yahweh said unto me, Go, prophesy unto My people Israel." [9] This passage is frequently rendered by present tenses, and understood to be a denial of prophetic status by Amos, and it is sometimes stated, with complete inaccuracy, that the words can only be so rendered. Actually, the ordinary rendering of the English Version, followed above, is the more natural rendering, and in closer accord with the normal usage of the Hebrew tense of the clause " and Yahweh took me." Moreover, the passage Amos iii. 7 is the clearest evidence that Amos did not really repudiate the title of prophet: " Surely the Lord Yahweh will do nothing, but He revealeth His secret unto His servants the prophets." What Amos is really saying to Amaziah in the passage that refers to his call is that he is not prophesying for reward, as Amaziah bitingly suggests, but because the constraint of Yahweh, imperious and irresistible, had been laid upon him. The authentication of his prophetic status is his call.

One of the most familiar passages in the Old Testament records the call of Isaiah. Confronted with the vision of God in the Temple, he is at once conscious of the overwhelming holiness of God and of his own uncleanness. Mingled trembling and elation fill his soul, but with the greater emphasis on the trembling, until his lips are touched with a live coal from the heavenly altar, and his sin cleansed by its burning touch. And when he hears the voice saying, " Whom shall I send? " he responds, " Here am I; send me." That there is here no effort to escape the call, no pleading of unsuitability, does not alter the fact that Isaiah is a prophet by divine constraint. Just as Israel dedicated herself to Yahweh at Sinai in response to the salvation wherewith Yahweh had saved her from Egypt, so Isaiah consecrates himself to the prophetic service because Yahweh had chosen him by that act of cleansing. He could not withhold from His service the heart that had been cleansed, or the lips that had known the touch of the purifying coal. Here, as everywhere in the true and higher prophecy, the initiative is with God.

Even more compelling was the call of Jeremiah. A modern writer, who traces prophetic inspiration to no deeper source than the prophet's own heart, observes: " The manner in which Jeremiah expresses his inspiration is illustrative of the general prophetic habit to sublimate the facts of their inspiration. This deliberate subtilization of inspirational power . . . tends to cover up the commonplace nature of inspiration, or, at any rate, to conceal the prophet's own psychological ignorance of the source of his prophetic calling." [10] That the fount of Jeremiah's inspiration was not in himself is made clear by his repeated efforts to get away from his prophetic calling. When the constraint was first laid upon him, he tried to escape it by the plea of his youth and inexperience. Later, when he felt that he had been let down by God, and accused God of having seduced him into this ministry, and of having overpowered him by His might, he vowed that he would never prophesy again. But immediately he felt a fire burning in his bones and a constraint from within that swept him into prophecy. Here is a man who was conscious that the divine hand had been laid upon him, to claim him for the prophetic office, and who, least of all men, was a prophet because he desired to be.

The call of Hosea was of a very different kind. There are some who believe that the statement that " when Yahweh spake at first by Hosea, Yahweh said unto Hosea, Go, take unto thee a wife of whoredom and children of whoredom," [11] represents a reading back of what later became clear into an assumed divine purpose at the beginning. They suppose that Hosea had no idea when he married Gomer that she was anything but a chaste woman. Others believe that Gomer was a Temple prostitute, and that Hosea, who loathed with all his soul the fertility cult and all its practices, felt an irresistible constraint to marry her. The constraint laid upon him was not, in the first place, a constraint to speak, but a constraint to act. Yet it came to him as a constraint of God, and the experience to which it led became the medium of the word of God.

The first experience of the divine constraint is unique in its impression, because it is the first. Yet it is not to be supposed that once the call was received and accepted, a mere technique would suffice for the future. The relationship of the call must persist in true prophecy. The prophet must

[10] Ackerman, *Anglican Theological Review,* iv, 1921–1922, p. 102.
[11] Hos. i. 2.

1 of consecrated spirit, who lives in close in-
God, and who feels the constraint of God laid
n the immediacy of his fellowship.

.ngs xiii we have the story of the unnamed prophet
.urneyed from Judah to Bethel, and there uttered a
.necy and then set out to return. When the king in-
.d him to a meal, he declined, pleading " it was charged
.ie by the word of Yahweh, saying, Thou shalt eat no bread,
nor drink water, neither return by the way that thou cam-
est." But when an old prophet of Bethel followed him and
invited him to return, and supported his invitation by a lying story of a divine oracle, superseding the one on which
the visitor relied, he turned back with him. As they sat at
table the old prophet became the medium of another message, this time a genuine divine oracle, promising the other
death for listening to the old prophet's deceptive word. It is
interesting to observe that there is less condemnation of the
liar than of his victim, and a strange irony that the announcement of the punishment should come through the
lips of the deceiver. It is also interesting to find that the
lying prophet could shortly after become the medium of a
genuine oracle, which was duly fulfilled. To many readers
it has seemed unjust that the younger prophet should be
condemned and should reap such dire punishment, when
he obviously quite sincerely believed the false word of the
other. Yet that is to miss the whole essence of prophecy.
The younger prophet had, by his own statement, received a
direct message from God, and he allowed that to be over-
ridden by a message received through another. In the nature of the case, he could not have the same inner certainty
of the authenticity of the indirect word as of the direct, and
for the man who, in the immediacy of his fellowship with
God, has known the certainty of the divine word in his own
inner consciousness, to defer to any message inconsistent
with it on less immediate authentication is disobedience.

The prophet was, then, a man who was conscious of the presence of God, and sensitive to the message of God. He was a true prophet in the measure in which he was the medium of God's message, and that was the measure in which he was attuned to the spirit of God. That the difference between true and false was no simple one is evidenced by the preceding story, where the same man appears as both false and true prophet. Clearly the lying prophet, who uttered a word which he knew was out of his own heart alone, was a false prophet. His insincerity of spirit made him, for the time being at any rate, a wholly false prophet. But the wholly true prophet, who was absolutely attuned to the spirit of God, is hard to find, and even amongst the true prophets, truth is a matter of degree. Jeremiah, who most of all prophets felt the divine constraint laid upon him, found his predictions unfulfilled, and was perplexed to understand why. He felt that God had deceived him, and made sport of him, had driven him to speak and had then gone back on him. He prophesied a doom which did not fall. At first he thought it would fall at the hand of the Scythians, and then twenty years later he thought it was about to fall by the hand of Nebuchadrezzar. And neither time did it fall. That Jeremiah was not uttering wishful thoughts is clear. For his heart was wrung with the words that he uttered, and he longed to be spared the task that was so imperiously laid upon him. Yet equally clearly, he was not perfectly attuned to the spirit of God. Nevertheless the sequel showed that the measure of his attunement was far greater than the measure of his discordance. For yet another twenty years passed, and the doom fell with a ruthless severity that showed that Jeremiah's word had been fundamentally true after all. He had seen the character of God, and in its light he had seen all the moral and social and spiritual evil of his day. And that evil had weighed upon his soul with irresistible constraint, a constraint which was rightly felt to be a divine constraint, since it was born not so much of the things he saw around him as of the contact with God, in whose light he saw them. God was moving in his soul, and stirring him to prophesy. Yet, though he shared the anguish of God's spirit at what he saw, he did not share the patience of God, or realize how long was the opportunity still left to Israel to turn from her way to the way of God.

Even in true prophecy, therefore, human and divine factors are interwoven. For the message came through the organ of the personality of the prophet. The older view of prophecy, which regarded it as wholly of God, made the prophet a negligible factor in the prophecy, of no more importance to the content of the message than a wireless transmitting set is to the content of the broadcast word. Many moderns have swept over to the opposite view, and have regarded prophecy as a purely human process. They have traced the prophet's word no further than to himself, and have dissolved all revelation into discovery. In their hands the story of prophecy has become the story of men's interest in men, or of their search after a God who may or may not exist, but who is at best relevant only as the goal of the process, and not as an agent. In their hands instead of the prophet being a negligible factor in prophecy, God has become the negligible factor. Neither of these views seems to be sustained by the study of Old Testament prophecy. The human factors are writ large in all the story. Even the literary style in which the oracles are couched bears the marks of the prophet's individuality. Yet equally certainly, the divine factors are writ large in all the story. For if the essence of prophecy is found in the divine call to be the medium of the divine word, received in the immediacy of a living experience of God, and in the touch of God's spirit on the prophet's spirit, then the uniqueness of Israelite prophecy lies in the unique richness of the experience of God, and the unique intimacy of the fellowship with God, enjoyed by Israel's prophets. The measure of that experience and intimacy was the measure of the prophet's spiritual capacity to enjoy it, and of his willingness to respond to it, yet it was not born of that capacity and willingness, but only conditioned by it. It was born of God, who can never be ignored in any true understanding of prophecy. That is why all pictures of the Old Testament prophets as statesmen and social reformers are inadequate. They are messengers of God, extensions of the divine personality, bearing a word which has relevance to statesmanship and social life, indeed, but also to every other side of man's life. For God is not indifferent to any side of man's life, and His message concerns it all.

It is important to realize that the profound and vital experience which mediated the message of God might be outwardly simple and commonplace. When Isaiah received his call the vision which he saw was doubtless seen by him alone, and the voice he heard fell on no other ear, just as when Saul of Tarsus had his great experience on the Damascus road, it was his alone, and those who were with him neither saw what he saw nor heard what he heard. In the simplicity and the profundity of worship, amongst all the Temple crowd, Isaiah knew a solitary experience which turned him into the prophet of God.

Sometimes a chance sight or sound, arising out of some quite commonplace experience, became the medium of a message to the prophet. An almond tree in blossom, a seething pot set over a rough fireplace, a potter at his wheel, two baskets of figs, and similar common sights could stir in Jeremiah's soul a message which he was sure was of God. There was nothing in the almond blossom of itself to dictate a message of God's awakening to activity in human affairs, nothing in the seething pot of itself to speak of the coming doom, nothing in the potter's wheel to compel thoughts of

God, and nothing in the figs to carry the thought to the exiles and those they had left behind. The prophet was sure
that it was God who was carrying his thought from the
thing he saw to the message that filled his mind.

Sometimes the message came through the things the
prophet suffered, and came, perhaps, not in a swift flash of
illumination, but by the gradual penetration of what God
was saying to him by the experience. Hosea's message was
found through the sorrows of his home. The faithlessness
of the wife he loved so deeply rent his heart, not so much
at the wounds her faithlessness inflicted on him as at the
foulness her adultery brought on one who was so precious
in his eyes. And he was lifted by that experience to understand the love of God and the awfulness of the injury Israel
did herself by her faithlessness to Him. Jeremiah, by the
loneliness his prophetic ministry brought upon him, found
a new depth of experience of the presence of God, and became the medium of a message of the fundamentally inner
quality of true religion which was of the greatest importance to Israel. In neither case could the experience of itself
necessarily bring the message. A wife's adultery does not of
itself speak of the love of God, or lift to God; nor does utter
loneliness of itself throw a man back on God. More important than the experience is what God is saying through it to
the man who is sensitive to hear. And the prophets were
sensitive, and that is why they were able to be the extensions of the divine personality and the messengers of God
to men.

The prophet's message was always first and foremost a
revelation of God. In the intimacy of his experience he saw
God, and perceived something of the character of God.
Whatever side of human activity his oracles dealt with, they
always sprang out of his vision of God. When he dealt with
the political and diplomatic situations of his day, he did not
speak as a statesman but as God's messenger; when he dealt

with economic and social questions, he did not speak as an economist or sociologist, but as the prophet of God; when he dealt with moral problems, he did not speak as a moralist, but as the mouthpiece of God. His interest was always and through and through religious. He looked on the world in the light of what he had seen of God, and in that light he saw its true nature. His predictions of the future did not spring out of his cleverness in penetrating the secrets time holds in store, but out of the clearness with which he saw the present in the light of the vision of God. Apart from the more general prophecies of the messianic age and the goal of history, which will concern us below, and which sprang out of religious principles, his specific predictions were always of the future as it should arise out of the present, and not of a distant future that was unrelated to the present. He penetrated the situation of his day, and saw to the end the processes on which men were embarking, because he saw them spiritually and perceived their inner essence.

Moses perceived that God was gracious and compassionate, and a saving God, and that He had chosen Israel to reveal these qualities of His heart in His dealings with her that she might serve Him and fulfil His great purposes through her. It is that perception of God which gives the key to all his work, and, as has been said, it was in establishing the Covenant on the basis of gratitude for the grace and salvation of God that he placed Israelite religion on a fundamentally ethical basis, and Israelite ethics on a fundamentally religious basis.

Samuel is sometimes called a second Moses. He does not appear to have perceived any great new fundamental truth of God's Being, but rather to have seen afresh what Moses had seen and to be the medium of a fresh deliverance of Israel from oppression. God's choice of Israel was not to be frustrated by the Philistines, and the religion that Moses had established become lost to the world in the submersion of Israel. Hence he was moved to call Saul to leadership against the Philistines. It was not mere nationalism, with a dash of religion to give it drive. It was an effort to quicken the nation with religious faith, to remind men that Yahweh was a saving God, and to ensure that His elective purpose should be fulfilled. He declared that God's compassion was stirred when He looked upon His people now, as it had been stirred when He saw their sufferings in Egypt. Yet deliverance now, as then, carried corollaries and involved conditions. In Egypt they had to trust the word of Moses and follow him, and then to commit themselves to the God who had saved. Now they had to know a renewed confidence in God ere they could know a resurgence of the national spirit, and deliverance would lay a constraint to continued loyalty.

The ethical strain in Israelite religion from the days of its foundation by Moses is seen all along. Nathan rebuked David for his adultery with Bathsheba; and Elijah, Ahab for the murder of Naboth. The eighth and seventh century prophets greatly developed this strain in their denunciation of all the moral and social evils of their time. Yet it was never merely the sturdy uprising of free men's souls at injustice and wrong, and the insistence on the rights of man. It was always insistence on the will of God. They perceived what God was like, and therefore what man must be. Man's rights were his, not because of what he was in himself, but because God willed them, and God willed them, not because this happened to be His pleasure, but because of what He was in Himself. If justice and mercy are of the essence of God's Being, then in these things He must delight, and men who honour Him must honour Justice and Mercy, which inhere in Him.

The promises of doom at the hands of Assyria and Babylon which the eighth and seventh century prophets uttered came from men who were as deeply patriotic as Samuel and the other prophets, who had kindled the ardour of the people against alien oppressors. These prophets did not size up the strength of the mighty empires of Assyria and Babylon, and penetrate the weakness of the resources and equipment of Israel and her neighbours, and base their word on such things. They saw the life of their day, and they saw it whole. And they knew that the life of a nation springs from its spirit. When the heart of a nation is right with God, then every aspect of its life is guided by His spirit, but when God is shut out from the heart then every side of life withers and decays. All the moral and social iniquity of their day showed that men were out of harmony with the spirit of God, and it was certain that their political life was equally out of line with His will. The hollowness of all their religious observance was proved by the character of their life, and it was therefore vain to expect that the national enterprises would prosper. The disease of spirit was cursing every side of the national life, and unless the spirit were brought to God to be healed dire troubles were inevitable.

It is frequently supposed that the prophets were utterly opposed to the cultus, and in particular to sacrifice, and that all they demanded was brotherhood and fair dealing. To the writer this seems quite without justification. The great canonical pre-exilic prophets denounced sacrifice that was not the organ of obedience to God, but we have no means of knowing what they would have said of sacrifice that was the organ of obedience. Their denunciation does not seem to have sprung out of any hostility to the cultus as such, but out of deep spiritual principles which were not being expressed in the cultus in their day.

In the days of Amos sacrifices were abundant, but injustice abounded on all sides. The rich were oppressing the poor, and the restraints of law and of custom were taken off. Bribery determined the verdicts of the courts, and all humanity was forgotten in the grim selfishness that ran through society. But if, as Amos perceived, God is just, then His people must be just, and all injustice is an inherent offence against God. What meaning could there be, therefore, in any sacrifices offered unto God, however splendid? If men do not in their hearts desire justice, then they cannot desire God, and any profession of desire for Him is a hollow pretence. Sacrifice must be validated by the spirit that accompanies it. He who offers a sin-offering that ostensibly carries a plea for the forgiveness of his sin, and at the same time loves his sin in his heart, and has no intention of turning from it, by his spirit stultifies his own offering. And sin is whatever is an offence to God, and so if He is just, then all injustice is sin. He who offers to God a sacrifice that expresses a desire for communion with God, but who has no desire for that communion in his heart, makes a mockery of his sacrifice. And if God is just, then all who love injustice can have no communion of spirit with Him. What Amos perceives is that the spirit denies the professed meaning of the act, and robs it of all meaning. That is why he has no use for the sacrifice. "I hate, I despise your feasts," he cries, speaking as the mouthpiece of God, " and I will take no delight in your solemn assemblies. Yea, though ye offer me your burnt offerings and your meal offerings, I will not accept them: neither will I regard the peace offerings of your fat beasts. . . . But let justice roll down as waters, and righteousness as a perennial stream." [12] It was the lack of justice, and the lack of any desire for it, that reduced the sacrifices to a hollow sham.

In all the many similar passages in the prophets, what they are really saying is just that they who worship God must realize what manner of Being He is, and must perceive that the great end of worship is that men may become like Him. Hosea calls for the quality of *hesed* in men, because this quality is of the essence of God's heart. This word

12 Amos v. 21 ff.

is perhaps the most untranslatable of all Hebrew words. It is often rendered *lovingkindness,* or *mercy,* yet it includes more than both of these. The qualities of *loyalty, love,* and *grace* are all included in the rich amalgam of this word. It is not to be supposed, of course, that Hosea was the first to perceive this quality of God's heart. It is probable that Exod. xxxiv. 6 is older than the time of Hosea, and it declares, " Yahweh, Yahweh, a God full of compassion and gracious, slow to anger, and plenteous in *ḥesed* and truth." Hosea's experience enabled him to appreciate more deeply this quality of God, and by the same token it led him to demand this quality of man. The message he brings to men from God is, " I desire *ḥesed* and not sacrifice, and the knowledge of God rather than burnt offerings." [13] The first half of this is often pressed in a literalistic way, to yield the meaning that sacrifice as such is alien to God's wish, but it is often the Hebrew way to express comparison by a sharp antithesis, and in any case the comparative character of the parallel second half confirms the view that comparison is in mind in the first half. To know God, and to reflect His character is the purpose of worship, and the purpose is of greater importance than all its forms.

The same thing comes out from the great denunciation of the diligent observance of the ritual uttered by Isaiah. " To what purpose is the multitude of your sacrifices unto Me? said Yahweh: I am full of the burnt offerings of rams, and the fat of fed beasts; and I delight not in the blood of bullocks, or of lambs, or of he-goats. . . . When ye spread forth your hands, I will hide Mine eyes from you: yea, when ye make many prayers, I will not hear: your hands are full of blood. Wash you, make you clean; put away the evil of your doings from before Mine eyes; cease to do evil: learn to do well; seek judgment, relieve the oppressed, judge the fatherless, plead for the widow." [14] It is in no sense because

[13] Hos. vi. 6.   [14] Isa. i. 11 ff.

sacrifices are an offence *per se* that they are here condemned, but because they are offered by men whose hands are full of blood, and who are unwilling to be cleansed and to turn from their evil ways, and reflect the character of God in their lives.

Or again, in the great passage in Micah: " Wherewith shall I come before Yahweh, and bow myself before the high God? Shall I come before Him with burnt offerings, with calves of a year old? . . . He hath shewed thee, O man, what is good; and what doth Yahweh require of thee, but to do justly, and to love *ḥesed,* and to walk humbly with thy God? " [15] It is the lack of justice and *ḥesed,* and the unreadiness to walk humbly with God in the way of His will that turns the sacrifices into an offence to Him. There is nothing here to indicate that men who showed the qualities asked for would not also desire to offer sacrifices. The sacrifices condemned are the sacrifices that are unreal, that mock God by asking for a boon that men are unwilling to receive.

The book of Deuteronomy is commonly held to rest on the teaching of the eighth century prophets. Its deep affinity of spirit with the prophets, and its inculcation of the high principles of life and conduct that were so dear to them, are obvious to every reader. Humanity and brotherhood are commended throughout. Yet Deuteronomy also prescribes the offering of sacrifices. It finds no inherent conflict between the obedience of the spirit and the observance of the ritual, and we are therefore the more justified in supposing that the prophets on whom this book rested, and who may be presumed to have been as well understood by its compilers as by us, found no such inherent conflict. When Deuteronomy prescribes sacrifices, that does not imply that it is indifferent to hands full of blood, or injustice, or oppression, and when the prophets denounce these

[15] Micah vi. 6 ff.

things it no more implies that they were hostile to the institution of sacrifice as such.

It is sometimes felt that whatever may be the case with the other prophets, there can be no doubt that Jeremiah was absolutely and inexorably opposed to the whole institution of sacrifice. That he more than any other prophet stresses the inner qualities of true religion is certain. He could contemplate without alarm the destruction of the Temple, and therefore the cessation of sacrifice, and in his own experience he had learned to know the depth of a fellowship with God that was apart from the cultus. But if Jeremiah knew that religion could survive the loss of the cultus, that is not to say that he believed it could only exist where it was divorced from the cultus. Stress is laid sometimes on his word: " I spake not unto your fathers, nor commanded them in the day that I brought them out of the land of Egypt, concerning burnt offerings or sacrifices: but this thing I commanded them, saying, Hearken unto My voice, and I will be your God, and ye shall be My people: and walk ye in the way that I command you, that it may be well with you." [16] This is taken to be a categorical denial that sacrifice had ever had any legitimate place in the religion of Yahwism. It is quite incredible that Jeremiah should have meant any such thing. We read in the Gospel that Jesus said: " If any man cometh unto Me, and hateth not his own father, and mother, and wife, . . . he cannot be My disciple." [17] It is impossible that He who taught love of enemies should really have demanded the hatred of the nearest of relations, and quite certain that what He really meant was that His disciples must love Him with a love that took precedence over all earthly affection. And similarly Jeremiah was expressing in terms that were formally absolute the relative importance of sacrifice and obedience. What he means — and the meaning is undeniably true —

[16] Jer. vii. 22 f.   [17] Luke xiv. 26.

is that the supremely important thing that happened at Sinai was not sacrifice, but the establishment of the Covenant, and the sacrifice that Moses instituted there was not sacrifice that had validity in itself alone, as a mere *opus operatum,* but sacrifice that was organically related to the Covenant, and that expressed the spirit of the Covenant.

On another occasion Jeremiah declared, " Your burnt offerings are not acceptable, nor your sacrifices pleasing unto Me." [18] But the context makes it clear that it is not because they are burnt offerings and sacrifices, but because they are not the organ of the spirit, but are offered by men who will not hearken unto the voice of God. " Behold, I will bring evil upon this people, even the fruit of their thoughts, because they have not hearkened unto My words; and as for My law, they have rejected it. . . . Your burnt offerings are not acceptable, nor your sacrifices pleasing unto Me."

The significance of prophecy is therefore to be found in its mediation of the revelation of God, and in its unfolding of His character no less than of His will, and Hebrew prophecy, which began where other prophecy began, is distinguished from all other prophecy by the heights of revelation it attained. In its great succession of prophets were men who by the sensitiveness of their spirit and by the richness of their consecration were able to be led into the secrets of God's heart, that they might unfold His will to men. Yet none perceived all the glory of God, and none was the perfect medium of the divine revelation. The prophetic word came through the organ of fallible human personality.

Such a view has theological and practical consequences of the greatest importance. If God could make human personality the organ of His spirit, He can still do so. Men today can still live in such rich and intimate fellowship with Him that they may be stirred in the depths of their being, to become the instruments of His will and purpose. The

[18] Jer. vi. 20.

prophets were such instruments because they responded to the divine call and were consciously and utterly consecrated to Him. It was not that an immanent God was unconsciously in all their striving of spirit, but that the transcendent God, to whom they surrendered their powers in the dedication of their will, became immanent in them, and expressed Himself through them. We in our day are living in times when the spirit of man is yearning for new and better things, and restlessly striving to find its Utopia in new economic and social conditions. The only sound principles of Utopia are expressed in the Lord's Prayer: " Thy kingdom come; Thy will be done on earth as it is in heaven." And men who are dedicated to that will may become the instruments of that will, to be, as the prophets were, extensions of the divine personality, and to call others to a like dedication. For ultimately the will of God can be done only in a society of men who desire to do His will, and who yield themselves to His purpose. Far more than conduct is involved. For the spirit that directs the conduct belongs also to the act, to give it its quality and value. The prophets were ever complaining that men performed as mere *opera operata* acts which were deemed to be virtuous. But the prophets called for something deeper, for the spirit that should inspire and infuse the act. Their cry was not, " Not sacrifice but justice," for justice is no more an end in itself than sacrifice. The justice they called for was the reflexion of the spirit of God, and it could prevail only amongst men who desired to do the will of God, and who were yielded to His spirit. It was justice which had a fundamentally religious basis, and which was infused with the spirit of consecration to the will of God.

VII. THE RISE OF JUDAISM

THE DESTRUCTION of the Temple by the Chaldaeans and the Babylonian exile might have been expected to spell the end of the religion of Israel. The broken and dispirited community left in Palestine lay at the mercy of its neighbours, while it would not have been surprising if the exiles had been gradually absorbed in the society around them, and had vanished from history. But He who chose Israel to be His people would not suffer that. His purpose could not be defeated. By history and by His servants He had revealed Himself and instructed Israel in days past, and by history and by His servants He was continuing to do the same. It was probably in no small part by the teaching of Jeremiah that He had prepared Israel to face this experience, whereby He was to teach her many new things. Jeremiah had been little listened to when he had spoken, but the complete and tragic vindication of his message must have affected men deeply. And while they had regarded it as blasphemy when he had declared that the Temple was not essential to religion, now that the Temple had gone and they were in a strange land, they began to explore the possibilities of keeping alive their religion through fellowship, and without the ritual. The work of Jeremiah bore fruit in Babylon. Yet it is improbable that anyone dreamed of a religion which should be permanently without the sacrificial ritual.

The exile provides the great dividing line of Israelite history and religion, and to the religion of post-exilic days we give the name Judaism. Superficially Judaism is the antithesis of the spiritual religion of Jeremiah, and so it has commonly been regarded. Its genius has been found to lie in the punctilious observance of the ritual of the cultus and the minutiae of the Law. That the Law and the Prophets stand over against one another symbolizing wholly opposed conceptions of the essence of religion has seemed axiomatic, and in no need of demonstration. To the Jew, with his profound veneration for the Pentateuch, the Law has seemed to tower high above the Prophets, while in modern times such Christians as have had any inclination to study either the Law or the Prophets, if they have had any acquaintance with modern expositions of the Prophets, have reversed these estimates. From the foundation of the Christian Church, indeed, the Law has been at a discount as compared with the Prophets, for from the beginning the Christians believed that the Law was superseded in Christ, whereas the Prophets had earned undying honour by testifying of Him. That, however, was quite different from the modern attitude, which finds the Law, in its present form, to be later than the great prophets, and to represent a tragic decline from the heights of the ethical faith of the prophets.

The affinity of the Law and of Judaism is with Ezekiel, and Ezekiel was in some respects a strange character, not very attractive to us, and consequently apt to receive rather less than justice at our hands. In the last generation much attention has been paid to the book of Ezekiel, and widely varying theories have been propounded. It has been assigned to various hands and to various dates, and of those who would retain at least a part of the book for a sixth century Ezekiel some would place him in Palestine, rather than amongst the exiles. To go into all these questions here would carry us too far afield; nor is it necessary for our purpose. Ezekiel is commonly called the Father of Judaism, and what is in the mind of those who so call him is the sketch of the organization of religion in the future, found in the last nine chapters of the book. That these chapters date from the sixth century and come from the hand of an exile in Babylon is agreed by some of those who deny them to Ezekiel, and they are then held to be from the hand of a disciple of Ezekiel. These chapters conceive of the restored community as centred in the worship of a restored Temple, with a carefully regulated priesthood, and a carefully regulated ritual of sacrifice. But whereas the old shrines had led men astray from Yahweh, and the Temple itself had contained much that was an offence to the purer Yahwism of the prophets, this writer dreams of a purified Temple, which shall be free of all such things. Something of the hardness of spirit that we commonly associate with the Judaism that appears in the Gospels can be seen in him, and we fail to see him in the setting of his times, or to recognize the real service he rendered. For it was no little achievement to keep men's hope alive, and to dream of the future and plan for it, in such a time, and the gross laxity of the shrines, against which the pre-exilic prophets had protested, provided some justification for the rigidity of this writer's spirit.

The fulfilment of this dream and the establishment of Judaism came with the work of Nehemiah and Ezra. The superficial reading of the books that bear their names would suggest that these two men were contemporaries, but that Ezra came to Jerusalem some years before Nehemiah. It has been already observed that for half a century the view has been gaining ground that Nehemiah preceded Ezra by more than a generation. Both of these men are associated with the rearing of the wall of particularism around Judaism, while Ezra brought the priestly Law and imposed it upon the community. It is common to regard their work in both respects as retrograde. For a century before Nehemiah, the great Deutero-Isaiah had set before men the world mission of Judaism, which will command our attention be-

low, and the narrow outlook and rigid spirit of Nehemiah
and Ezra stand in marked contrast with this. Yet let us be
just to them. Through all this century Deutero-Isaiah's
grand vision had borne no fruit, and the state of the Palestinian community that Nehemiah and Ezra found could
have inspired little hope of the success of any renewed call
to such an enterprise. Instead they addressed themselves to
the practical problems of the hour. And here they had very
enduring success, and it is probable that but for their work
we should never have heard of Deutero-Isaiah's.

Particularism must have begun in Babylon, and it was
from Babylon that it was brought to Palestine by Nehemiah
and Ezra. In Babylon the only way to preserve the faith of
Judaism was for its holders to keep themselves to themselves
as much as possible, to resist the influences of the culture all
around them, and to nurture one another's spiritual life.
And Nehemiah and Ezra sought to bring that spirit into the
Palestinian community. By intermarriage with the surrounding people alien religious influences, of the kind that
had called forth the condemnation of the pre-exilic prophets, were still being brought into the heart of the community. Hence they denounced and forcibly dissolved
mixed marriages. This was not due to any hatred of foreigners as such. For Judaism in its most particularistic days was
always ready to receive proselytes — foreigners who would
genuinely embrace the faith of Israel, and who would not
imperial the purity of that faith. It was the purity and preservation of that faith that so exercised these founders of
Judaism, and their work rested on no basis of nationalism
or racialism, but on a basis of religion. They were passion-
ately concerned for the maintenance of the religion of Yahwism, and they feared that the faintly burning flame of
Judaism might be quenched altogether. Even a slight acquaintance with the conditions of the times must convince
the student that there was real ground for this fear, and of-

fer some excuse for the severity of the measures they took.

It has also to be remembered that the establishment of particularism was timely, and that in the providence of God it had a very real part to play in the fulfilment of the purpose of Israel's election. About a century after the time of Nehemiah the Persian empire was succeeded by the Greek empire of Alexander and his successors. Hellenism now came into the Jewish world as an aggressive force, and even with the barrier of particularism Judaism was to be subjected to a greater peril than it had yet known. The conscious purpose of Alexander, symbolized by his own marriage with Roxana, was the marriage of oriental and Greek culture, and his successors continued to carry his purpose into effect.[1] Nor was the purpose unwelcome to all the Jews. The glamour of Greek culture made Greek customs attractive to many. For despite a century of particularism, not all Jews were marked by that spirit. In many quarters there was a tendency to sit very loosely by Judaism and its customs, and a great readiness to show what was doubtless regarded as breadth and liberality of spirit. Inevitably all who clung to the way of Judaism became increasingly marked by the spirit of particularism, and met the new peril by a hardening of the shell into which they retired. Of the grim fight between Judaism and Hellenism which took place in the second century B.C. it is unnecessary to treat here, or of the nationalist revival under the Maccabees to which it gave rise. It should never be forgotten, however, that that conflict was not one between an alien king and a united Jewish nation. It was a conflict within the nation as much as with foreign elements. For there was the deepest cleavage between the lax hellenizers and the *hasidim,* or " pious ones."

1 The aggressiveness of Hellenism was mainly due to its inherent attractiveness, and there is no evidence that it was forcibly imposed on the world. The conflict of Judaism with Hellenism in the Maccabaean age was due to complex political as well as religious factors.

But what of the other side of the work of Nehemiah and Ezra? The latter's promulgation of the priestly Law was not unrelated to the establishment of particularism. At the heart of the Law lay the conception of religion as the centre of the life of the nation, just as Ezekiel or his disciple had conceived it. It was to be a carefully regulated religion, the rigidity and splendour of whose organization should be a safeguard against the perils of the past. It is very doubtful if Ezra thought of this religion as in any way the antithesis of prophetic religion. He doubtless thought he was serving the ideals of the prophets, and embodying them in the Law, that they might achieve more than the preaching of the prophets had hitherto achieved. For the priestly Law was not intended to be the substitute for faith, but its organ. The essence of particularism was not narrowness, but loyalty, and by the Law that spirit of loyalty was offered something around which to crystallize, that it might continue.

That the common antithesis of Law and Prophets is not really justified may be established by a number of considerations. It has already been said that the hostility of the pre-exilic prophets to the cultus should not be exaggerated and converted into a complete opposition to all sacrifice, nor should the loyalty of the pre-exilic law of Deuteronomy to the prophetic ideals be forgotten. One of the greatest expressions of prophetic teaching is found in Deuteronomy, in words that nobly crystallize much of the message of the pre-exilic prophets: " Hear, O Israel: Yahweh is our God, Yahweh alone: and thou shalt love Yahweh thy God with all thine heart, and with all thy soul, and with all thy might." [2] But this great word cannot be set down as merely a Deuteronomic word, unrelated to the Judaism that Ezra established and coming from the " prophetic law-book." For Judaism has singled out this word for unique honour and esteem, and its love for all the minutiae of the Law has

[2] Deut. vi. 4 f.

never dimmed its regard for this summary of prophetic teaching.

Another great and familiar prophetic word is found in the Holiness Code. That Code is by general agreement older than the body of the Priestly Code which Ezra introduced, but it appears to have been embodied in that Priestly Code, and in any case it has been part of the Law of Judaism from the time of the compilation of the Pentateuch. It declares: " Thou shalt love thy neighbour as thyself." [3] The whole context of these words expresses the demand for humanity, social righteousness and justice, which was characteristic of the prophets. Moreover, it bases this demand on religion, precisely as did the prophets. " Thou shalt not oppress thy neighbour, nor rob him: the wages of a hired servant shall not abide with thee all night until the morning. . . . Ye shall do no unrighteousness in judgment: thou shalt not respect the person of the poor, nor honour the person of the mighty: but in righteousness shalt thou judge thy neighbour. . . . Thou shalt not hate thy brother in thine heart . . . but thou shalt love thy neighbour as thyself: I am Yahweh."

On the other hand, the character of the post-exilic prophets and their attitude to the cultus in general and to sacrifice in particular should be remembered. Haggai and Zechariah urged on the rebuilding of the Temple, and were therefore quite clearly not opposed to the cultus. " I will fill this house with glory, saith Yahweh of hosts," cried Haggai; . . . " the latter glory of this house shall be greater than the former." [4] And Malachi rebuked the people for the half-heartedness of their obedience to the demands of the cultus, and for the meanness of the sacrifices they offered. They were offering in sacrifice the blemished and the second-rate, and so were dishonouring God, for whom nothing but the best would do. For all this the post-exilic proph-

3 Lev. xix. 18.   4 Hag. ii. 7, 9.

ets are often contrasted with the pre-exilic prophets, and their attitude to the cultus and to sacrifice is thought to mark them as very unworthy successors of the great pre-exilic figures. That they were lesser men than Amos and Hosea, Isaiah and Jeremiah, is undoubtedly true, but that they are in strange company amongst them is not true. For the contrast so often remarked is more apparent than real. It is a contrast of form rather than of essence. When the great prophets of the eighth and seventh centuries denounced the splendid sacrifices of their day, they were declaring that sacrifices without true loyalty and submission of spirit, sacrifices that were not the organ of such a loyalty and submission, were meaningless and vain. When Malachi denounced the meanness of the sacrifices of his day, he was declaring that true loyalty and submission of spirit must have as their organ worthy sacrifices. There is no shadow of contradiction here. The man who does not do justly and love *ḥesed* and walk humbly with God can only mock God by all his sacrifices; but he who brings less than his best to God dishonours Him and demonstrates the hollowness of any profession of his loyalty.

What Judaism, as represented by the Law, sought to do was not to establish sacrifice as an end in itself. Nowhere does it declare that so long as sacrifices are offered men may live how they will, or that men's hearts may be indifferent to God so long as they adhere to the ritual. The sacrifices for which it calls are sacrifices that express the deep and sincere spirit of the officers. Nowhere is there a word to suggest that clean hands and a pure heart are matters of indifference to the Law, or that justice and *ḥesed* and the humble walk with God can be dispensed with. Lying behind all the teaching of the prophets was the perception that what God is His worshippers must become. And the same perception lies behind the Law. " Ye shall be holy; for I Yahweh your God

am holy " is a word from the Law,[5] and it proclaims the
same principle. The sacrifices for which it calls must be offered in a profoundly humble spirit. They must be the sacrifices of men who hate sin with a deep hatred and desire
to be cleansed of it, and who desire communion with God
that they may be like Him.

It is often pointed out that the Law's stress on unconscious sin and on purely ritual and involuntary uncleanness distinguishes it from the Prophets, and implies that
the fineness of the ethical religion of the prophets has sunk
to the mere ritualism of the priests. For while there are
great ethical and spiritual words in the Law, such as those
which have been quoted above, it is undeniable that there
is a weight of emphasis on the ethical in the greater pre-
exilic prophets which is not found in the Priestly Law, and
a weight of emphasis on the ritual in the Priestly Law
which is wholly lacking in those prophets. That this emphasis on the ritual brought peril in its train may be agreed.
For it was ever easy for those who did not appreciate the
spirit that inspired the Law to suppose that moral offences
were no more heinous than technical offences. But that was
not really the point of view that inspired the Law. What it
sought to do was to foster the spirit that found the most
trivial technical offences to be anything but trivial, since
they contravened the will of God. And that deep sensitiveness of spirit really prevailed in Judaism at its best. " Be
heedful of a light precept as of a weighty one," said Rabbi
Judah the Prince.[6] His intention was not to bring weighty
precepts into contempt, or to reduce moral offences to the
level of the technical, but to elevate the technical to the
height of the moral, and to show the profundity of his regard for the whole Law. To suggest that there is anything
in such an attitude which would have shocked the pre-exilic

5 Lev. xix. 2.   6 Pirqe Aboth ii. 1.

prophets would be ludicrous. For it is poles asunder from the things they condemned.

Nor did the Law anywhere teach that there was hope of forgiveness for the man who sinned deliberately, and who so far from hating his sin offered sacrifices with a heart that was resolved to renew its sin. The sincere confession of sin was essential to its expiation. " It shall be, when he shall be guilty in one of these things, that he shall confess that wherein he hath sinned; and he shall bring his guilt offering unto Yahweh for his sin which he hath sinned, . . . and the priest shall make atonement for him as concerning his sin." [7] This confession was something more than a mere statement of fact; it was an expression of penitence. The sinner was required to make restitution to his neighbour, against whom he had sinned, in a way that would certainly have commanded the full approbation of the prophets. " When a man or woman shall commit any sin that men commit, . . . then they shall confess their sin which they have done: and he shall make restitution for his guilt in full, and add unto it the fifth part thereof, and give it unto him in respect of whom he hath been guilty." [8] But for deliberate sin the Law offered no cleansing. " But the soul that doeth aught with an high hand, whether he be homeborn or a stranger, the same blasphemeth Yahweh; and that soul shall be cut off from among his people." [9] This was the kind of sinner whose sacrifices the prophets found to be of no avail, the man who proudly pursued his own cruel and selfish way, who knew not how to humble his soul before God, and in whose heart was the firm resolve still to pursue his way even when he was engaged in the act of sacrifice. For such a man the Law held no comfort, any more than the prophets. Nor did the leaders of Judaism, the men who entered most deeply into its spirit and meaning, ever soften the condemnation of such men. In the Mishnah we read:

[7] Lev. v. 5 f.   [8] Num. v. 6 f.   [9] Num. xv. 30.

" If a man say, I will sin and repent, I will again sin and repent, he will be given no chance to repent. If he say, I will
sin and the Day of Atonement will clear me, the Day of
Atonement will effect no atonement." [10]

Let it never be forgotten that the profound sense of sin
which marks the Law was born of the sense of the overwhelming majesty of God. No sin could be trivial which
contravened His holy will, or by its polluting touch unfitted one to come into His holy presence. But this was
perceived by Isaiah as clearly as by any devotee of the Law.
When at his call the prophet saw Yahweh exalted upon His
throne, and heard the seraphim hymn the holiness of God,
his soul was overwhelmed with the sense of his sin, which
unfitted him to stand in that holy presence. " Woe is me!
for I am undone! " he cried, " because I am a man of unclean lips, and I dwell in the midst of a people of unclean
lips: for mine eyes have seen the King, Yahweh of hosts." [11]
His attitude of heart was precisely that which the Law was
designed to foster.

Nor should it be forgotten that there is a sense in which
the prophets, no less than the Law, belong to the post-exilic
age. Many of the usages of the Priestly Law doubtless go
back far into the past, but it was in the post-exilic age that
the Law was compiled, to be made the vehicle of utter loyalty to the pure religion which had derived from Moses
through the prophets. It was also in the post-exilic age that
the prophetic books were compiled. This is much too commonly forgotten. These books cannot have assumed their
present form until long after the times of the prophets
whose names they bear, although it is quite certain that
many of the oracles they contain are the genuine utterances
of the men to whom they are ascribed. The variety of the
materials they contain shows that they are posthumous com-
pilations. For in addition to actual oracles, they contain au-

---

[10] Yoma viii. 9.   [11] Isa. vi. 5.

tobiographical material and also biographical material related in the third person. We know that Jeremiah prepared a collection of his own oracles during his lifetime, and subsequently added to it, and this collection is doubtless one of the sources of our present book of Jeremiah. Yet it cannot be the sole source, and the combination of material from this source with material from other sources may most reasonably be assigned to a later age, when there was a profound interest in gathering together the works that should preserve all that was known of the life and utterances of these great figures of the past. Moreover, the fact that some oracles are independently ascribed to two different prophets would suggest that the books were compiled some considerable time after their own day. Still more certain is it that the collection of the prophetic books into what now forms the second division of the prophetic canon of the Hebrew Scriptures belongs to the post-exilic age. Since the book of Malachi is included in that division, and since Malachi belongs to the fifth century B.C., it is quite certain that the prophetic books were not all gathered together before the time of Ezra, and it is probable that the compilation did not assume its present form until a good deal later. This means that the age that laid so much stress on the observance of the Law was the age that revered and collected the oracles of the prophets.

It is unlikely that these formed two quite separate and unrelated interests of different sections of the people. Indeed the fact that the books of Haggai, Zechariah and Malachi are found in the same collection as the oracles of Amos and Hosea is the clearest testimony to the fact that the post-exilic circles which delighted to treasure the sayings of the pre-exilic prophets, with their denunciation of the sacrifices of their day, also delighted to treasure the sayings of these other prophets, which called for sacrifices. They do not seem to have been conscious of the contrast which is now so commonly drawn between them, and we clearly cannot set the circles which were interested in the cultus over against those who were interested in the spiritual teaching of the prophets. This means that Judaism was more profoundly spiritual than is often supposed, and it is clear that what the creators of Judaism aimed to do was to make the strict observance of the Law the organ of the spirit that prophets had called for, and the protection of prophetic religion from all the contamination of the influences that had so often prevailed in earlier days. They hated all the iniquities of the high places as much as the prophets had done, and they were as deeply opposed to all the evils that corrupted the life of society in the days of the pre-exilic prophets.

Nor should we forget that the synagogue was the creation of post-exilic Judaism. The origins of the institution of the synagogue are veiled in obscurity. It is commonly believed that it was in Babylon in the time of the exile that it took its rise. There can be no certainty about this, but it seems a likely view. The exiles could not let their religion centre in the cultus of a sacrificial altar, for there was no Yahweh altar in Babylon, and no thought of erecting one. If they were to maintain their religious life and their corporate consciousness it was desirable that they should meet together, and that their religion should be at the heart of their fellowship. To read the writings that enshrined the traditions of their race, in so far as they were available, to offer prayer together to the God of their fathers, and to exhort one another to cherish the faith of Israel and to resist all the lure of the life and culture that lay around them, would be not unnatural ways of expressing their fellowship. And when with Nehemiah and Ezra, who came from Babylon, Judaism was formally established in Jerusalem, it would not be surprising for the synagogue also to be introduced in Palestine, if it had not already taken its rise there. The probability, however, is that it had already begun to appear. For if it had been introduced in any datable fashion, or had been associated with the work of either of those leaders, we should have expected to have some record of its introduction preserved. It is therefore likely that it began in some simple way, without any idea that anything of enduring importance to the world was being begun, and began in Palestine because it could minister to needs comparable with those it ministered to in Babylon. For with the disappearance of all the " high places " the experience of worship at the Temple could be but a rare experience of most of the people, and some local centres for the nurture of religious life were needed.

All of this is purely speculative. But what is not speculative is that at some time in the post-exilic age, in the age of Judaism that is, the synagogue came into being and became one of the characteristic institutions of Judaism. Later it influenced the worship of the Christian Church and of the Mohammedan mosque, and its mark is therefore deep and abiding on three great religions of the world. The worship of the synagogue did not centre in the altar of sacrifice, and had no elaborate cultic rites. It was a simple worship, and purely spiritual. Yet its establishment quite certainly took place in the period that is supposed to have been marked by the antithesis of its spirit. Here again, therefore, we find reason to beware of the too ready assumption that Judaism is to be equated with the formal observance of rites and ceremonies as ends in themselves.

It is also pertinent to remember that it is to Judaism that we owe the gathering together of the Canon of the Old Testament. So far as we know it was not until the end of the first century A.D. that the Canon was definitely fixed by the decision of an authoritative council of Jews. But that was the end of a process, and the only questions at issue there were whether certain books should be excluded or not.

What that Council did was to give formal recognition to the place the books admitted had long held in the esteem of men. For we know that long before that the recognition of the sanctity and authority of the books of the Old Testament had been very widely and generally won. In books of the New Testament, written before the Council of Jamnia was held, there are ample references to the existence of the Old Testament as a collection of sacred literature to establish this. All that the Council of Jamnia did was to define the limits of Sacred Scripture, not to create the concept of such Scripture or to initiate a collection.

Very few of the books of the Old Testament are older than the exile in their present form. This is not to deny that they contain a great deal of material that is older. There are fragments of poetry and extensive poems embedded in the Pentateuch and in the historical books that are older — in some cases very much older — than the exile. The great prose account of the reign of David found in 2 Sam. ix–xx is probably one of the oldest pieces of historical narrative in the world. The Judahite and Ephraimite collections of the traditions of Israel, and the bulk of the book of Deuteronomy already existed, and collections of oracles of the pre-exilic prophets. Many of the psalms already existed. No doubt a good deal of literature of the type that is found in the Old Testament, including many of the sources on which the Old Testament draws, and other lost works, were in existence. Nevertheless, with few exceptions, the final editing of the Old Testament books in their present form must be assigned to the post-exilic age. That this is so of the prophetic canon has been said above. It is also true of the Pentateuch — which is compiled not alone of the Judahite and Ephraimite documents and of Deuteronomy, but also of the Priestly document that Ezra appears to have promulgated — and still more true of the final division of the Hebrew Canon, the Writings.

Doubtless the exiles in Babylon treasured such literature as they possessed, and before the exile the beginnings
of the veneration which led to canonization must be placed.
The book of Deuteronomy had been accepted as the authoritative basis of Josiah's reform. But when Ezra brought
the Priestly Law and secured the acceptance of its authority, the compilation of the Pentateuch seems to have soon
followed, and it must have assumed its present form not
long after the time of Ezra. This is clear from the fact that
the Pentateuch forms the Scripture of the Samaritans as
well as a part of the Scripture of the Jews. The Samaritans
are not likely to have adopted it from the Jews after their
breach with them, and we must therefore conclude that it
had already achieved a place of authority and veneration
before the Samaritan schism. That schism cannot be precisely dated, but is probably to be assigned to the fourth
century B.C.

The completion of the prophetic canon was probably
somewhat later, though by completion it is not here meant
that it was fixed and defined in any formal way. What is
meant is that the prophetic books, which each seem to have
had a history and not to have been written *tout d'un trait*,
seem all to have reached substantially their present form
by a date about 300 B.C. The miscellaneous works which
comprise the Writings had probably already begun to be
collected by that time, but received additions to a much
later date.

The threefold character of the Hebrew Canon has sometimes given rise to the idea that first the Law was canonized, then the Prophets were collected and canonized, and
then a third collection was formed, into which alone any
additions could now be received. It is more likely that there
was much overlapping in the process, and that the collection of Law, Prophets and Writings was going on side by
side, but that the Law attained its completed form before

the Prophets, and the Prophets before the Writings. Once a collection had achieved stability, by usage and not by enactment, the way of additions would not be easy, and hence, for instance, the books of Chronicles, Ezra and Nehemiah found entrance into the Writings easier than into the collection of Former Prophets, with which they stand in our Bibles.

By the collection and elevation to veneration and esteem of the books of the Old Testament post-exilic Judaism rendered a lasting service to mankind, deserving of more recognition than it commonly gets. This was not the achievement of a spiritually decadent age, which is to be contrasted with the splendid heights of the great prophetic days as obsessed with pernickety ritual.matters and blind to great moral and spiritual issues. The books that a man gathers and treasures on his shelves are a clue to his interests and his spirit, and the Judaism that compiled and collected and treasured this wonderful library, which is without equal amongst the spiritual treasuries of mankind, deserves the respect of all who have spiritual penetration.

Within its compass there is an astonishing range and variety of literature. Legends, tales, history, poetry, discussion, biography, addresses, pithy aphorisms, religious and civil law, and what not besides, may be found here. Its sheer literary distinction would entitle it to immortality, and there are great passages which deserve a place in any anthology of the world's prose or poetry. Yet it was not written merely as literature, but as religious literature, and still more was it as religious literature that it was collected and treasured. For every variety of its contents derives its real quality from religion. The whole is an incomparable record of the religious experience and thought of Israel, whose unique mission in the purpose of God lay in the field of religion. Every mood of the human spirit is reflected here, and for every mood there is a message. For it must be remembered that it is as religious literature that the Old Testament has survived, and as religious literature alone that it can continue to survive. All our study of it must be dominated by that recognition. And on that recognition there should be erected the shrine of honour to the men whose insight dictated its compilation, and to the age which saw it gathered.

In particular it would be well for all who think creative and spiritual religion came to an end with the pre-exilic prophets, and post-exilic Judaism was hard and formal, to remember all that the psalms have been to men and still are. That many of the actual psalms were written in pre-exilic days is much more widely agreed to-day than it would have been a generation ago. Nevertheless, it is still generally believed that the majority of our psalms come from the post-exilic age, and the compilation of the Psalter is certainly to be placed in that age.[12] Few scholars to-day would assign large numbers of psalms to the Maccabaean age in the way that was common at the beginning of the century. Most would hold that a large number of the psalms come from the Persian period, the period that saw the birth of Judaism, but that there is a core of pre-exilic psalms also in the Psalter. There is less disposition to attempt to relate the psalms to particular historical situations, and a much greater desire to recognize that the psalms are religious poems, and hence to relate them to the religious use that they were written to serve.

Mowinckel has tried to relate very many of the psalms to ritual and magical purposes. He views the Psalter as a collection of potent spells, whose recitation released power, rather than as the expression of a spiritual faith. He thinks that any unfortunate Israelite sufferer would immediately assume that some enemy had put a spell on him, and all the

---

[12] Engnell goes to the opposite extreme with the view that Ps. cxxxvii is the only post-exilic psalm in the Psalter.

references to " workers of iniquity " in the psalms have the sorcerers who cast these spells in mind. The sufferer would repair to the shrine and invoke the services of the appropriate type of priest to counter the spell by the recitation of the proper antidote. Mowinckel also believes that there was an annual Accession Festival in Israel, when the Ark was carried in sacred procession through Jerusalem, and when Yahweh reascended His throne. He then associates with this festival, as part of the ritual of the day, a number of the psalms, including especially all that contain such phrases as " Yahweh reigns," or " Yahweh is King." The purpose of the ritual here again is held to be magical. For it is believed that the ritual of this Accession Festival provided a technique for the ensuring of the welfare of the community and the state during the ensuing year, whose due performance was supposed to be fundamental to the well-being of the state.[13]

That magical ideas and practices had a place in pre-exilic Israel is undeniable, since even the pre-exilic law of Deuteronomy forbade such practices. It may well have been, too, that Israel had an Accession Festival, something after the pattern of the Babylonian one, though there is no conclusive evidence for it. Nor is there any very conclusive evidence that all the psalms on which Mowinckel relies are of pre-exilic origin. Certainly it would be a singular turn of fortune if psalms which had been written to serve as the liturgy of magic found a place in a post-exilic collection of religious poetry, when the ideas on which they rested were decisively rejected by the leaders of Judaism, and a surprising circumstance that poems which were born of such a primitive faith should be able so richly to express the spiritual life of many generations of people who have no use for sorcery and its ways. Clearly the assumed original and

13 Engnell would carry this farther and maintains that the psalm heading " To David " should be rendered " For the king," and that every psalm which bears this heading belongs to the ritual of the annual festival whereby the divine kingship was renewed in Israel.

primary purpose of the poems can be stamped but lightly upon them.

But whatever measure of truth may be in these theories of Mowinckel's, they have a purely antiquarian interest. It has been said above that whatever the original significance of the Passover may have been, from the time of the Exodus its meaning for Israel had reference to that great deliverance. In the same way, even if some of the psalms were written to serve a magical purpose, it was not to serve any such purpose that the post-exilic collectors gathered them into the Psalter. For it must be repeated that whatever pre-exilic elements may be in the Psalter, it is a post-exilic collection. And the collectors intended it to serve spiritual interests, and to spiritual needs it has ministered to our own day. The Psalter provides the clearest evidence of the fundamental spirituality that could be found in Judaism. And since it is probable that the singing of the psalms by the Temple choirs gave them a place in the official liturgy of the Temple, and certain that at a later date the psalms had a place in the worship of the synagogue, the evidence of their spirituality is valid not alone for pious circles within Judaism, but for the appreciation of Judaism as a faith. Any sound estimate of Judaism must judge it as a whole, and not concentrate on its sacrificial ritual alone.

One other indication of the spiritual richness of post-exilic Judaism may be mentioned. This is the supreme production of the school of the Wisdom writers. The Hebrew mind did not run much to abstract speculation in philosophy. Its genius was quite other than the Greek. And when the Jew did speculate, it was not on the problems of existence and on the nature of the ultimately real, but on practical questions, usually related to his religion. The Old Testament contains certain books, known as the Wisdom literature, and there are some other works, not found in the Hebrew Canon of the Old Testament, which belong to the same class. None of these are profoundly philosophical in the Greek sense. Proverbs contains many shrewd observations on life, but its most speculative section is concerned with the nature of Wisdom itself. Ecclesiastes is more concerned with the nature of reality, and finds it in a ceaseless flux in such a way that some students have been led to trace it to the influence of Greek schools. The Song of Songs is commonly treated as a work of the Wisdom writers. This is due to the allegorical meanings that have been traditionally found in it by Jews and by Christians. It is more probable that it is a collection of love songs, not properly associated with the Wisdom school at all. In the hands of some modern writers it becomes a liturgy of the old fertility cult, but it is difficult to suppose that in post-exilic days Judaism would have treasured with its sacred literature a liturgy of the cult that called forth so much prophetic opposition in pre-exilic days, and that was certainly completely repudiated by Judaism itself.

The Wisdom literature doubtless had its origins in preexilic days, and it is probable that some sections of the book of Proverbs, in particular, go back to those days. All of the Wisdom books seem to have reached their present form, or to have been wholly composed, in post-exilic days. This is true in particular of the most notable Old Testament Wisdom book, the book of Job, which must date from postexilic days. This is the greatest work of genius in the Old Testament, and one whose rich spiritual message must be taken into account in any just appraisal of Judaism. It deals with a great speculative problem, the suffering of the innocent, yet its interest is rather practical and spiritual than speculative.

It had been the view of Deuteronomy that obedience to the will of God brings prosperity, and disobedience is sure to entail calamity. The thought of Deuteronomy was primarily of the nation, for it never was the teaching of any part of the Bible that individual fortune and individual merit were rigidly bound together and perfectly matched. Abel was not murdered for his sin, but despite his righteousness and God's approval of his offering. Naboth is not supposed to have received what he deserved when he was judicially murdered. The sufferings of the downtrodden at the hands of the oppressive and evil classes of the people would not have called forth the championship of the prophets if they had conceived of those sufferings as the rightful entail of their sin. The individual's share in the common suffering of the nation, brought upon it by its corporate wickedness, did not raise any problem. For the Hebrew recognized the solidarity of society to a much greater extent than is characteristic of ourselves. He was carried in the tide of the nation's life, and his fortunes were involved in the fortunes of society.

Then Jeremiah and Ezekiel had emphasized the personal responsibility of the individual, and in days when men were attributing the cause of the national calamities to others, these two prophets directed them to look into their own hearts and to find in their sorrows the fruit of their sin. It is sometimes said that individualism was born with Jeremiah and Ezekiel. This is an exaggeration. Never in Biblical thought was the individual looked on solely as a member of the corporate group with no individual responsibility and no individual religious experience. Nor is it likely that Jeremiah and Ezekiel regarded him solely as an individual, with no social ties that made him also but a fragment of the social whole. Man has both individual and social aspects, and any complete view of him recognizes both. What happened with Jeremiah and Ezekiel was that the individual aspect came into greater prominence. The Covenant of Sinai was a covenant the corporate society of Israel made with Yahweh. But Jeremiah spoke of the New Covenant that God would make with individual souls. Its law should be inscribed not on tables of stone, but on the living tables of human hearts and personalities, and it should command the individual loyalty of each heart.

In some sections of the people this stronger emphasis on the individual was linked with the Deuteronomic teaching of the nexus between desert and experience to yield a hard and fast idea that the individual always reaped what he deserved, and that therefore outer fortune was a true measure of inner worth. This never was the orthodoxy of Judaism as a whole, though it appears to have been the orthodoxy of certain circles — presumably of successful people. The first purpose of the book of Job was to protest against such an idea. It is sometimes thought that its purpose was to offer a solution of the problem of innocent suffering. This is very improbable, and it is certain that in its original form it did not achieve a solution. That the problem was troubling serious minds may be readily believed. But the book of Job attempted something deeper and more profoundly spiritual than the intellectual solution of this problem. And for its attempt the first essential was to insist that there is a problem, and that the shallow orthodoxy of the circles that denied its existence was unsound.

The book consists of a prose prologue and epilogue, with a poetic dialogue in between. It is probable that chapter xxviii, the Elihu speeches and the second speech of Yahweh do not belong to the original form of the book, and that there has been some derangement and loss from the text of the third round of speeches. For the poetic part of the book probably once consisted of an opening speech by Job, and then three rounds of speeches, each of the friends speaking in turn and being answered by Job, and then Yahweh addressing Job and producing his submissive response.

In the prose prologue the reader is told that Job is plunged into suffering, not because of his sin, but to vindicate God's trust in him. He is a man " perfect and upright, one who feared God and eschewed evil." He therefore does not deserve to suffer, and the reader is told here quite unmistakably that his suffering is not self-entailed, but utterly innocent. God has staked Himself upon Job, so that in his suffering Job is vindicating God's trust in him. Naturally he cannot know this, and neither can his friends. To disclose it to the reader was essential, so that he might know beyond a peradventure that Job was not suffering for his sin. Yet it was equally essential not to disclose it to Job. Others must suffer without knowing the cause of their suffering, and a Job who had been given the explanation of his sorrows would have had no message for them. What the author wished to say, then, is that there is such a thing as innocent suffering, and though the cause cannot be deduced by the sufferer, there is a cause hidden in the counsel of God. He does not wish to explain suffering. The explanation is given to the reader in Job's case, because it was necessary to give it. But there is no suggestion that it is always the same. It is always hidden from the sufferer and from his friends, and its baffling intellectual problems must therefore remain unsolved.

The friends believe that Job's suffering is the proof of his sin, and the clear evidence of his isolation from God. Job denies that his sin can explain his suffering. It is not that he is self-righteous, or claims to be sinless. He has no consciousness of any sin so heinous and so notable as to explain the overwhelming measure of his suffering. He denies that his sin and his suffering are matched, though he feels that they ought to be, and he makes many wild charges against God and accuses Him of injustice. For Job sometimes feels that his sufferings prove that he is isolated from God, though at other times he reveals a confidence that God will somehow vindicate him. Then God speaks to him from the whirlwind. Job is rebuked, but not for any sin which had produced his sufferings. He is rebuked for the wild charges which he had made in his ignorance, and these are in no sense the explanation of his troubles. Humbly Job bows before God, repenting of his folly, and crying: " I had heard of thee with the hearing of the ear; but now mine eye seeth thee." [14] That is to say, he declares that his experience had brought him a deeper knowledge of God, which was as the experience of sight compared with a rumour when set against the knowledge he had had before. God then declares Job vindicated on the issue which had been put to trial by his sufferings, and Job's prosperity is restored. Many readers feel that the epilogue spoils the book and throws away the whole case of Job. Prosperity does become the reward of righteousness, after all, and so the friends are right. This is a very mistaken apprehension of the meaning of the epilogue. In the prologue Satan had accused Job before God, and God had delivered Job over to be tested. After he had come through the test, and had demonstrated the falsity of the accusation — for Job nowhere breathes a word of regret for his integrity and loyalty to God — he could hardly be left still in the torments of Satan. The termination of his sufferings and the restoration of his prosperity are not the reward of his righteousness, but the indication that the trial is over.

One of the most dreadful consequences of the view that sin and suffering were always matched was the torture of the sense of isolation from God it produced in the sufferer. And the message of this book that there is innocent suffering meant that the sufferer was not by the mere fact of his suffering cut off from God. He might even be serving God, as Job was serving, and God might come to him in his very suffering, to bring a a deeper spiritual experience, as He came to Job. This is a very profound religious message, of enduring significance to men. It says that of more importance than the experience is what a man draws from it for

[14] Job xlii. 5.

his spiritual enrichment, and what he draws from it depends on how far he finds God in it.

Very abundant is the evidence, therefore, that the post-exilic age was not just an age of decadence and negligible achievement, and the creators of Judaism were not so immersed in sterile forms that they were incapable of perceiving the riches of the spiritual and ethical faith of the pre-exilic prophets. They were men to whom the world owes an immeasurable debt, the transmitters of a faith they shared, and the collectors of a literature that richly enshrined that faith. They are entitled to our sympathetic understanding and to our gratitude, and to our appreciation of the spiritual purpose they intended to serve by the ritual and by sacrifice. For this, too, was intended to enshrine their faith, and to carry that faith forward into the future and preserve it from contamination.

VIII. THE REVELATION OF GOD
AND ITS COROLLARIES

IN AN EARLIER chapter the growth of monotheism in Israel has been briefly reviewed. But the Old Testament has much more to say about God than that He is One. It says much about the character of God which is abidingly true. At the same time it says much that we can no longer accept as true. For many outgrown beliefs about God were entertained by Old Testament writers and characters, and we must distinguish between the continuing thread and the passing elements.

When the Danites migrated to the north and fell suddenly and without provocation on the unsuspecting city of Laish, for no better reason than that they coveted their land, they were encouraged by an oracle which assured them that Yahweh favoured their enterprise, though it was a plain violation of the tenth commandment. When the Israelites entered Canaan, they were moved with the same motive of land hunger, and they believed that their unprovoked attack on the land, and the ruthless slaughter of its inhabitants, had the fullest approval of Yahweh. Sometimes, as at Jericho, they massacred the entire population of a captured place, both male and female, old and young, and they did this as an act of religion, because they thought it was well-pleasing to Yahweh. Samuel believed that Yahweh wanted Israel to make a sudden attack on the Amalekites as a reprisal for something that had happened some centuries before, and to massacre them to a man. When Uzzah died suddenly at the time the Ark was being moved to Jerusalem, his death was believed to be due to the fact that Yahweh was angry with him because he had touched the

Ark, which had been entrusted to his care. David believed that God sent a famine on Israel in direct punishment of an act of Saul, committed many years earlier, and that He was pleased when seven of Saul's descendants were publicly hanged to expiate the crime. If the character of God is unchanging, and if that character is truly revealed in the Person of our Lord, or, indeed, in other passages of the Old Testament, these things can only represent men's false ideas about God. Here, as everywhere, we must preserve the historical sense, and remember that much has been outgrown. For the abiding message of the Old Testament can be apprehended only by him who reads it with discrimination, to separate the transient and the false from that which is enduringly true.

On the first page of the Bible we are told that man was created in the image of God. This is not to be understood in physical terms. There are many passages which think of God in physical terms, passages which represent Him as moulding man or building woman with His hands, or taking a walk in the Garden of Eden in the cool of the day, or coming down to see with His own eyes what is going on at Babel, or paying a call on the patriarchs and having His feet washed. But these things are not in the document which says that God created man in His own image. For this is the least anthropomorphic of all the documents. Anthropomorphism cannot be altogether dispensed with, indeed, and we are conscious of no impropriety when we speak of the heart of God, or of the voice of God, or of the eye of God. But we are only using the language of our experience to represent what we recognize to transcend our experience, and we are in no danger of forgetting that God is a Spirit. Nor was the writer of the first chapter of Genesis behind us in this. God was to him transcendent and spiritual, and man was not thought of as a physical replica of the divine Being. His thought was much deeper than that. For he was expressing his profound sense that man is by his creation akin to God.

For man has not merely a body, like the beasts of the field, though somewhat different in the details of its form. He is capable of fellowship with God, who is a Spirit, for he was created to be a spiritual being.

This is not to belittle the difference between man and God. Nothing could have been farther from the thought of the compilers of the Priestly document of the Pentateuch than such a belittling. In our day there is much emphasis in some quarters on the otherness of God, and He is frequently termed the " Wholly Other " than man. This was the result of a much-needed reaction from the view that so emphasized the divine element in man, and the immanence of God in man, that it sometimes led men to think they need look for no God beyond their own heart and nature. Neither extreme, however, represents the enduring message of the Old Testament. That God is other than man is its invariable teaching. He is man's Creator, before whom man must bow in adoration and awe. He is far beyond and above man. Even the seraphim veil their faces in His presence, and man is overwhelmed at the sense of the gulf that separates him from God. Yet God is not *wholly* other than man. The Old Testament, as well as the New, speaks of God as Father, and calls men His children. The Old Testament speaks of God's spirit clothing itself with a man's personality, even as the New speaks of His spirit dwelling in men and directing all their life. The prophets, as has been said, believed that they were extensions of the divine personality. All of this means that in the teaching of the Old Testament, no less than in that of the New, truth is found to lie in the tension between man's kinship with God, and God's otherness than man.

Moreover, the Old Testament teaches that God is a Being with a moral character. He is not merely a Spirit, with whom we can have spiritual intercourse. He is a good Spirit. There are passages in the Bible which conceive of God as Power, somewhat arbitrary and inexplicable. He first moves

David to number the people, and then blazes forth in anger against him for numbering them, and carries off great numbers of the people by plague. These are the passages that reflect the ideas that became outgrown. The more profoundly significant passages recognize that God's power is controlled by His character, and that there are things that God cannot do, not because He has not the means, but because He would be false to Himself if He did. Many religions impose various taboos upon men. These taboos must be observed, whether they are understood or not. And the Old Testament has many such taboos. Whatever historical origin they may have had, or whatever ideas may at one time have been embodied in them, does not matter. They must just be observed in blind and unquestioning obedience. But it is not for these that the Old Testament survives. Beyond these it lays, as we have seen, ethical constraints upon men. And all of these ethical constraints spring out of the view of God. They have a theological basis. When God calls men to be righteous, it is not because it is His whim to have men so. It is because He is righteous, and He who made man in His own image would have men reflect His own righteousness. When God calls men to manifest a tender and gracious spirit towards the weak, it is because He Himself manifests such a spirit in Himself, as the deliverance from Egypt showed. And through the course of the years the growing perception of the character of God brought growing demands upon men, for what God is men are called to be. " Be ye therefore perfect, as your heavenly Father is perfect," said our Lord,[1] in words that aptly represent the teaching of the Old Testament, as well as of the New. And it is teaching that would be the sheerest nonsense, if man were wholly other than God, and equally nonsense were man not other than God.

In another connexion we have recalled the familiar word

[1] Matt. v. 48.

in Micah vi. 8, in which the demands of God are formulated: " What doth Yahweh require of thee, but to do justly, and to love *ḥesed,* and to walk humbly with thy God? " In this great verse we have expressed those corollaries that we have drawn from the creation of man in God's image. Man must reflect the justice and the *ḥesed* of God, and must walk in His fellowship. He is the child of God, and must therefore be like God; he is by his creation capable of fellowship with God, and he must therefore experience that fellowship, if he is to attain the goal of his creation.

But the Old Testament teaching about God did not rest merely on speculation. It was not attained by men who withdrew from the turmoil of the world into the isolation of their own thought. It was rather attained by men who played a part in the affairs of their own day, who found God in common life as well as in great affairs, and who were led into the secrets of God's counsels by the things they witnessed and the things they experienced. When Amos perceived that God is a God of justice, demanding that men should practise justice in their dealings with one another, it was not because he was dreaming of Utopia, or because he saw that a world in which strict justice prevailed would be to the general interest of men. It was because his indignation was stirred at the injustice and the suffering he saw around him, and because he believed that it was the spirit of God that was stirring his emotions. In the setting of all the oppression and corruption of his day he saw God, and in the light of his vision of God he saw the true hatefulness of the things that went on around him. When Hosea penetrated so deeply into the love of God, and saw the sacredness of the demands of love for utter loyalty, it was not because he had the soul of a poet, and was moved with the thought of the rich and beauteous depths of love. It was because he was a sufferer, knowing a deep agony of spirit at the faithlessness of his wife, yet at the same time knowing a profound love for her. He knew in his own heart how deep is the demand of love for loyalty, not because it is selfish but because it is love. And he believed that it was the spirit of God moving in his spirit, and lifting him to share the secrets of God's heart that he might unveil them to men. When Jeremiah perceived that worship was not confined to the sanctuary and its cultus, he was not carrying through a dialectic process, and arguing that if God was Spirit, then His contact with the spirit of men was not conditioned by things material, but only by the receptiveness of men's spirit, and His worship could be the enriching experience of all who would offer it in spirit and in truth, wherever they might offer it. His teaching rested on his own vivid experience. He who was alone amongst men, and excluded from the worship of the Temple, experienced the presence of God and knew the joy of worship. It was not that he attained an intellectual persuasion that God could be worshipped apart from the Temple; it was that he had known the experience of worship apart from the Temple. His faith was born of his experience, and he declared his faith that it might be the basis of a like experience in others.

In this and in so much more of the same sort that could be drawn from the Old Testament we are reminded that God enters into the experience of men, and teaches them of Himself when they are sensitive to learn. In that fact there is a revelation of the character of God. He is not aloof and remote, the haughty monarch, but the Father, sharing the life of His children. He approaches men by the things they suffer, as He approached Hosea and Jeremiah; He also approaches them by simple daily experiences, by the things they see around them and the common tasks of life. By the early beauty of the almond tree in flower He could stir in Jeremiah thoughts of Himself, and by a basket of summer fruit he could stir in Amos the thought of approaching judgement. The great messages that these men learned

through their experience are true for us, and the understanding of God which they obtained through their experience is for us as well as for them. But beyond this, there is
abiding significance in the record of the way in which their
understanding was reached. It declares that our experience
may be the medium of God's approach to us, and that
through it He may teach us continually of Himself.

It has already been sufficiently indicated that God's message did not alone come through individual experience. In
corporate experience, too, He revealed Himself. For His
hand appears in all the course of history, and by its course
He teaches men of Himself and of His will. Old Testament
religion is throughout deeply rooted in history and experience. It was not built of the stuff that dreams are made of.
And Israel's religious leaders and prophets continually expounded unto her the meaning of history, and the things
they had themselves learned in their private experience,
which were ever at bottom things about God Himself, and
the corollaries for human conduct of their perception of
the nature of God.

Nor does the Old Testament ignore the corollaries of
monotheism. If God is One, and there is no other, then He
must be the God of all men, and Israel's election is not for
herself alone, but that she may be a blessing to all men. It
is by no accident that the corollaries of monotheism are
clearly perceived by Deutero-Isaiah, who first set forth in
unmistakable and explicit terms the truth of monotheism
itself. " There is no god else beside Me: a just God and a
saviour; there is none beside Me. Look unto Me, and be ye
saved, all the ends of the earth: for I am God, and there is
none else. By Myself have I sworn, the word is gone forth
from My mouth in righteousness, and shall not return, that
unto Me every knee shall bow, every tongue shall swear." [2]
Here the truth that Israel's God is not hers alone is set forth

2 Isa. xlv. 21 ff.

with the utmost emphasis as the inevitable corollary of monotheism. Yet Deutero-Isaiah does not for a moment abandon the thought of Israel's election. Indeed, he lays peculiar emphasis on that election in a whole series of passages. For the sole God of all men does not leave men to find Him of themselves. He has chosen Israel, that she might lead them to Him. " I Yahweh have called thee in righteousness, and will hold thine hand, and will keep thee, and give thee for a covenant of the people, for a light of the Gentiles; to open blind eyes, to bring out the prisoners from the dungeon, and them that sit in darkness out of the prison house. I am Yahweh; that is My name: and My glory I will not give to another, neither My praise unto graven images." [3] Here it is clearly declared that Yahweh is not content to leave the Gentiles to the worship of the not-gods, and that the fundamental purpose of His choice of Israel is that she should mediate His revelation unto them. She is thought of as charged with a mission to carry the faith which is her glory to be the glory of all men.

That mission reaches its greatest heights in the Servant Songs. It is disputed whether these are by the author of the rest of Deutero-Isaiah, or whether the Servant here is the nation Israel as elsewhere in Deutero-Isaiah, or an individual figure of past or contemporary history, or the ideal messianic figure of the future. It is probable that there was much fluidity in the author's thought, and it could pass without difficulty from the Servant-community of Israel to an individual who should supremely in himself embody its mission, and who should carry that mission to a point no other should reach.[4] On this view a messianic interpretation is neither to be wholly excluded nor made the sole in-

---

[3] Isa. xlii. 6 ff.

[4] The writer's view of the Servant, outlined in *Israel's Mission to the World*, 1939, and *The Missionary Message of the Old Testament*, 1945, owes much to H. Wheeler Robinson, and is closely similar to the view of F. B. Denio (*American Journal of Theology*, 5, 1901, pp. 322–327).

terpretation. In so far as a messianic interpretation is given to the Servant, the Songs are not to be thought of as a specific prediction of the life and work of our Lord, but as the enunciation of a great and creative idea which He clothed with reality. That idea was not alone of the mission to lead all men to the God of Israel, but of the means whereby the mission should be achieved.

In the first of the Songs we read: " Behold My Servant, whom I uphold; My chosen in whom My soul delighteth: I have put My spirit upon Him; He shall bring forth judgment to the nations." [5] In so far as the Servant is Israel, here as elsewhere in the Servant Songs there is an emphasis on her election that is unsurpassed anywhere in the Old Testament. For the election of Israel is in no sense inconsistent with the thought of Yahweh as the God of all men. For the purpose of the election is the service of God through the service of men, and the making known to the Gentiles of the character and will of God. The privilege and honour of Israel in being chosen of God is great indeed, but it is the privilege and honour of service. This is brought out even more clearly in the second of the Songs: " He said to me, Thou art My Servant; Israel, in whom I will be glorified. . . . And now saith Yahweh that formed me from the womb to be His Servant, to bring Jacob again to Him, and that Israel might be gathered unto Him: . . . it is too light a thing that thou shouldest be My Servant to raise up the tribes of Jacob, and to restore the preserved of Israel: I will also give thee for a light to the nations, that My salvation may reach to the end of the earth." [6] Here again the mission is based on the election. It is a mission to herself as well as to others. For Israel is called to lead all her children to her God, and beyond that to carry her service to the ends of the earth.

If the author of the Servant Songs had gone no farther

<hr />

[5] Isa. xlii. 1. [6] Isa. xlix. 3 ff.

than this, he would have reached a notable height, which was rarely reached by other Old Testament writers. There are many passages which recognize the implications of monotheism, and declare that Yahweh is to be worshipped of all men. Some of these are found in the collections of the oracles of pre-exilic prophets, though in every such case many scholars attribute these sayings to later days, and there can be no certainty of their authorship or date. Others are quite certainly of post-exilic date, and later than Deutero-Isaiah. Yet none of them, with a single exception, rises to the heights of Deutero-Isaiah and the Servant Songs already noted. For they think less of Israel's mission to the nations than of the spontaneous flow of the nations to Israel's God, and of the honour Israel will receive in the eyes of the nations and the service that will be rendered unto her.

There is a verse found in Isaiah,[7] and also in Habakkuk,[8] which presents the idea of the universal worship of Yahweh: " The earth shall be full of the knowledge of Yahweh, as the waters cover the sea." Similarly we read in the Psalter: " All the ends of the earth shall remember and turn unto Yahweh: And all the kindreds of the nations shall worship before Thee. For the kingdom is Yahweh's: And He is the ruler over the nations; "[9] and " All the nations which Thou hast made shall come and worship before Thee, and magnify Thy name, O Lord. For Thou art great and doest wondrous things: Thou alone art God."[10] In a number of passages it is made more explicit that this universal recognition of Israel's God was conceived of as involving the spiritual leadership of Israel, and the elevation of Jerusalem to be the spiritual centre of mankind. An oracle attributed independently to Isaiah[11] and to Micah[12] declares that " it shall come to pass in the latter days, that

7 Isa. xi. 9.
8 Hab. ii. 14.
9 Ps. xxii. 27 f. (Heb. 28 f.) .

10 Ps. lxxxvi. 9 f.
11 Isa. ii. 2 f.
12 Micah iv. 1 f.

the mountain of Yahweh's house shall be established as the chief of the mountains, and shall be exalted above the hills; and all nations shall flow unto it. And many peoples shall go and say, Come ye, and let us go up to the mountain of Yahweh, to the house of the God of Jacob; and He will teach us of His ways, and we will walk in His paths: for out of Zion shall go forth instruction, and the word of Yahweh from Jerusalem." In the book of Zephaniah, in a passage which is generally thought to come from a later hand, we read: " Then will I turn to the peoples a pure language, that they may all call upon the name of Yahweh, to serve Him with one consent. From beyond the rivers of Ethiopia My suppliants, widely dispersed, shall bring Mine offering." [13] A passage in the book of Jeremiah, which is similarly attributed to a secondary source, says: " At that time they shall call Jerusalem the throne of Yahweh; and all the nations shall be gathered unto it, to the name of Yahweh: neither shall they walk any more after the stubbornness of their evil heart." [14] The same thought inspires a passage of Trito-Isaiah: " Also the strangers, that join themselves to Yahweh, to serve Him and to love the name of Yahweh, to be His servants, every one that keepeth the sabbath without profaning it, and holdeth fast by My covenant; even them will I bring to My holy mountain, and make them joyful in My house of prayer; their burnt offerings and their sacrifices shall be accepted upon Mine altar: for Mine house shall be called a house of prayer for all peoples." [15] Or again, in Zechariah we find: " In those days it shall come to pass, that ten men shall take hold, out of all the languages of the nations, shall even take hold of the skirt of him that is a Jew, saying, We will come with you, for we have heard that God is with you." [16]

In these, and in several other passages that could be cited,

[13] Zeph. iii. 9 f.
[14] Jer. iii. 17.

[15] Isa. lvi. 6 f.
[16] Zech. viii. 23.

despite the nobility of their conception, there is little trace
of any mission of Israel to the Gentiles, and their expected
conversion to the faith of Israel is thought of rather as the
corollary of the prestige of the Jews, and the glory of Jerusalem. And the prestige of the Jews and the glory of Jerusalem should be still further enhanced by that conversion.

The prophet Malachi gives expression to a much more
remarkable thought. He rebuked the Jews, as has been said,
for the poverty of their sacrifices, holding that they reflected
the poverty of their spirit and the weakness of their loyalty.
He declares: " I have no pleasure in you, saith Yahweh of
hosts, neither will I accept an offering at your hand." [17] And
then he continues: " For from the rising of the sun unto its
setting My name is great among the Gentiles; and in every
place incense is offered unto My name, and a pure offering:
for My name is great among the Gentiles, saith Yahweh of
hosts." What he is here saying to his fellow Jews is that the
quality of the worship derives from the spirit that infuses
it, and not from its form, or from the God in whose name it
boasts. And he accepts the corollary of that thought. When
men of other nations offer to gods that are in truth no-gods
a worship that is infused with a pure spirit, the only God of
all men accepts it as offered unto Himself. By the sincerity
and exaltation of its spirit it is elevated above the half-
hearted worship Malachi saw all around him. Here there
is involved no bringing of worship to Jerusalem, and no
mission of Israel to the nations; nor even the acknowledg-
ment of Yahweh by that name, or any instruction in His
will and purpose.

None of this rises to the height of Deutero-Isaiah, with
his strong sense of the vocation of Israel to carry her faith
to all men. Nor have we yet exhausted the greatness of the
thought of the Servant Songs. For with the third of the
Songs we begin to see the means whereby the Servant is to

[17] Mal. i. 10.

accomplish His mission. " I gave My back to the smiters, and My cheeks to them that plucked off the hair: I hid not My face from shame and spitting." [18] Here there is no thought of a mission effected through honour and prestige, but through dishonour and suffering. It is by one who is looked down upon that the mission is carried through, not by one who inspires the envy of men. And in the fourth of the Songs, which rises to heights far surpassing the other three, this comes out yet more clearly. " He was despised and rejected of men; a man of sorrows, and acquainted with grief: and as one from whom men hide their face He was despised, and we esteemed Him not. Surely He hath borne our griefs, and carried our sorrows: yet we did esteem Him stricken, smitten of God, and afflicted. But He was wounded for our transgressions, He was bruised for our iniquities; the chastisement of our peace was upon Him; and with His stripes we are healed." [19] The speaker here represents the Gentiles, and the whole poem presents the great conception of a suffering which is redemptive, and which redeems not merely because it is suffering, but because of the spirit in which it is endured. If these four Servant Songs are by the author of Deutero-Isaiah, as seems to the writer most probable, he has travelled far beyond the simple corollary of monotheism in the thought that God is the God of all men. He has perceived that the end of Israel's vocation is to spread the knowledge of His name. The one God of all the earth is too wonderful a treasure for Israel to keep to herself. His truth and His fellowship, the knowledge of His nature and will, carry the sacred responsibility to share them with all His creatures.

It would, perhaps, be pressing the familiar Micah vi. 8 too far to find in it a suggestion of universalism. There we read: " He hath shewed thee, O man, what is good; and what doth Yahweh require of thee, but to do justly, and to

love *hesed,* and to walk humbly with thy God? " The
strangeness of the words " O man " here have often been
noted, and it is possible that they carry the suggestion that
the prophet is enunciating a principle which is of wider
validity than the bounds of Israel, expressing God's demands of man as man. A similar suggestion can be found
in the first chapter of Genesis, where the statement that
man was created in the image of God is certainly of wider
reference than the people of Israel, and implies that man
as such is capable of fellowship with God, for he is a spiritual being. It is equally implied that He who created man
in His own image is the God of all men.

It has been said that there is one other Old Testament
writer, besides Deutero-Isaiah, who entered into the thought
of the mission of Israel to the nations. This was the author
of Jonah. Yet here that mission is not set forth as a programme. The book of Jonah is quite unlike the other prophetic books of the Old Testament, and is rather of the
nature of a story about Jonah, who was called to preach to
the city of Nineveh and tried in vain to evade the call.
When he went to Nineveh and preached there, the city repented, to the disgust of the preacher, who had no pity in
his heart for the people to whom he proclaimed the message
of God. For this disgust and lack of pity he is rebuked by
God. It is commonly recognized to-day that the purpose
of the book is to condemn the narrow spirit of some of the
writer's contemporaries. It is not a call to Israel to embark
on a mission to the world, or even to Nineveh, which had
long since been destroyed when the story was written. It is
rather a declaration of the universality of the love of God,
and of His willingness to receive and to bless all who turn
to Him in humble repentance and obedience. That is a
great and gracious message, and one which ranks this writer,
alone of Old Testament writers, with Deutero-Isaiah. It is
possible that the book reflects something of the writer's

own spiritual pilgrimage, and that in his account of Jonah's reluctance to answer the call, and disgust at the sparing of Nineveh when it repented, there is reflected his own surly unwillingness to receive the message which he sets forth. He could have found it easier to contemplate the judgement of the nations than the repentance and pardon of the nations. Yet he was driven by the inner dynamic of his belief in the unity and love of God to the apprehension of the truth that he sets forth. Moreover, while the book is scarcely the programme of a world mission, it implies that through Israel alone can the preaching of God's message be done, and through its story of Jonah's mission to Nineveh, however unhistorical it might be, it familiarized men with the conception of such a mission.

It nevertheless remains true that Deutero-Isaiah, and especially in the third and fourth of the Servant Songs, reaches ideas of unique sublimity in this connexion in the Old Testament. That God is the universal object of man's rightful worship is implied in the concept of monotheism, and if *hesed* is of the essence of His nature, then He must be expected to manifest it in His interest in all men. But this can offer no clue to the source of the concept of the Suffering Servant. It is quite improbable that this was in any sense derived from the contemplation of Israel's sufferings in the exile. In the first place the pre-exilic prophets had declared that her sufferings were self-entailed by her disloyalty to her God, and it is improbable that Deutero-Isaiah disapproved of their view. Indeed, the opening verses of the prophecies of Deutero-Isaiah recognize that Israel has suffered for her sins. They bring a message of hope and comfort because that suffering is now ended, and her sin pardoned. " Comfort ye, comfort ye My people, saith your God. Speak ye comfortably to Jerusalem, and cry unto her that her time of service is accomplished, that her iniquity is pardoned; that she hath received of Yah-

weh's hand double for all her sins." [20] The historical sufferings of Israel in the exile can therefore have nothing
whatever to do with the sufferings of the Servant. For he
was not suffering for his sins, and his own pardon was not
the goal of his sufferings. " He was wounded for our transgressions, He was bruised for our iniquities; the chastisement of our peace was upon Him; and with His stripes we
are healed . . . although He had done no violence, neither was any deceit in His mouth. . . . Yet He bare the
sin of many, and made intercession for the transgressors." [21]
This great idea was not the deduction from any historical
suffering of Israel, for history knows of none that could sus-
tain it. Moreover, if Deutero-Isaiah had supposed that the
sufferings of the exile would prove potent to lead the world
to Israel's God, he would have made a grim and tragic mistake. His message to Israel was that her sufferings were
over and she was about to experience a great deliverance,
that He who was overthrowing her oppressor as a prelude
to a second Exodus was calling her to be a light to the Gentiles, and that mission was linked in the person of the Suffering Servant to an experience of cruel but innocent suffering. The sufferings of the Servant would therefore
appear to have lain in the future as the prophet saw it.

It is possible that this concept owed something to the
teaching of Hosea. Just as universalism is the corollary of
the unity of God, so the concept of vicarious suffering is in
some measure the corollary of Hosea's perception of the
character of God. Hosea loved his wife, and because he
loved he suffered in her unfaithfulness. Yet his love continued, and he deeply yearned to save from the corrupting
power of her sin the wife whose conduct caused him his
pain. And Hosea through his experience came to know
what God was like, and what the inner quality of the *ḥesed*
of God was. All the pain of his heart was but a pale copy of

[20] Isa. xl. 1 f.   [21] Isa. liii. 5 ff.

the pain of God's heart, and all his yearning for the redemption of Gomer but a reflection of God's yearning for the redemption of Israel from her sin. It is the nature of love to suffer, and to go on loving its object even when its love brings the suffering. But if God is the God of all men, then that love is not confined to Israel, and the same yearning and the same pain mark God's thought of all men. Moreover, if the essential demand of religion is that men shall reflect the character of God, then Israel was called not alone to be loyal to Him, but to reflect His spirit and to share His love. She, too, must yearn to see all men loving and serving Him, and must realize her mission to be the extension of the divine personality in leading them to Him. And she will assuredly enter into the pain of His love, for her love and service will be scorned and trampled on, to make her heart bleed, not with her sufferings so much as with her pity and her love. None can enter into the love of God without also entering into the sorrows of His heart. By her entering into that sorrow Israel could alone hope to fulfil her mission.

Yet if Deutero-Isaiah was thus borne on the inner dynamic of his own full and explicit monotheism, linked with the message of Hosea, it was probably not by rational processes that he was carried. There was the moving of the spirit of God in his spirit, lifting him to express the things he perceived in a way that transcended any mere logical deduction from already apprehended truth. For, as has been said above, there was fluidity in his thought, and if in some measure the Servant stood for Israel, it equally stood for some individual who should carry the mission of the Servant to a unique point. And this is especially true of the fourth Song, where he seems to be thinking less of a personalization than of a person. It was in a Person, too, that it found its supreme fulfilment. In that Person the love of God was shared, and the divine yearning over men was manifested. And that He saved by suffering has been the faith and the experience of the Church. Yet it was not by the physical sufferings of crucifixion that He saved. Many have been crucified besides Jesus of Nazareth, without achieving any service of men. It was because His crucifixion was the consequence of His love, and because its deepest agony was not the physical agony of the pain He endured, but the agony of the love that loved even when it was rejected, and that knew an infinite pity for those who inflicted a deeper injury on themselves by their rejection of Him than any they inflicted on Him. It was because in His crucifixion He entered perfectly into the love and the suffering of God that He so gloriously fulfilled the prophecy of the Servant.[22]

The Early Church became a missionary Church, and to-day the Church is essentially missionary. It is to us a matter of course that the Christian faith is not something given to us to corner, but a Gospel of universal import. Yet we cannot truly fulfil the mission entrusted to us, unless we enter in some measure into the suffering of the Servant. For if the fulfilment of that vision in the Cross of Christ is of the essence of the message the Church proclaims, there is a sense in which we are called to enter into the experience of the Cross, and to " suffer with Him." [23] We do not merely proclaim the love of God in Christ objectively; we enter into that love, and know its yearning, and feel the pangs of God's rejected love. Without that sympathy, in the proper sense of the word, that suffering with God, we cannot fulfil the mission to the world which Israel passed on to the Church; with it we cannot be indifferent to that mission.

We are the inheritors of the faith and message of the Old Testament, and our debt to this Book for the lasting worth

[22] This paragraph stands almost verbatim as the penultimate paragraph of Chapter III of my small book on *The Missionary Message of the Old Testament.*

[23] Rom. viii. 17.

of its faith and message is immeasurable. It is true that Judaism never became a missionary faith in the sense in which Christianity has. Deutero-Isaiah thought of his people as charged wth a message to all men, and in his clear perception of the unity of God and the love of God felt an exuberant sense of the wonder of the treasure entrusted to Israel, and the wonder of her responsibility to share it with all men. Yet in the post-exilic days no such mission was undertaken. The exiles who returned found a dispirited community in Palestine, hard to arouse and with scanty resources, completely unfitted spiritually to enter into the vision and the mission that had so inspired Deutero-Isaiah. And in the next century Nehemiah and Ezra felt that the pressing problem was to preserve the faith of the community from complete extinction. It was threatened in many ways, as has been said earlier, and they believed that only by the withdrawing of the community within itself, and the complete cutting off of contact with all alien influences as far as possible, could its faith be maintained. Instead of an exuberant spirit and an aggressive influence, they saw the aggressive cultural and spiritual influences around them, powerful and hard to resist.

Yet it has to be remembered that Judaism was never wholly forgetful of her mission. To use a metaphor which the writer has elaborated elsewhere, if Judaism erected the wall of particularism around the garden, it was to prevent ways had a gate in the wall to admit friends. For Judaism She therefore always welcomed proselytes, who were ready did not swerve from her monotheism, or forget its corollary. the garden from being trampled down; and Judaism al- to share her life and faith. And the New Testament brings its evidence that there were not a few proselytes and other interested Gentiles found in the synagogues of the Jews. Even though Judaism never embarked on a conscious mission to all men, she did not entirely forget that mission; and she certainly preserved the message of Deutero-Isaiah, and passed it on to Christianity, where it bore fruit. For the Church regarded itself as the heir of Judaism, entering into the heritage of her election and her mission alike. And so the Church embarked on the stupendous enterprise of carrying its message anywhere and everywhere. It conceived of itself as charged with a Gospel of universal significance, and therefore as charged to carry it to all men. In this it was but carrying into effect the corollaries of faith which the Old Testament had taught.

There is a further corollary of the revelation of God which calls for mention. It has already been said that in the Old Testament teaching that man was made in the image of God there was implicit the recognition of man's kinship with God and otherness than God. This is even more clearly the corollary of the divine use of human personality as the medium of revelation. For it has been sufficiently said in earlier chapters that if God could reveal some things of Himself through history and through external experience, it was through the organ of human personality that the richest and clearest revelation came. Indeed, even the revelation in history and experience required the medium of personality for its interpretation.

It is frequently observed that an artist is always limited by the medium through which he expresses himself. The sculptor, the painter, the musician, and the poet may all deal with the theme of Spring, but each is limited in the expression of his thought by his medium. And when God speaks through Nature, through history, and through personality He is in each case limited by His medium. But because personality is the most akin to Himself it is the medium of His highest word, and it is personality He uses to set before men His positive will for them, and the ideals whereby alone they may truly live.

The theological consequence of the view that human

personality may be the organ of the divine Spirit is that recognition of man's kinship with God and otherness than God already noted. If the spirit of God can penetrate and possess the spirit of man, while the one may be rightly recognized to be profoundly other than what it penetrates and possesses, it cannot be wholly other. The heresy of the view that God is wholly other than man seems to be especially exposed in the Christian view of the Person of Christ. For the Christian view is that our Lord was one Person, and that He was truly God and truly Man. Godhead and Manhood are united indissolubly in a single Person. Wholly other, then, they cannot be; yet other they must be. The necessity for Christ would seem to be involved in the true reading of the Old Testament. For its perception that human personality may be the organ of divine revelation both prepares for the doctrine of the Incarnation, and demands the Incarnation as the goal and climax of revelation. For revelation through the organ of human personality means that God is limited in His self-revelation by the spiritual imperfections of the organ. Perfect revelation requires the perfect organ. And since nothing short of a perfect revelation can be believed to satisfy a self-revealing God, the perfect Man, in whom God perfectly reveals Himself, who is thus wholly One with God, may reasonably be expected. This is not to reduce Christ to but one of the prophetic line, any more than Paul's reference to Him as the " first-born among many brethren " [24] reduces Him to but the *primus inter pares* of the Church. He in whose true and perfect Manhood God perfectly reveals Himself is alike of us and beyond us. He is of us and beyond us precisely because God is of us and beyond us, our Kinsman and our Creator, our Father and our God.

[24] Rom. viii. 29.

IX. THE NATURE, NEED,
AND DESTINY OF MAN

IN WHAT HAS been already said there is involved something of the Old Testament conception of man. For it has been said that he is a creature of God, made in the image of God, and that this is not intended to minimize the difference between man and God or the likeness between man and God. For already Jeremiah, before the date of the Priestly document that declares man to be in the image of God, had asked, " Am I a God at hand, saith Yahweh, and not a God afar off? Can any hide himself in secret places that I shall not see him? saith Yahweh. Do not I fill heaven and earth? said Yahweh," [1] and there is no reason to suppose that the priestly writer would have disagreed with Jeremiah's answers to these questions. Physically, then, there can be little likeness between man and God, and it is in the spiritual quality of his being that he is made in the image of God.

This is not to ignore the oft-noted fact that in Hebrew thought man is an animated body. The Hebrew did not think of man as a spirit inhabiting a body, in the sense that the real man consisted of the spirit, while the body was but its casket. Body and spirit belonged together in the unity of personality. In the totality of his personality, therefore, man cannot be in the image of God, and that wherein he is akin to God cannot be isolated from the totality of his personality. A sculptor may carve an image of a man so that all must recognize the likeness. Yet the totality of his manhood is not transferred to the stone, and the likeness is not separable from the stone. It is the reproduction of one aspect of an indivisible whole in another indivisible whole,

[1] Jer. xxiii. 23 f.

whose otherness is as obvious as its likeness. And in a comparable way the spiritual quality of that animated body which the Hebrew conceived man to be showed him to be made in the image of God, who nevertheless, in the totality of His Being, is very different from man. In his spiritual attainment man is quite other than God; but in that he is a spiritual being, capable of fellowship with God, and capable of reflecting something of the character of God, he has a measure of affinity with God. And this measure of affinity is God's gift to man in the act of his creation, and not something that man has achieved for himself.

While, therefore, man is a creature of dignity and honour, when he truly understands the source of that dignity and honour his heart is filled with humility and awe at the wonder of his privilege. " When I consider Thy heavens, the work of Thy fingers, The moon and the stars, which Thou hast ordained; What is man, that Thou art mindful of him? And the son of man, that Thou visitest him? For Thou hast made him but little lower than God, And crownest him with glory and honour." [2] He can take no pride unto himself for his high status amongst created things, but is filled with wonder that he should be singled out for such honour. And in that honour privilege and responsibility are knit together indivisibly. That he is in the image of God opens up to him the infinite privilege of fellowship with God, and at the same time lays upon him the sacred obligation to enjoy that fellowship, and so fulfil the purpose of his creation. The oldest Creation story the Bible contains narrates with simple naïveté how God strolled through the Garden of Eden, calling out for Adam and Eve, who had hidden from His face and fellowship. Behind that story lies the profound and enduring thought that fellowship with God is alike man's privilege and duty. The idea of a man priding himself in the thought that he is the

[2] Ps. viii. 3 ff. (Heb. 4 ff.)

crown of creation, and self-sufficient without God, would
have been ludicrous to the writers of the Old Testament.
His assumption of self-sufficiency would have indicated that
he was missing the goal of his creation, and was therefore
insensitive to the real meaning of the glory in which he
took pride.

Stress is often laid on the social character of the Hebrew
conception of man, and it is of the utmost importance to
remember that he was not thought of simply as a separate
individual, responsible for his own life, but also as a part of
the social whole. Yet we should beware of overstating the
facts. It is sometimes supposed that Jeremiah and Ezekiel
discovered the individual. This is a gross exaggeration. It
is true that with Jeremiah and Ezekiel the individual came
into much greater prominence, but it is not true that hitherto man had been regarded solely as a member of the community. Nor did those two prophets regard him solely as
an individual. With them there came a new emphasis on
the individual, rather than a discovery of the individual.

That man is a social figure was never doubted by Israel.
He is a member of a family, and therefore involved in the
life of the family. In the present, expanded form of the
Decalogue, it is said that Yahweh is " a jealous God, visiting the iniquity of the fathers upon the children, upon the
third and upon the fourth generation of them that hate "
Him,[3] and the same thought is found elsewhere in the Old
Testament. Man is also a member of the tribe or nation,
and again he is involved in its history. When David sinned
by numbering the people, it occasioned no surprise that
the punishment should fall upon the whole people. It occasioned no more when the private sin of Achan entailed
the community in defeat until the sin of Achan was purged
by the destruction of him and all his family. It is true that

[3] Exod. xx. 5.

the law of Deuteronomy lays it down that " the fathers shall not be put to death for the children, neither shall the children be put to death for the fathers," [4] but this does not mean that the authors of Deuteronomy failed to see that children are inevitably involved in the consequences of their fathers' sins, and in the consequences of the sins of the community, whether the corporate sin that marks the general life of an age, or the representative sin of the king. These are plain facts that are established by the experience of every age. For even though only the sinner be put to death for his sin, his children may be involved in poverty, and will certainly be involved in disgrace, in consequence, while sins that do not bring formal punishment may bring hatred or disease upon a family, as well as upon the sinner; while so far as the wider community is concerned, days of war bring grim evidences of the way in which men and women may be swept out of the chosen way of their lives into new, and oft-times tragic experiences, by no act of their own. We are certainly parts one of another, and knit together with bonds that we did not create and cannot escape.

It is sometimes supposed that this represents some radical injustice of the nature of things. In a recent book S. J. Case says: " In the processes of history one generation's mistakes saddle troubles upon the children, while the sinning ancestors escape scot-free. In primitive times one could say that the iniquity of the fathers was visited upon the children to the third and fourth generation. In those days it was a vengeful Deity whom men revered, but that conception can no longer be tolerated where a modern sense of justice prevails. . . . Can we believe that God is so arbitrary a monarch, or so vindictive a feudal noble, that he could find satisfaction in executing punishment upon guiltless sons and daughters of sinful parents who are peacefully

[4] Deut. xxiv. 16.

reposing in their tombs? Calamity is not a divine judgment but is the natural consequence of failure to embrace
opportunity." [5]

The modern sense of justice that lies behind this appears
to be based on the conception of man as only an individual.
The fact that children do suffer for the sins of their fathers
is recognized, but it is supposed that the character of God
is preserved by attributing this to natural consequences,
and not to God. But if God is the Author of the universe
and all that is, and if there is a fundamental injustice in the
very nature of things, then the character of God is not
saved, and the advance upon the beliefs of primitive times
would not appear to be conspicuous. In so far as Israel believed that in arbitrary ways God took pleasure in the punishment of children for the sins of their fathers, her belief
has been outgrown; but if in natural and inevitable ways
children do share in the fruits of their fathers' sins, a place
must be found for this in the divine justice, if God is indeed to be accounted just. Nor is this difficult, when man
is recognized to be both an individual and a member of
various social units, whose experience he must share. For
then the recognition of the will of God operating in the
natural consequences of human action is seen to be no expression of His vengeful character, but the expression of the
divine benevolence. For the operation of these natural
principles must be viewed as a whole before their real character can be seen, and before their revelation of the character of God can be truly estimated.

In a passage which is commonly attributed to the earliest
of the Pentateuchal sources we read: " Yahweh, Yahweh, a
God full of compassion and gracious, slow to anger and
plenteous in _hesed_ and truth; keeping _hesed_ for thousands,
forgiving iniquity and transgression and sin: and that will
by no means clear the guilty; visiting the iniquity of the fa-

[5] _The Christian Philosophy of History_, 1943, p. 181.

thers upon the children, and upon the children's children, upon the third and upon the fourth generation." [6] Here, in these primitive times, we find a surprising wholeness in the view of things. The divine beneficence and the involving of children in the consequences of their fathers' sins are treated as the obverse and reverse of the one and undivided character of God. In their wholeness, indeed, the very natural principles which bring evil consequences bring also incalculable blessings upon succeeding generations. To isolate the evils and to ignore the blessings can lead to no sound judgement.

If man were but an individual, it were unjust that he should be involved in the fruits of any action but his own. He could not then expect to enter into the inheritance of knowledge and culture and freedom achieved by the generations that have gone before. He could only expect that his life would be as wholly isolated as if he were placed at birth on a desert island, without any inherited capacities beyond those enjoyed by the first man. He could not expect to put on a gramophone record and hear a famous orchestra interpreting a great symphony; he could not even expect to use electricity or gas, unless he had first discovered their possibilities wholly for himself; he could not even eat an omelette unless he had first learned of the possibility of an omelette when he found out for himself the secret of its making; in his world literature would be quite inconceivable, save such as he wrote for himself and for no other, and speech would be an irrelevance; the rights of citizenship would be unmeaning, for there could be no citizenship. Barren indeed would be the world of pure individualism, and few would desire to live in it. But all who desire to enter with enjoyment into all the inheritance of good wrought for them by their fathers should pause before they claim in the name of justice to be freed from all the

6 Exod. xxxiv. 6 f.

inheritance of evil. For both are brought to them by the operation of the same principles, and the good of their inheritance infinitely outweighs the evil. It is more profitable for them to reflect that in so far as there is evil in their lives it is a curse not alone to themselves, but to the society to which they belong, and to the children who shall come after them.

If man's oneness with the generations that have gone before him calls for recognition, his oneness with the contemporary society of which he forms a part needs no arguing. In our day we are witnessing a sustained debate between those who hold the individual and those who hold the social view of man. In the reaction from the older individualism, which too often regarded any claims upon him by society as subject to his ratification, there is the swing to the opposite extreme, which recognizes the claims of society upon him as absolute, and divests him of all rights save such as the community chooses to allow him. Israel had a more balanced view, and her emphasis on man's sociality and on man's individuality offers a vital message to the modern world.

The common idea that prior to Jeremiah and Ezekiel the individual was thought of solely as a fragment of the social whole is not borne out by the study of the Old Testament. He had individual rights which were inalienably his, and which not even the king could invade. That was why Nathan rebuked David for the adultery with Bathsheba, and Elijah rebuked Ahab for the murder of Naboth. The prophets were all fundamentally individualists. They refused to regard themselves as merely fragments of the community, bound to reflect the will and spirit of the community, and wholly caught up into the life of the community. Elijah could believe that he was in a minority of one who remained loyal to the will of God, but his belief did not shake his resolve to remain loyal. There were obligations more sacred than any laid upon him by the spirit of his day. Micaiah could see all the other prophets of his time taking a line which he could not share, while still unashamedly maintaining the individuality of his position.

But what is commonly meant when the rise of individualism is ascribed to Jeremiah and Ezekiel is that prior to these prophets religion was the affair of the community rather than of the individual. Yahweh was the God of Israel as a whole, rather than of individual Israelites. It was the nation Israel that was His child, whom He called out of Egypt. Vital to the religion of Israel was the obligation to keep the great festivals, when all who belonged fully to the community should repair to the shrines. It is true that a multiplicity of individual sacrifices were offered there, but these represented the individual's sharing in the social festival. His sacrifice had not meaning for himself alone. It was rather the recognition that he belonged to the community, and that its history and its life were for him, and that therefore its religion claimed his devotion. All this and more is true. Yet it is also true that religion functioned on more than festival days. Even at the festival time Hannah could bring her individual prayer to God, and religion had a meaning for her as an individual and not merely as a fragment of Israel. She believed that God could enter into her bitterness of spirit, and could take compassion on her, a helpless woman of no importance. Moreover, on other than festival days a man might celebrate some event in his own home by a sacrifice at the shrine, followed by a sacrificial meal, such as that at which we find Samuel when Saul first came to him at Ramah. Here we find that others were invited to the meal, so that it was given a social character. But here it was not that he by his sacrifice was entering into the social experience, but that he was inviting others to enter into his experience and to share its joy.

Moreover, in all that has been said in an earlier chapter of the call of the prophets, it is clear that this was a pro-

foundly individual experience. His call might have significance for the community, and for succeeding generations.
But it was ever an individual experience of God, marking
the prophet as not merely one among the thousands of Israel, but as an individual, claimed by God for a unique
service, and responsible to God as an inividual for the exercise of his ministry.

The sociality and the individuality of man were therefore held together in the unity of a single view of the nature of man. The fundamental unity comes out most
clearly in what Principal Wheeler Robinson has frequently
called attention to as the Hebrew concept of corporate
personality. The group could be thought of as function-
ing through an individual member, who for the time being
so completely represented it that he became identical with
it. By the study of this concept Wheeler Robinson has
thrown light on the use of the pronoun " I " by the Psalmists, and on the Suffering Servant of Deutero-Isaiah. There
was a fluidity of thought which seems strange to us, whereby
the speaker could pass from the community to the individual who represented it, and from the individual back to
the community, without any apparent consciousness of the
transitions.

Here, as everywhere, a historical perspective must be preserved, and it must not be supposed that all of the deductions which Israel drew from her conception of man were
justified. The practices of blood revenge and of the levirate
marriage were based on that conception, as were many of
the actions that are most repugnant to us. The destruction
of Achan's family, and the hanging of Saul's descendants in
Gibeah, were justified by the sense of the solidarity of the
family, past, present and future. But these events took place
before the newer emphasis on the individual had redressed
the balance of the excessive emphasis on the corporate unity
of the family and the tribe. Nevertheless, while we may

rightly reject many of the false deductions, which Israel herself outgrew, we may find enduring truth in her recognition of the individuality and the sociality of man, and we may seek to hold both firmly together in a unity which subordinates neither to the other.

Even more vital to the Old Testament than its conception of the nature of man is its view of his need. He is not alone a creature of dignity and high estate; he is a creature of deep need. And his need is for salvation from sin. There are many terms for sin in the Bible, and it is variously thought of as a missing of the mark, rebellion against God, moral perversion, or obtuseness of character. But however conceived, sin comes between man and God and holds man back from the attainment of the goal of his being. It is often said that it is the later post-exilic Judaism which is obsessed with the thought of sin, and which provided in the stately ritual the means of disposing of sin. It is undoubtedly true that sin figures more largely in the later Law, where there was combined with the prophetic ethical emphasis an emphasis on techical offences which quite certainly has ancient roots in Israel. But it is not true that the idea of sin belongs in any sense only to the post-exilic age. At the beginning of the oldest of the Pentateuchal sources sin figures as the curse of man, causing him to be driven from the Garden and separating him from God. In the great court history of the reign of David, that is probably extracted from the most ancient of the sources of the books of Samuel, we find that when David is rebuked for his adultery with Bathsheba, he replies, " I have sinned." Nor was involuntary and unconscious sin the creation of post-exilic days. In the oldest of the sources of the history of Saul's reign, we find that on the evening of the battle of Michmash when Saul consulted the oracle no response was forthcoming. And Saul said, " Draw nigh hither, all ye chiefs of the people: and know and see wherein this sin hath been this day." [7] And when the " sin " was located, it proved to be that Jonathan, who had not been present when his father prohibited the eating of food that day, and who therefore had no knowledge of the interdict, had tasted a little honey in the forest. What is new in the post-exilic Law is no fresh conception of the existence or the nature of sin, but a greater emphasis on the exceeding sinfulness of sin.

For sin was always thought of as essentially sin against God. It might be individual or it might be corporate, it might be the transgressing of some ritual precept or it might be some moral offence; but it was always first and foremost sin against God. Often, indeed, man's sin against man is denounced, but it is always conceived of as also and primarily sin against God. When David confesses his sin in the matter of Bathsheba, he does not merely say, " I have sinned," or, " I have sinned against Bathsheba, or against Uriah," or, " I have violated the moral law," but " I have sinned against Yahweh." So too in the psalm which has been traditionally associated with this incident, but which is to-day more generally regarded as quite unconnected with it, the Psalmist cries, " Against thee, thee only, have I sinned, and done this evil in thy sight." [8] For sin against man is not the infringement of rights which are man's by nature, but the infringement of rights which are his because God willed that they should be his. To deny those rights was of course to injure man; but it was also to rebel against God. Justice and morality were never thought of as principles to which even God Himself must bow, and which He must acknowledge, or which He takes under His guardianship, but principles which inhere in God's character, so that the denial of them is *ipso facto* the denial of God and rebellion against Him.

This was always the point of view of the prophets. They denounced moral iniquity in the name of God, and not in

[7] 1 Sam. xiv. 38.   [8] Ps. li. 4 (Heb. 6)

the name of humanity. When Amos found the rich grinding down the poor, and ruthlessly exploiting all the resources of the law for their own enrichment, he believed that the heartless indifference to the sufferings of others and the implicit denial of the spirit of brotherhood was an offence against God. When Isaiah, with a deeper and more spiritual ethical sense, cried, " Woe is me! for I am undone; because I am a man of unclean lips, and I dwell in the midst of a people of unclean lips," [9] he was responding to the vision of God. It was in the light of that vision that uncleanness was seen to be unclean, and the prophet's trembling of heart was before God. When Jeremiah called for circumcision of heart, and penetrated to the springs of human thought and action, and carried thither his ethical demands, he was but drawing out what he perceived to be the significance of the Covenant that bound Israel to God. It is always ethics springing out of religion and vitalized by religion that the prophets inculcate, for in their view all sin is sin against God.

It is precisely the same with the later Law, where we read: " If any one sin, and commit a trespass against Yahweh, and deal falsely with his neighbour in a matter of deposit, or of pledge, or of robbery, or have oppressed his neighbour," [10] and again: " When a man or woman shall commit any sin that men commit, to do a trespass against Yahweh," [11] where the sequel makes it plain that the trespass is also a trespass against man. Everywhere in the Old Testament sin is perceived to be against God, and its growing understanding of the character of God carried with it a profounder penetration of the nature and the range of sin, to lead in its turn to a deeper insight into the depth of human need for salvation from sin.

But if all sin is sin against God, it is also true that all sin

9 Isa. vi. 5.
10 Lev. vi. 2 (Heb. v. 20).

11 Num. v. 6.

is sin against man. No sin is the private concern of a man. If he sins against God in sinning against his neighbour, clearly his sin also concerns his neighbour. If he defrauds his neighbour, or oppresses his neighbour, or wrongs his neighbour by such adultery as David's or by such iniquity as Jezebel's elimination of Naboth, manifestly his sin is not merely a private matter between himself and God. But even if no direct wrong is done to his neighbour, his sin yet concerns others. Achan's sin in preserving what should have been destroyed was no direct sin against man, but against God alone. No man was impoverished by what he had done. Yet its consequences concerned the whole community, for it brought a curse upon all Israel. Similarly Jonathan's involuntary sin in tasting honey involved consequences upon others, in the failure of the oracle to give any response when the king, as the representative of the community, consulted it. Many of the ideas that appear in these incidents belong to the transcended past, and are in no sense valid for us. Yet there is something abidingly true in their message. No man's character or acts are his alone. He is a member of a community, and he lives his life not to himself alone. In countless ways the most private acts of his life concern others. He may not alone sin, but by his example lead others to sin, like Jeroboam the son of Nebat. He may transmit the fruits of his sin to his children in a diseased body or in a character which is all too prone to repeat his sin. At the least by his sin he lowers the moral and spiritual worth of the community to which he belongs, just as by his righteousness he may enrich the whole community. In the story of Abraham's intercession for Sodom it is indicated that a handful of righteous people might have been the salvation of the city. By the same token every man who sins lowers the tone of the community, demeans his personality and therefore willy nilly reduces the quality of his influence, whether conscious or unconscious. Morally and spiritually he is a social liability instead of the social asset he might be.

Man's deepest need, therefore, is for deliverance from sin. There are passages in the Old Testament which think of salvation from physical and political subjection, and at some of these we have already looked. But such salvation was never thought of as the deepest and most fundamental need of men. Salvation from the sin that separated him from God, and that cursed him by its corrupting touch, and restoration to the favour and fellowship of God, were of greater significance and importance.

In an earlier chapter it has been observed that it is often supposed that in the thought of the Old Testament, apart from the prophets, and especially in the post-exilic thought, salvation is achieved by the mere offering of sacrifice. It is true that both in pre-exilic and in post-exilic days there were some in Israel who supposed that they could attain salvation by the mere performance of ritual acts. But it has been already insisted that that was a heresy to both prophets and the creators of Judaism alike. For in the thought of the Old Testament salvation is effected by no human act, but by God alone. Whether salvation is from physical and political servitude, as in the case of deliverance from Egypt, or whether it is from sin, it is conceived of as God's act. This is a message of abiding significance, and in few ages more needed than in ours, when the heresy condemned by the prophets is so widespread amongst those who fondly believe they are the disciples of the prophets.

The prophets found men cherishing a magical view of the ritual. Such a view has prevailed in many religions, and it is the constant peril of a ritualistic religion that men shall regard the ritual act as an end in itself, and as the source of power instead of the channel of power. When the prophets found men diligent in keeping feasts and lavish in sacrifices, yet living lives which they perceived to be the very antithesis of the will of God, they roundly declared that their religiosity, so far from bringing them salvation, was an offence to God and a curse to themselves. Their emphasis on social righteousness, however, which in the last generation has come into new prominence in what is sometimes thought to be a re-discovery of the prophets, has led not a few to suppose that it is by social righteousness that man is saved. To the prophets that would be as gross a heresy as the faith in the ritual which they condemned. For man is not saved by man's act, whether that act be the offering of sacrifice, or conformity to a high ethical code.

The prophets were fundamentally religious leaders, calling men to the springs of religion as the basis of their conduct. It was only men who walked humbly with God who could do the will of God, only men on whose hearts God had inscribed His law who could reach the goal set before men in the prophetic witness. Obedience to God in daily life was called for, not as the substitute for sacrifice, but as its validation; or perhaps it would be truer to say, as the evidence of the reality of sacrifice. It was not that only the good could sacrifice, but that only those who were ready to be made good could truly sacrifice. When sacrifice has any meaning at all, it presents to God man's plea for help and equally the pledge of his willingness to receive it. And when he has received it, he is so lifted into the fellowship of God that the will of God must triumph in all his life. For salvation is not alone from but to — salvation from sin and to renewed fellowship with God. Nor is that fellowship with God ever thought of merely in terms of mystical ecstasy. It issues in goodness. It has a positive end, which is naturally and necessarily the antithesis of the sin from which man is saved. For if sin is disobedience to the will of God, then salvation must issue in obedience to His will. But it is God who grants the boon of this salvation and the obedience to which it leads, in response to the true submission of spirit of him who rightly seeks it. Salvation is always and wholly of God; it is equally salvation unto God.

Many who bear the Christian name in our day conceive of salvation as something to be enjoyed. They suppose that it brings them deliverance from the penalties of sin and a guarantee of immortal bliss, a peace and poise of spirit amidst all the vicissitudes of life, and an assurance of their continued eixstence beyond the grave. And they have no conception of a salvation which lifts them into the will of God, and makes them living centres of divine influence, linking them with the purposes of God to infuse all the purposes of their life, and enabling them to present the character of God in all their activities. In the thought of the Bible salvation is dynamic. It is a gift to be humbly received and gratefully enjoyed; it is also power for the fulfilment of the high obligations it lays upon those who receive it. It is not alone something which God does for man, but something which He achieves in him.

On the destiny of man the Old Testament has less to say. It believed that man was not made for death, but that death came by sin. This is the significance of the story of the Garden of Eden. The real end of man's being was to live for ever in the fellowship of God, but sin came between him and that end. Sin therefore not alone brought death, but destroyed his fellowship with God. Hence death is commonly conceived of as complete and utter isolation from God. The doctrine of Sheol which is found in most of the Old Testament pictures the departed as continuing to exist, indeed, but in a colourless sort of existence, without God, and without joy. It held out the dreariest prospect to men and contained no glimmer of comfort for them. " My soul is full of troubles," cried the Psalmist, " and my life draweth nigh unto Sheol. I am counted with them that go down into the pit; I am as a man that hath no help: Cast off among the dead, Like the slain that lie in the grave,

Whom thou rememberest no more." [12] This is the cry of the man who is only conscious of his loyalty to God, and it reveals his idea of the prospect of the faithful, and not of the wicked. They are wholly isolated from God. " Shall Thy lovingkindness — Thy *hesed* — be declared in the grave? " he continues, " Or Thy faithfulness in Abaddon? Shall Thy wonders be known in the dark? And Thy right-eousness in the land of forgetfulness? " Similarly in the psalm which is attributed to the good king Hezekiah we read: " For Sheol cannot praise Thee, death cannot cele-brate Thee: They that go down into the pit cannot hope for Thy truth." [13] Job refers to the gloom of the life of Sheol by piling up the terms for darkness: " Before I go whence I shall not return, Even to a land of darkness and deep shade; A land of thick darkness, like darkness itself; Of chaotic deepest darkness; And where when it shines most brightly, it is but as pitch darkness." [14] There the dead are in ignorance of all that goes on in the world they have left, and conscious alone of their misery. " His sons come to hon-our, and he knoweth it not; And they are brought low, but he perceiveth them not. But his flesh upon him hath pain, And his soul within him mourneth." [15]

It is not seldom regarded as surprising that we have to wait till so late in Israel's history before we find traces of a belief in the resurrection. For Israel's neighbours show larger traces of such a belief from early times. In particular the fertility cult, that belonged not alone to the world of Is-rael's neighbours, but had its roots so deeply in Israel her-self, portrayed in its great annual festival a death and a resurrection. The myth that interpreted the ritual told of the divine descent into the grave and resurrection there-from, and hence presented the idea of resurrection from the dead. Yet it has to be remembered that neither myth nor

[12] Ps. lxxxviii. 3 ff. (Heb. 4 ff.) .   [14] Job x. 21 f.
[13] Isa. xxxviii. 18.   [15] Job xiv. 21 f.

ritual had any relevance to human resurrection. It was concerned with the annual resurrection of Nature and the revival of the springs of fertility, and by the ritual it sought to bring about the resurrection of the divine beings on whom that fertility depended. It created in its devotees no strong faith in any resurrection to richness of life; still less could it create in the exponents of the higher religion of Israel, who eschewed the fertility cult and all its ways, any such faith. When the belief in a resurrection appeared, it arose in a very different way.

Sometimes a verse in Hannah's song is made to serve as evidence of faith in the resurrection. " Yahweh killeth, and maketh alive: He bringeth down to Sheol, and bringeth up." [16] It is supposed that this means that Yahweh killeth and bringeth to life again. This is in the highest degree improbable, and it would be in complete disharmony with the general thought of the passage, which is that God is the Author of all the vicissitudes of life. Death and birth, the sweeping out of life and the bringing into life, are alike His work. For us it would be more natural to mention birth before death, since birth precedes death in the course of a life. But normally death comes to the aged, and birth always to the very young! To place the experience of the aged before the experience of the babe would seem to the oriental more in keeping with the relative honour due to them. Hence no suggestion of resurrection should be read into such passages as this.

Occasionally we do find, however, glimpses of a richer faith than the barren Sheol doctrine, and men break through the clouds of this grim and depressing belief. " God will redeem my soul from the power of Sheol," cried one of the Psalmists, " For He shall receive me." [17] " Thou shalt guide me with Thy counsel," sang another, " And afterward receive me into glory." [18] And in a famous and fa-

[16] 1 Sam. ii. 6.   [17] Ps. xlix. 15 (Heb. 16) .   [18] Ps. lxxiii. 24.

miliar passage, Job, who normally was held fast in the grip of the Sheol belief, reached out beyond it to the verge of a greater faith. " I know that my kinsman liveth," he cried, " And that he shall stand at the last upon the earth: And after my skin hath been thus destroyed, From my flesh [or, Without my flesh] shall I see God." [19] These and other texts can be culled, rarely without difficulties of text and interpretation, and not to be overpressed, yet probably witnessing to a yearning desire for something more satisfying than Sheol could offer. It is of the utmost importance to observe that that desire was not for a life of enjoyment, but for a life that should not be isolated from God. It was therefore religiously based. It was no philosophic speculation based on the thought of the immortality of the soul, no longing for such a sensuous heaven as Islam promises to the faithful, and still less the haunting sense of the inescapable round of life that appears in Indian thought. It was the faith that man who was made for the fellowship of God might continue to enjoy that fellowship, in which alone true life is found.

When the idea of a resurrection from the dead appears in the Old Testament, it does not have the form of a universal resurrection to judgement in a spiritual realm. In Ezekiel's vision of the valley of dry bones, it is made clear that what is in mind is not the resurrection of dead Israelites to life, but the restoration of the nation from the death of the exile to renewed life in Palestine. " Then said He unto me, Son of man, these bones are the whole house of Israel. . . . Behold, I will open your graves, and cause you to come up out of your graves, O My people; and I will bring you into the land of Israel." [20] It is in the book of Daniel that we find a clear instance of individual resurrection. Here it is the resurrection of some of the righteous and some of the wicked to reap the fruits of their deeds on earth. " Many of

19 Job xix. 25 f.   20 Ezek. xxxvii. 11 f.

them that sleep in the dust of the earth shall awake, some to everlasting life, and some to shame and everlasting contempt." [21] It was by the inner dynamic of his own earlier teaching that the author was carried to this hope. In the time of the Maccabaean persecution he had encouraged men to resist the attack on their faith by Antiochus Epiphanes and the hellenizing Jewish circles. He had encouraged them by stories of dauntless men who stood faithful to God in burning fiery furnace and lion's den, and who were delivered. They were not men whose faithfulness was born of the confidence that they would be delivered, indeed. They were fully assured that God could deliver them if He would, but they were determined to be faithful, whether He delivered or no. And many showed such a spirit in those Maccabaean days. They stood unflinchingly by the faith of their fathers and the God of Israel, even though many were not delivered but met a martyr's death, or gave their lives in the battle for freedom. The author of the book of Daniel profoundly shared the faith that God could have delivered them. He also profoundly believed that God would bring to triumph the cause for which they stood, and he looked for the establishment of the enduring kingdom of God in the immediate future. Little wonder, then, that he was carried by the dynamic of this belief to the hope that they who had given their lives in the service of the kingdom would not be denied a share in its glories, and that the God who had not delivered them purposed a more signal vindication and honour in their resurrection, while some of the most notable of their adversaries should be raised to receive a more terrible doom than they appeared to have received. The whole outlook of this conception is bounded by the circumstances of the writer's day. It is no universal or speculative belief to which he gives utterance, and it is to a resurrection on earth in the flesh that he looks. Important as

21 Dan. xii. 2.

this passage is, therefore, as a moment in the development of thought on the afterlife, it would seem to be of far less enduring validity than those other passages, noted above, which testify to a fundamentally spiritual yearning for an unbroken fellowship with God. Nevertheless it, too, is religiously based. It is not born of its author's view of the nature of man, but of his faith in the power and the character of God.

There is another important passage where the idea of the resurrection is found. This is in Isa. xxvi. 19. Here the context makes it clear that no resurrection for the unrighteous is in mind, but only the resurrection of the righteous. " This passage of Isaiah," says Charles, " presents us with a truly spiritual doctrine of the future life; for that life stands in organic and living relation to the present life in God, which the faithful enjoy on earth. And since the faithful alone stood in this relation, only the resurrection of the righteous was conceivably possible. This limitation of the resurrection to the righteous is the primitive form of this conception." [22] This passage would appear to contain the earliest reference to the idea of the resurrection, in the sense of the restoration of the individual to life after death, in the Old Testament. It is definitely richer in content than the already quoted passage from the book of Daniel, and in its richness it would seem to be in line with the most profoundly religious thought of the Bible.

For, as has been noted, in the thought of the Bible man was created for immortal fellowship with God. But sin came in and broke that fellowship, isolating man from God. If, then, sin is swallowed up in the salvation of restored fellowship, immortality should ensue. The Old Testament never actually works this idea out in this way, because it is not speculative. Yet it is implicit in its thought. And it of-

---

[22] *A Critical History of the Doctrine of a Future Life*, 2nd ed., 1913, p. 133.

fers the deepest and most truly religious of all reasons for faith in the immortality of the redeemed. The eternal God is the source of the life which is mediated through His fellowship. It is therefore eternal. The belief in the inherent immortality of human personality can never be convincingly demonstrated on purely speculative grounds, and if it could it would have little religious value. But a belief in the abiding quality of the life that derives from the fellowship of the abiding God is essentially religious. It is not speculatively based, but based on faith in God and the belief that He is eternal. Yet it is no belief that is contrary to reason. Indeed it is an eminently reasonable belief, if the idea of God is itself accepted.

It is of interest to note that all this is in the fullest harmony with the teaching of the Fourth Gospel, in which the thought of our Lord finds its deepest and most spiritual expression. Here much is said of eternal life, but this is not thought of as the life of the undying spirit of man. It is eternal because its source is the eternal God, mediated to men through the Son. It is the gift of God to those in whom He lives, and who find the spring and fount of their life in Him. " Labour not for the meat which perisheth, but for the meat which endureth unto eternal life, which the Son of man shall give unto you." [23] " This is the will of My Father, that every one which seeth the Son, and believeth on Him, should have eternal life." [24] There is no suggestion that eternal life is the natural inheritance of man. For eternal life is clearly something far richer than immortality. It is not merely length of life but quality of life. And of far more importance than to assure man that his spirit will endure for ever is it to offer him the rich and infinite fount of life that is to be found in the fellowship of God. That is what the Old Testament was feeling after, and it was yearning for this that made the Old Testament writers dissatis-

[23] John vi. 27.   [24] John vi. 40.

fied with the Sheol doctrine. " Thou hast made us for Thyself," said Augustine, " and our heart is restless till it find its rest in Thee." [25] It is precisely this that gives the clue to the source and character of the life beyond the grave to which Israel was moving. The destiny for which man was created was the fellowship, and therefore the service, of God. He can fulfil his destiny only in so far as he is lifted out of his sin by the divine act of salvation, and shares that fellowship and that service.

[25] *Confessions,* Book I, Chap. i.

X. THE MEANING OF WORSHIP

No PEOPLE HAS contributed more richly to the worship of mankind than Israel. In ancient times that worship centred in the shrines that abounded in the land, but in postexilic times, when there was a single legitimate sanctuary, synagogues came into being, and in the New Testament we find synagogue and Temple ministering in complementary ways to the spiritual needs of the Jews. The synagogue has largely influenced the form of worship in both Christianity and Islam, and some branches of the Christian Church show a varying measure of the influence of the Temple, while others disclaim any debt to it. The latter commonly conceive of worship wholly in prophetic terms — though there was nothing prophetic about the worship of the synagogue — and associate the Temple with a priestly worship that has been altogether superseded in Christ. Yet with a sound instinct they are sometimes found worshipping in buildings that are called Temples, or Tabernacles — and the Tabernacle is represented in the Bible as the prototype of the Temple. The breaking down of the sharp antithesis between prophet and priest may be expected to lead to a deeper recognition of that debt to the Temple preserved in these names, and preserved more largely in the forms of worship of other branches of the Church.

In the origin of the Temple there is nothing uniquely Israelite. Many of the shrines that were found in the land were almost certainly ancient Canaanite shrines taken over by the Israelites, and associated in some measure with the worship of Yahweh. Each may well have had its own local variety of usage, though in the main their forms of worship were alike. Comparable shrines, with largely similar forms, were found in other lands, and in particular in the lands whose life and culture form the background of Israel's. When the Jerusalem Temple was built, it was not designed to be the sole sanctuary of the land, to supersede all the multiplicity of shrines that abounded. It was built to be the royal sanctuary, attached to the king's palace. It surpassed all other shrines of the kingdom in its splendour, but for a time it is probable that the prestige it enjoyed as the royal sanctuary was out-matched in the popular esteem by the ancient associations of other shrines, though its possession of the Ark would do much to offset these. For long the Temple was little better than the other shrines in the spiritual quality of its worship. Its erection by Tyrian artificers brought into its ornamentation motifs that were associated with non-Yahweh religion, while there are frequent references in the Old Testament to practices within its precincts that arouse the opposition of prophets, and that called forth the condemnation of the writers. It is rather for what it became that the Temple is important. For when reforming circles planned to purify the forms of worship in Israel, they proposed to tolerate but a single legitimate sanctuary, where practice could be more easily regulated. The Jerusalem Temple was the obvious choice for this sanctuary. For by this time it had doubtless acquired associations of its own, and its attachment to the palace made it more easy to regulate its practice. Both in the reign of Hezekiah and in that of Josiah the plans of the reformers soon broke down. But in post-exilic days, when Israel's life centred more largely in its religion, and under the more rigid discipline of Judaism, the Second Temple became the home of a purer worship, and it is to that Second Temple that we must look for all that is of enduring worth in the worship of the shrines of Israel.

In many of the older shrines, and in the pre-exilic Temple, ritual fornication was one of the forms of worship. The ritual dance and the drinking of wine belonged also to the essence of worship. All of this, of course, belonged to the

fertility cult, which at bottom had nothing to do with the religion established by Moses, and which was opposed by
the great prophets. In recent years much attention has been
directed to the ritual incantation of spells, and priestly div-
ination, which are likely to have had a place in Israelite, as
in Babylonian and other, worship. With none of these
things need we concern ourselves. For to whatever extent
we may discover them in Israelite practice, they came out
of the past and have now perished with the past. They speak
no word of enduring worth on the meaning of worship.

On sabbaths and feast days large numbers of people must
have assembled at the shrines, but not for ordered and con-
ducted corporate worship. They were probably in groups in
the open court, which was noisy with the hubbub of the
throng, save at certain moments of the ritual when the hush
of silence would fall upon them. On other days individuals
or small groups of people would repair to the shrines for
the direction or help of the priests, or for a sacrificial meal.
For many things besides sacrifice went on in the local
shrines and in the Jerusalem Temple. In a real sense the
shrine was the centre of the life of the community, and not
merely of its worship. It is nevertheless true that the due offering of private and public sacrifices provided in all ages
the most important of the priestly duties, while in the great
days of Judaism, when the Temple was purged of all ignoble practices such as had marred it in older days, and when
the ritual of sacrifice attained its stateliest forms, this was
especially true.

To say this would seem to many tantamount to saying
that the Temple offers no enduring contribution to worship, save perhaps in ways we have not yet examined. For
sacrifice was abolished for Christians in the death of Christ,
and neither priest nor altar is any more required for the
offering up of oblations. Christ is our High Priest and we
need no other; the sacrifice offered once for all at Calvary
has swept away the need for any further sacrifice. And so

the Temple lost its chief *raison d'être* when sacrifice was superseded. Little wonder that a Temple that had thus become an anachronism within a few years ceased to exist, albeit by violent hands and not because it had become an anachronism. Little wonder that even the Jews, who failed to recognize the supersession of sacrifices in the death of Christ, have been compelled by the grim hand of circumstance to live without sacrifices since that destruction of the Temple.

Yet this is less convincing than to many it may appear. For the moment we may pause to observe that to say this is to record the importance of the Old Testament for the New Testament understanding of the place and work of Christ. For if He has superseded for us the High Priest, we can only understand Him in the light of the High Priestly function; and if His death is the final sacrifice, rendering obsolete all the sacrifices of the Law, it can only be understood in their light. Yet all such understanding has been out of vogue in modern times. The interpretation of the Cross in terms of sacrifice has been eliminated from the thought of many, and there has been a widespread idea that sacrifice was superseded by the Old Testament prophets, rather than by the death of Christ. The latter idea has been sufficiently examined above, but it is necessary to ask whether the whole sacrificial character of Old Testament religion is unmeaning for Christianity and irrelevant to us.

It scarcely needs to be said that all who refuse to allow any sacrificial significance to the Cross part company with the New Testament, as well as cut adrift from the Old. Their refusal springs from a variety of reasons. Sometimes it is a form of humanism, which believes it can exalt man by reducing the stature of Christ to the level of a mere hero and example, and which finds the springs of man's redemption in himself, and in his own effort to follow a great Leader. Sometimes it is born of a desire to safeguard the

love of God, and a feeling that a sacrificial view of the Cross
implies that it was God who needed to be won over. Any
view of the Cross which merely sets Christ and God over
against one another, and depicts God as stern and wrathful
while Christ is gentle and loving, is to be rejected as dishonouring to God and Christ alike. For if in the supreme
moment of redemption Christ is in any sense the antithesis
of God, it is hard to see how His divinity can be affirmed.

The New Testament teaches unmistakably Christ's unity
with God. " I and the Father are one," we read,[1] and " He
that hath seen Me hath seen the Father." [2] Nor was that
unity broken in the hour of redemption. " God was in
Christ, reconciling the world unto Himself; " [3] " God com-
mendeth His love toward us, in that while we were yet sinners Christ died for us; " [4] " God, who is rich in mercy, for
His great love wherewith He loved us, Even when we were
dead in sins, hath quickened us together with Christ. . . .
And hath raised us up together in heavenly places in Christ
Jesus." [5] The love of God shines forth in the Cross of Christ,
and reaches there the climax of its expression. It was not
God who needed to be changed, but man, for the obstacles
to fellowship lay not in the heart of God but in the sin of
man.

Nevertheless any interpretation of the Cross merely in
terms of the revelation of the love of God and the sinfulness
of sin, and which represents the effect of the Cross but as
the breaking of man's proud heart in repentance by the unveiling of his need and the moving love of God, is insufficient. Man is saved not by his own repentance, but by the
power of God. It is not that the Cross is the organ that produces faith in us, and then we are saved by our faith. Our
repentance and our faith are the indispensable conditions
of our salvation, but in no sense the organ of our salvation.

[1] John x. 30.   [3] 2 Cor. v. 19.   [5] Eph. ii. 4 ff.
[2] John xiv. 9.   [4] Rom. v. 8.

When a man travels by train he has faith that he will reach his destination. Yet it is not his faith that brings him to it. It is his faith that brings him to entrust himself to the train, and that entrusting of himself is a necessary condition of his journeying. But it is the engine which conveys him to his goal. Man's repentance and faith but make possible a redemption they in no sense achieve, a redemption which is God's act and which is achieved in Christ.

None of this yet touches any sacrificial significance of the Cross. For sacrifice is man's offering unto God. Yet how can the death of Christ be said to be man's offering unto God? They who nailed Him to the Cross performed no sacred act of sacrifice, and they who clamoured for His death or handed Him over to die found no blessing in their sinful deed. The New Testament distinguishes between the physical death of Christ as the climax of human sin and the spiritual offering of Himself to God, of which that physical death became the organ. It speaks of Christ as the High Priest of this sacrifice as well as the victim, and declares that He " hath given Himself for us an offering and a sacrifice to God." [6] That is to say that we who are redeemed by Him are the ones whose sacrifice He offers in Himself. To ignore this element of the significance of the Cross is to impoverish our understanding of its meaning.

Nor is there any real inconsistency between the recognition of the sacrificial meaning of the Cross and the recognition that in Christ crucified the love of God is incomparably revealed. For in the New Testament Christ is described as " the one Mediator between God and men." [7] A mediator is essentially one who represents each party to the other, and therefore while Christ, as God's representative, is not to be set over against God, as our representative. He is to be set over against God.

It has already been said that in the deepest teaching of

[6] Eph. v. 2.   [7] 1 Tim. ii. 5.

the Old Testament sacrifice had no meaning or validity unless it was the organ of the spirit of the offerer. It could not
mediate the divine fellowship to the man who did not really
desire to walk with God; it could not mediate the divine
forgiveness and cleansing from sin to the man who loved his
sin and was determined to cling to it. In all such cases it
was a hollow sham, and therefore an offence to God. But
where it was the organ of the spirit it was believed to have
rich efficacy. It not alone presented to God the offerer's plea
for the boon he sought. It bore to God the pledge of his
loyalty and obedience, and where the boon it sought was
cleansing from sin, it bore his penitence of spirit and his
surrender of himself to be cleansed. Yet it was more than
the token and pledge of his spirit. It was the organ of God's
grace unto him. Of itself it could no more convey to him
the divine blessing than it could carry a valid plea from
him. But when he made it the organ of his spirit, God
could make it the organ of His approach to the offerer, and
by the touch of His Spirit upon man's could cleanse him
in the innermost springs of his being.

In this view of sacrifice the Old Testament fitly prepares
for the New Testament conception of the Work of Christ.
Nowhere is it taught that His death is a sacrifice that has
validity for men as a mere *opus operatum,* independently
of their spirit. He died once for all long years ago, yet it is
in the moment when we make that death the organ of our
surrender and faith that it becomes effective for us. So long
as we cling to our sin we are numbered with His crucifiers,
but when in penitence we cast ourselves at His feet, His
death is our sacrifice. We become identified with Him in a
richer way than men could ever become identified with an
animal sacrifice that was made the organ of their spirit. For
He who is the crown and climax of manhood can most
worthily bear our spirit to God, and represent us in our
humble submission unto Him. And similarly He who is

the effulgence of the divine glory can most perfectly convey the divine blessing unto us. He is our representative when we are truly one with Him, and He is the perfect Mediator between God and man because He alone is in Himself one with God.

This mystical or sacramental view of sacrifice is condemned by some because it is open to the abuse against which the prophets declaimed, and because men are apt to forget that it is not as an *opus operatum,* but as the organ of the spirit, that it is found to be charged with power. And in days when the otherness of God is so much insisted on in some quarters, there is some reluctance to recognize the validity of the mystical element in religion, and some disposition to deny that in any sense man may know the *unio mystica* with God. That mysticism has forms which are not Christian, and that it sometimes reaches great extravagances and becomes a selfish luxury, is undoubtedly true. Yet in the clear teaching of the New Testament and in true Christian experience there is a mystical element that is not to be ignored.

The man who turns with loathing from the self that is numbered with Christ's crucifiers becomes one with Him in His death. His " old man is crucified with " Christ,[8] and henceforth ceases to be. When the New Testament speaks of Christ " who His own self bare our sins in His own body on the tree," [9] it does not mean simply that Christ bore the penalty of our sins. It means that our sins themselves were laid on Him, to perish with Him, so that " we, being dead to sins, should live unto righteousness." [10] And this can only be when we yield up the self of sin unto Him, to die with Him. But it is not alone the self of sin that is yielded up to Him. It is the penitent and submissive self, which is now brought into oneness with the obedience of Christ, and borne by Him into the presence of God. And there is

[8] Rom. vi. 6.   [9] 1 Peter ii. 24.   [10] *Ibid.*

received from God in Christ a new self, cleansed and purified. He who is crucified with Christ becomes one with Him
not alone in death, but also in life. He is born anew, and
the new self knows the mystical experience of union with
the risen and living Christ. " I am crucified with Christ:
nevertheless I live; yet not I, but Christ liveth in me: and
the life which I now live in the flesh I live by the faith of the
Son of God, who loved me and gave Himself for me." [11]
The new self is not something that a man achieves for himself by turning over a new leaf. It is something which God
achieves in him by the power of the Cross. He who bears
our penitence to God mediates unto us the divine activity
and the divine presence in our hearts. " If any man be in
Christ, he is a new creature." [12] He is " created in Christ
Jesus unto good works, which God hath before ordained
that we should walk in them." [13]

While this may indicate the importance of the Temple
ritual for Christian theology, and may suffice to show that
to regard sacrifice as superseded in the prophets is an impoverishment of our understanding of the New Testament,
it may seem still to be irrelevant to the subject of worship.
In almost every branch of the Christian Church, however,
one of the greatest acts of worship centres in the sacrament
which is variously called the Lord's Supper, Holy Communion, the Eucharist, or the Mass. Each of these terms
brings out one element of the significance of the sacrament,
but the Mass, which is associated with its sacrificial meaning, was firmly rejected by the Reformers. To them this
sacrament was the memorial of a sacrifice, rather than the
renewal of a sacrifice. For Christ offered Himself once for
all at Calvary, a sufficient sacrifice potentially for all, and
actually for all who believe.

That the sacrament is a memorial of Christ's death is
plainly stated in the New Testament. In the Pauline form

[11] Gal. ii. 20.   [12] 2 Cor. v. 17.   [13] Eph. ii. 10.

of the words of institution we read: " This do in remembrance of Me." [14] Yet it is much more than a memorial. Paul declares that whoever eats unworthily " is guilty of the body and blood of the Lord." [15] By this he would seem to mean that whoever fails to bring to the sacrament the spirit which is fitting, instead of entering into the benefits it should confer, enters into the guilt of those who crucified Christ. His view of this sacrament has this in common with the prophetic view of sacrifice, that it is the spirit of the worshipper which makes valid for him that which his act implies, and the lack of the right spirit turns his act into the organ of a curse instead of the organ of a blessing. It is not merely that without the right spirit he fails to appropriate the blessing which might be his; he adds to his guilt and positively injures himself. He numbers himself with the crucifiers of Christ, and repeats the essential iniquity of that act.

For while it is true that " we are sanctified through the offering of the body of Jesus Christ once for all," [16] and that " Christ hath once suffered for sins," [17] so that there is no need for this sacrifice to be repeated, it is nevertheless possible to " crucify the Son of God afresh." [18] There is a sense in which that which is unrepeatable may be repeated. And if it is possible to crucify afresh the Son of God, not in a historical and physical sense, but in a spiritual act of inner rejection, it is equally possible to renew the offering of that sacrifice of Christ unto God, when it is made the organ of our spirit. It has been above argued that this is what happens in the moment of conversion, when the new self is born. It happens again in the corporate experience of worship, when we rightly partake of the sacrament. For while we need to be born again into Christ but once, by the paradox of faith we need to be continually reborn into Him.

---

[14] 1 Cor. xi. 24.   [16] Heb. x. 10.   [18] Heb. vi. 6.
[15] 1 Cor. xi. 27.   [17] 1 Peter iii. 18.

We there renew our union with Christ in His death and resurrection, and make His death afresh the organ of our surrender unto God and find in it anew the organ of divine blessing unto our souls. At this table we may by our spirit either be guilty of the body and blood of the Lord, or find that sacrifice of Christ on Calvary essentially renewed for the purification and quickening of our hearts. That is why we need a sacrament. To remember the death of Christ as a mere historical celebration, or even to remember it with gratitude for all the wonder of its significance for the world and for us, is insufficient. We need to remember it that its work may be renewed in us, and that it may become anew our sacrifice unto God, and the power of God unto us. Its spiritual enrichment is apprehended in the renewed consecration of ourselves unto Christ, and in the renewed dying unto self; yet is its spiritual enrichment in no sense self-attained. It is the gift of God in Christ, which is but apprehended by faith. And faith is that which carries us into Christ, to be united with Him.

The Fourth Gospel represents our Lord as discoursing to His disciples as they sat at the Last Supper of the True Vine, and calling them to abide in Him and to experience His abiding presence in their hearts, in a union as close and fundamental as the union of the vine and the branches. Whether the discourses of the Fourth Gospel are historically reliable or not, it is with profound spiritual penetration that this stands here, to emphasize that it is as we sit at the table of the Lord that that rich experience of surrender unto Him and identification with Him, in which His death becomes our sacrifice, must here be renewed if we truly enter into the experience this sacrament mediates.

Here, then, at the supreme point of Christian worship we find values which derive from the Temple and its ritual of sacrifice taken up into our faith. and the words of the prophets that proclaimed the hollowness of the sacrifices of

their day may bring a relevant message to us as we apply
their spirit to our experience. If we cherish in our hearts
the love of those things that are alien to the spirit of Christ
we cannot know the mystical union with Him whereby the
sacrifice becomes valid for us, and His death becomes a
" vain oblation " so far as we are concerned, and our presence in that holy place an offence to God.

It is not to be supposed, however, that sacrifice is the only
element of the worship of the Temple with an enduring
message. Other elements were incorporated in the worship
of the synagogue, and may be considered in relation to both
Temple and synagogue. They include worship on the Sabbath, sacred song and prayer.

We have already seen that the origins of the synagogue
are obscure, but that it probably came into being in the
exilic and early post-exilic period, in the first place, perhaps, in Babylonia, and then, either independently or under the influence of the returning exiles, in Palestine.
While there is little direct trace of the synagogue in the Old
Testament, it must have been steadily growing in influence
during the later pre-Christian centuries, and in the New
Testament we see that it was firmly established both in Palestine and amongst the Diaspora in the first Christian century.

The worship of the synagogue was especially associated
with the Sabbath day. We read that our Lord " as His custom was, went into the synagogue on the Sabbath day," [19]
and that Paul and Barnabas " went into the synagogue on
the Sabbath day," [20] while at Corinth Paul " reasoned in
the synagogue every Sabbath." [21]

The Sabbath was one of the oldest institutions of Israel,
and it figures not alone in the Decalogue of Exod. xx, which
may with probability be attributed to Moses in its original
form, but also in the Decalogue of Exod. xxxiv, which prob-

[19] Luke iv. 16.   [20] Acts xiii. 14.   [21] Acts xviii. 4.

ably derived from the stream of tradition which had nothing to do with Moses. This means that in its origins the Sabbath is older than the time of Moses. The association of new moon and Sabbath in the Old Testament has led to the view that it was connected with the phases of the moon, while evidence from Babylonia has provided a wider background for the discussion of its origin. Into all that there is no need for us to go here, since we are less concerned with an antiquarian interest in origins than with the significance for worship with which the institution became invested.

In the Ritual Decalogue of Exod. xxxiv we read: " Six days shalt thou work, but on the seventh day thou shalt rest." [22] Here there is no mention of any obligation to spend the day in worship. It is merely a day of rest from labour, whose taboo is given the authority of religion. In the Ethical Decalogue of Exod. xx and Deut. v this is expanded and reinforced, in Exod. xx by a consideration which derives from the priestly account of the Creation, and in Deut. v by a consideration which derives from the essentially Deuteronomic point of view. The former reads: " Remember the Sabbath day to keep it holy. Six days shalt thou labour, and do all thy work: but the seventh day is the Sabbath of Yahweh thy God: in it thou shalt not do any work, thou, nor thy son, nor thy daughter, thy manservant, nor thy maidservant, nor thy cattle, nor thy stranger that is within thy gates. For in six days Yahweh made heaven and earth, the sea and all that is therein, and rested the seventh day. Wherefore Yahweh blessed the Sabbath day and hallowed it." [23] The Deuteronomic form, however, reads: " Observe the Sabbath day to keep it holy, as Yahweh thy God hath commanded thee. Six days shalt thou labour, and do all thy work; but the seventh day is the Sabbath of Yahweh thy God: in it thou shalt not do any work, thou, nor thy son, nor thy daughter, nor thy manservant, nor thy maidservant,

[22] Exod. xxxiv. 21.   [23] Exod. xx. 8 ff.

nor thine ox, nor thine ass, nor any of thy cattle, nor thy stranger that is within thy gates; that thy manservant and thy maidservant may rest as well as thou. And remember that thou wast a servant in the land of Egypt, and that Yahweh thy God brought thee out thence by a mighty hand and by a stretched out arm: therefore Yahweh thy God commanded thee to keep the Sabbath day." [24] In both of these the only obligation laid on men is the abstention from labour. This is in accordance with the meaning of the root from which the word probably comes, which means *to rest*, or *to desist*.

That the day was from early times associated with worship, however, is rendered probable by many considerations. In his denunciation of the empty observances of the Temple cultus of his day, Isaiah couples new moons and Sabbaths with the offering of sacrifices, the burning of incense and the calling of assemblies. The whole context of this reference would suggest that the Sabbath was a day in which people commonly repaired in large numbers to the Temple, and the same thing is clear from the story of the proclamation of Joash as king. This proclamation was made on the Sabbath day, when the Temple courts were thronged, and it would appear that it was usual for the royal guards to be disposed in three companies, of which two were on duty at the palace on ordinary days and at the Temple on Sabbath days, while the third company reversed these roles. There are some references to Sabbath offerings in the Old Testament, and while these are all from the later, post-exilic period, there is no reason to doubt that such offerings were customary in pre-exilic times. Finally, we may observe that Trito-Isaiah looks forward to the day when " from one new moon to another, and from one Sabbath to another, all flesh shall come to worship." [25] What he here seems to mean is that worship shall not be confined to Sabbaths and other special days, or be limited to Israel alone, and it would appear to be implied that in his day the Sabbath was a day of worship. Nor is it in any way surprising that a religious quality should be given to the observance of this day, seeing that the ordinance on which that observance rested was religious.

Hence, when the synagogue came into being, it would be natural to transfer to it the Sabbath assembly, which was now no longer possible in Temple or shrine. And apart from this, if there was any disposition to meet together at all to keep alive faith and worship, practical considerations would cause this to be done on the day when ordinary business was laid aside. And the sacredness of the day, which at first consisted in the abstention from any secular work, came more and more to consist in prayer and meditation, and in the cultivation of the spirit, in corporate worship of God and mutual encouragement to walk in His way.

The modern world is enthusiastic to expand the Sabbath as a day of rest from ordinary labour into a day and a half, or even two days, out of every seven, though its rest days often differ *toto coelo* in their feverish restlessness from the inactivity of the ancient Israelite and Jewish Sabbath. But it has great need to re-discover the Sabbath as a day of worship and of spiritual renewal, through which it may find God and be found of Him.

In the worship of both Temple and synagogue there was song and prayer. When Isaiah speaks of " a song as in the night when a holy feast is kept," [26] he makes it clear that there was singing at the great festivals, and Amos includes the singing of the Temple in the same condemnation with the meaningless sacrifices of his day: " Take away from me the noise of thy songs; for I will not hear the melody of thy viols." [27] In the work of the Chronicler there are many references to the music of the Temple, and while we cannot

[26] Isa. xxx. 29.   [27] Amos v. 23.

safely rely on these for the practice of the pre-exilic days with which they ostensibly deal, we can quite safely find in them the reflexion of the practice of his own day, and be sure that in the Second Temple music had an assured and not inconsiderable place, and that it was led by choirs of singers.

Many writers speak of the Psalter as the " Hymn Book of the Second Temple." How far it was a hymn book, in our sense of the term, is far from certain. At the beginning of the present century it was common to hold that a large number of the psalms were not composed until the Maccabaean period. Such a view made the compilation of the Psalter so late that it could hardly be supposed that the Temple choirs of the Chronicler's day could have used this Hymn Book. To-day there is a general tendency to find few, if any, Maccabaean psalms, but on the contrary a good deal of ancient and pre-exilic material, though it is unlikely that any part of our Psalter was collected in its present form before the return from the exile. Whatever the age of individual psalms, the compilation of the Psalter must be placed in the age of Judaism, and it has already been noted that this is a fact which should not be forgotten in our estimate of the quality of Judaism.

Mowinckel, as has been said above, has advanced the view that many of the psalms were spells, or counter-spells, for individual use by diseased or unfortunate persons. Such people would assume that their troubles were due to the magical devices of their enemies, and the spells which had been cast over them, and they would go to the appropriate priest, who would either recite over them or cause them to recite the proper psalm to break the spell. On this view large parts of the Psalter consisted of a corpus whose effective use required the expert knowledge of the priest. The psalms were not the vehicle of praise and devotion, but sources of power, to be ritually used for the liberation of the power. Other psalms, he holds, belonged to the ritual of an annual festival similar to the Babylonian New Year's Feast, when there were sacred processions, and the Ark was carried round the city, and again magical power was released by the correct ritual use of the psalms. How far these views are to be accepted need not here concern us. It would certainly be a surprising thing if psalms which were created to serve no higher purpose than to be magical spells became the vehicle of a spiritual worship that endured for many centuries, and that flourished amongst men who firmly repudiated all the magical ideas that were their inspiration. For the Judaism of the Second Temple condemned spells and all such practices as firmly as did the prophets, whose oracles it treasured. And certainly the Christian Church took over the use of the psalms as the vehicle of worship, and not as potent spells.

That the psalms were collected for liturgical use, whatever purpose may have inspired their composition, is the view of many, and the suggestion has been made that the compilation of the Psalter was carried through in order to provide for a triennial cycle of readings, to accompany the triennial cycle of readings from the Law and the Prophets. On this no certainty can be attained, and it may well be that the Psalter came into being as an anthology of religious poetry, expressing not alone praise and prayer, but every mood of the religious spirit, and that its own inherent suitability to be the medium of the expression of similar moods in others led to its use in worship. Some of the psalms may reflect historical situations, though they are rarely recoverable with any certainty, and if they were, the psalms would probably be the less suitable to express the emotions of men in other situations and other ages. Some are calculated to express the corporate thought and feeling of men in united worship, or on national occasions, while others are more calculated to express the individual spirit's feelings in some solitary experience of joy or sorrow. How they came to be used in worship can never be known with any assurance. Neither can it be known to what extent or in what form they were used in the Temple. It can only be held to be probable that at least some of the psalms were used in the public worship, and were chanted by the Temple choirs,[28] and that many psalms by their spiritual penetration attained so high a place in the esteem of men that they were commonly used to express private and public feelings on a wide variety of occasions.

Whatever degree of probability may attach to these various views, there can be only certainty that the Psalter is an incomparable enrichment of worship to this day, and if the Jews had had no other legacy for the world but this collection of sacred poetry, our debt to them would have been surpassingly great. That there are passages which fall below the Christian level, and others which express outgrown ideas, is not to be surprised at. What is to be surprised at is that there is so much that can nobly express our spirit, and that can become the garment of our praise and our prayer in an age so far removed from that in which it had birth.

That the Temple was a house of prayer appears from both the Old and the New Testaments. In the shrine of Shiloh Hannah's lips moved in private prayer, and Trito-Isaiah refers to the Jerusalem Temple as God's " house of prayer," and adds, " My house shall be called a house of prayer for all people." [29] And when our Lord begins one of His parables with the words, " Two men went up into the Temple to pray," [30] He makes it clear that in His day men still resorted to the Temple for this purpose. This is made even clearer elsewhere, where we read that " Peter and John went up together into the Temple at the hour of

28 Cf. Mishnah, Tamid vii. 4 (Tr. by Danby, p. 589).
29 Isa. lvi. 7.
30 Luke xviii. 10.

prayer, being the ninth hour." [31] To what extent ordered, corporate prayer entered into its worship may not be known. It is sometimes inferred that in pre-Deuteronomic days there were no such prayers, and that prayer was purely individual and spontaneous. That is very improbable. The law of Deuteronomy lays it down that on certain occasions when men came to the Temple they should recite the words of a specified prayer.[32] It is likely that many would recite them together, since many would come on the same day to recite the same words. Nor is it likely that the compiler of Deuteronomy was the first to observe that to many it is a boon to be guided in the expression of their desires, or that such guidance was limited to the occasions specified in the passage referred to. It is probable that prayers accompanying the ritual of sacrifice were uttered audibly in the hearing of the worshippers, in the solemn stillness that marked its supreme moments, and that these prayers were designed to lift the worshippers into the spirit they expressed.

Inevitably prayer would figure in some form in the worship of the synagogues from the start. For prayer has so vital a place in worship that it is inconceivable that it should have been dropped wholly out of the instrument of worship designed by the men who created the synagogue. If we are right in the surmise that the synagogue began in exile as a means of keeping alive the religion of Israel in isolation from the Temple cultus, it is likely that there was a corporate quality about its worship from the start. Men would sing together the songs of Zion, and keep alive their traditions by reading such books as they possessed and by the oral teaching of those who were able to give it. It is unlikely that that corporate quality would be lost in prayer. Yet the prayers of the Temple, in so far as there was corporate prayer in the Temple, apart from the chanting of psalms, in so far as psalms may have been chanted in pre-exilic days, would be imperfectly suited for their use. For the only such Temple prayers that we have any ground for inferring were those that accompanied ritual acts. It is likely that such prayers would be recited to keep alive the memory of the ritual, and in the worship of the synagogue such prayers have persisted. For forms of prayer are used whereby " the traditional liturgy provides a sort of parabolic and metaphorical fulfilment of sacrifice." [33] But beyond this the synagogue gradually developed its own forms and traditions of prayer, designed to express its own spirit and to serve its own needs, and we know that prayer came to occupy an important place in its worship.

Reference has already been made to yet another element of the worship of the synagogue in the reading of sacred books. This was probably original with the synagogue, and was not derived from the worship of the Temple. Clearly when the synagogue was first created there could not have been the reading of what we know as the Scriptures of the Old Testament, for these Scriptures were not yet in existence, and they had certainly not been canonized. It is possible that Deuteronomy was used, and perhaps elements of other books of the Old Testament, including some collections of prophetic oracles which have gone into the compilation of the existing prophetic books. With the growth of the sacred literature other books would be read, and the synagogue may have played no little part in developing that esteem for these books which led to their ultimate canonization as Scripture. We know that in New Testament times the Law and the Prophets were read in the synagogues. For in a speech attributed to James we read: " Moses . . . hath in every city them that preach Him, being read in the synagogues every Sabbath day," [34] while in

33 Oesterley and Box, *Religion and Worship of the Synagogue,* 2nd ed., 1911, p. 361.
34 Acts xv. 21.

the synagogue at Nazareth there was handed to our Lord the book of Isaiah, from which He should read.[35] On that occasion He followed the reading by an address, and while the character of His address was clearly unusual, both here and elsewhere when He spoke in synagogues, it was normal for an address to be given. And wherever Paul went in his journeyings, he attended synagogues and delivered his message there so long as possible.

In the addresses of our Lord and of Paul there was a direct and prophetic quality which may give us a false impression of the character of the normal addresses. For men commented on this unusual feature of our Lord's addresses, which contrasted with the ordinary scribal discourses. These consisted of citations of authorities for the interpretation of passages. Into their exegesis probably went a considerable measure of the fancifulness that marks some of the Pauline passages, and much of the argument of the Epistle to the Hebrews. While this may often be of no little spiritual suggestiveness, it is pseudo-logical and in no sense prophetic. But whatever its character, its aim was to interpret the word, and to minister to the understanding of its teaching.

All of these features were taken over into the worship of the Church. For here there was a weekly assembling for worship, though the Lord's Day was substituted for the Sabbath. Here too there was the reading of the Scriptures of the Old Testament, and later of the New as it came into being, with exposition and exhortation, and prayer. For all of these our debt to the people of the Book is both real and deep. Yet the supreme point of our debt is found in the Scriptures of the Old Testament, whose reading in public worship the Church took over from the synagogue. For the Old Testament, including as it does the psalms whose chanting is an enrichment of Christian as of Jewish worship, is an

35 Luke iv. 17.

unrivalled spiritual treasure, which is calculated to foster as well as to express the worship of men in all ages. Not alone do the forms of our worship rest on those of Judaism, but the content of our worship is in rich measure supplied from the wealth of its Scriptures.

Every element of worship here finds place, and to cite all the great and moving passages it contains would alone more than fill the present book. It must here suffice to indicate something of the variety of its contribution to worship, as distinct from its contribution to our understanding of the nature and will of God, and to refer in the briefest catalogue to a few of the great and familiar passages in which the various elements of worship are enshrined.

The stories of the call of Moses and Isaiah, when read in any spirit of understanding of their grandeur, are well calculated to kindle in the hearts of the hearers a sense of awe in the presence of a God who is high above us, and before whom we must tremble — not in terror, indeed, but in profound reverence. And such reverence is fundamental to all true worship. Or again, the familiar words of Ps. viii, when we enter into the spirit of the man who penned it, may foster in us the sense of adoration as we bow before the vast and beneficent power of God. The majestic music of Isa. xl delivers us from all sense of an easy familiarity with the God in the hollow of whose hand all things lie, and calls us to a waiting upon Him in which the deepest humility must mark our spirit. The great words of the Shema‘, " Hear, O Israel: the Lord our God, the Lord is one; And thou shalt love the Lord thy God with all thine heart, and with all thy soul, and with all thy might," [36] have stirred the souls of men for eighty generations and more with their message that the great and glorious God is One before whom we may not alone shrink, but draw nigh in adoring love. And the same is true of many another passage. " Thus saith the

[36] Deut. vi. 4.

high and lofty One that inhabiteth eternity, whose name is Holy; I dwell in the high and holy place, with him also that is of a humble and contrite spirit." [37] In His presence all worldly dignity and earthly treasure are of no moment, and all human wisdom fades into insignificance. " Let not the wise man glory in his wisdom, neither let the mighty man glory in his might; let not the rich man glory in his riches; But let him that glorieth glory in this, that he understandeth and knoweth Me, that I am the Lord which exercise lovingkindness, judgment and righteousness in the earth: for in these things I delight, saith the Lord." [38] Familiar are all these, and many other passages. Yet hackneyed they can never be, when read with penetration. And always will they call forth something of the spirit of worship they so nobly reveal.

Yet worship is more than adoration and reverence. It includes praise and thanksgiving. And these may be found in abundance in the pages of the Old Testament. " Bless the Lord, O my soul: and all that is within me, bless His holy name. Bless the Lord, O my soul, and forget not all His benefits." [39] We have but to hear these opening words, and all the melody of the song that follows, and we are transported into something of the spirit of the singer. " O sing unto the Lord a new song: sing unto the Lord all the earth; " [40] " O sing unto the Lord a new song; for He hath done marvellous things; " [41] " I will bless the Lord at all times: His praise shall continually be in my mouth." [42] Who can hear the psalms which begin with these words without some kindling of heart, and without making them the vehicle of his thankfulness for the common blessings of life, or for some signal blessing which may have been granted unto him, or to the community to which he be-

[37] Isa. lvii. 15.
[38] Jer. ix. 23 f. (Heb. 22 f.).
[39] Ps. ciii. 1 f.

[40] Ps. xcvi. 1.
[41] Ps. xcviii. 1.
[42] Ps. xxxiv. 1 (Heb. 2).

longs? God's hand is to be seen in every sphere of our life, and everywhere it calls for our song of praise and our glad thanksgiving. Nowhere are the singers of Israel so other-worldly and ascetic that they forget to give thanks for all the mercies of this life; yet nowhere are they so immersed in the blessings of this life that they forget the inner and spiritual gifts of God. For to their penetrating eye those inner and spiritual gifts belong essentially to this life, and give meaning and worth to all experience. " O that men would praise the Lord for His goodness, and for His wonderful works to the children of men! For He satisfieth the longing soul, and the hungry soul He filleth with good." [43] " The Lord is my shepherd; I shall not want. He maketh me to lie down in green pastures: He leadeth me beside the still waters. He restoreth my soul: He leadeth me in the paths of righteousness for His name's sake." [44] " Man doth not live by bread alone, but by every word that proceedeth out of the mouth of the Lord." [45]

Yet man that is unclean cannot come into the presence of God, who is " of purer eyes than to behold iniquity." [46] When he comes before Him, it must be with the consciousness of his sin, in confession and penitence. " Woe is me! for I am undone; because I am a man of unclean lips, and I dwell in the midst of a people of unclean lips." [47] " For Thy name's sake, O Lord, pardon my iniquity; for it is great." [48] But of all the penitential passages in the Old Testament, and especially in the Psalter, Ps. li stands out supreme in the profundity of its recognition of sin, and in the depth of its cry for the divine cleansing. " Have mercy upon me, O God, according to Thy lovingkindness: according to the multitude of Thy tender mercies, blot out my transgressions. Wash me thoroughly from mine iniquity, and cleanse me from my sin. For I acknowledge my

[43] Ps. cvii. 8 f.
[44] Ps. xxiii. 1 ff.
[45] Deut. viii. 3.
[46] Hab. i. 13.
[47] Isa. vi. 5.
[48] Ps. xxv. 11.

transgressions: and my sin is ever before me. Against Thee, Thee only, have I sinned, and done this evil in Thy sight. . . . Purge me with hyssop, and I shall be clean: wash me, and I shall be whiter than snow. . . . Create in me a clean heart, O God; and renew a right spirit within me." [49] How many worshipping souls have these words borne into that abasement of spirit that marked their author! As the instrument of worship, in one of its profoundest moments, their worth will never be exhausted. Nor does the Old Testament leave man with the agonized confession of sin upon his lips. It brings him the assurance of forgiveness, and the peace of the purified heart. " Though your sins be as scarlet, they shall be as white as snow; though they be red like crimson, they shall be as wool." [50] It brings him to share not alone the trembling cry of Isaiah, but the touch upon his lips of the live coal from the heavenly altar, and the heartening word: " Lo, this hath touched thy lips; and thine iniquity is taken away, and thy sin purged." [51] And then it pronounces blessing upon him, instead of woe. " Blessed is he whose transgression is forgiven, whose sin is covered. Blessed is the man unto whom the Lord imputeth not iniquity, and in whose spirit is no guile." [52] And there steals into the heart of the worshipper who has entered into the reality of true confession a new serenity of spirit that makes his worship a rich experience of grace.

He is filled with a great aspiration for the fellowship of God, for he realizes that the greatest of God's gifts is Himself. And innumerable are the passages that are calculated both to reflect his mood and to guide his spirit. " As the hart panteth after the water brooks, so panteth my soul after Thee, O God. My soul longeth for God, for the living God: when shall I come and appear before God? " [53]

[49] Ps. li. 1 ff. (Heb. 3 ff.) .
[50] Isa. i. 18.
[51] Isa. vi. 7.
[52] Ps. xxxii. 1 f.
[53] Ps. xlii. 1 f. (Heb. 2 f.) .

" O God, Thou art my God; early will I seek Thee: my soul thirsteth for Thee, my flesh longeth for Thee in a dry and thirsty land, where no water is; To see Thy power and Thy glory, so as I have seen Thee in the sanctuary." [54] " My soul longeth, yea, even fainteth for the courts of the Lord: my heart and my flesh crieth out for the living God." [55] " Thy mercy, O Lord, is in the heavens; and Thy faithfulness reacheth unto the clouds. Thy righteousness is like the mountains of God; Thy judgments are a great deep: O Lord, Thou preservest man and beast. How excellent is Thy lovingkindness, O God! Therefore the children of men put their trust under the shadow of Thy wings. They shall be abundantly satisfied with the fatness of Thy house; and Thou shalt make them drink of the river of Thy pleasures. For with Thee is the fountain of life: in Thy light shall we see light." [56]

In his fellowship with God he finds a fortification of his spirit, and a quiet trust which can triumph over all the trials of life. He is conscious that " he that dwelleth in the secret place of the Most High shall abide under the shadow of the Almighty," [57] and he shares the experience of the Psalmist who sang, " I have set the Lord always before me: because He is at my right hand, I shall not be moved." [58] He can say: " My soul, wait thou only upon God; for my expectation is from Him. He only is my rock and my salvation: He is my defence; I shall not be moved. In God is my salvation and my glory: the rock of my strength and my refuge is in God." [59] In times of peril, whether individual or national, he knows a poise of spirit that comes from his confidence in God, and in his worship there is born a tranquillity that nothing can disturb. " God is our refuge and strength, a very present help in trouble. Therefore will we

---

[54] Ps. lxiii. 1 f. (Heb. 2 f.) .
[55] Ps. lxxxiv. 2 (Heb. 3) .
[56] Ps. xxxvi. 5 ff. (Heb. 6 ff.) .

[57] Ps. xci. 1.
[58] Ps. xvi. 8.
[59] Ps. lxii. 5 ff. (Heb. 6 ff.) .

not fear, though the earth be removed, and though the mountains be carried into the midst of the sea. . . . The Lord of hosts is with us; the God of Jacob is our refuge." [60] I will lift up mine eyes unto the hills. Whence shall come my help? My help cometh from the Lord, who made heaven and earth. He will not suffer thy foot to be moved: He that keepeth thee will not slumber. Behold, He that keepeth Israel shall neither slumber nor sleep. . . . The Lord shall preserve thee from all evil: He shall preserve thy soul. The Lord shall preserve thy going out and thy coming in from this time forth, and even for evermore." [61] " He will keep the feet of His saints, and the wicked shall be silent in darkness; for by strength shall no man prevail." [62]

His worship is the organ of his response to God's approach, and if it merely brings him peace and poise of spirit, without holy resolve and consecration, it fails to fulfil its purpose. And again, there are passages whose high resolve and surrender to the will of God his heart can echo. Isaiah heard the voice of God in the Temple say, " Whom shall I send? And who will go for us? " And yielding himself in ready response he cried, " Here am I; send me." [63] And to many a soul the reading of that passage has been both a benediction and a call, lifting them to a like yielding of themselves to be the instrument of the divine purpose. Or the words of the Psalmist: " Let the words of my mouth and the meditation of my heart be acceptable in Thy sight, O Lord, my Rock, and my Redeemer," [64] have been adopted, not alone as the cry of the worshipper for purity of heart in the hour of worship, but as the expression of his yearning for a mind which is wholly attuned to the thought of God. " One thing have I desired of the Lord, that will I seek after," he cries in the words of another

[60] Ps. xlvi. 1 ff. (Heb. 2 ff.) .
[61] Ps. cxxi. 1 ff.
[62] 1 Sam. ii. 9.
[63] Isa. vi. 8.
[64] Ps. xix. 14 (Heb. 15) .

psalm; " That I may dwell in the house of the Lord all the days of my life." [65] Or he echoes the resolve of another: " I will dwell in the house of the Lord for ever." [66] And into the words he puts the meaning, not of a withdrawal from all the cares of life into the calm of the sanctuary, but of the carrying of the spirit of the sanctuary into the life of the world, in a spirit of consecration to the will of God. " Shew me Thy ways, O Lord; Teach me Thy paths." [67] " I delight to do Thy will, O my God; Yea, Thy law is within my heart." [68] " With my whole heart have I sought Thee: O let me not wander from Thy commandments." [69] So long as men with humble hearts hear or repeat such words in the hour of solemn worship, so long will they help to infuse that worship with the spirit of obedience to the divine will, and the dedication of the self and all it possesses to be the instrument of God's purpose.

It is only when such a spirit has been reached that petition for all the countless boons that men seek can wisely be made. For no longer will they suppose that their prayer is a means of controlling God, or that they have a right to the things they ask of Him. Their petitions will be the earnest pleadings of humble souls that realize that if God grants their boons it is of His grace, and that if He withholds them they may yet find in His sovereign will their peace. " Into Thy hand I commend my spirit " [70] and " My times are in Thy hand " [71] are the words of a man who was crying unto God out of the depths of his agony. For when a man has reached this spirit he may bring to God all his needs and all his desires. In his pains and sorrows and disappointments, in all his anxieties and fears, in his material and spiritual needs alike, he can come to God and plead with freedom that is without trace of presumption, as men who come before us in the Old Testament prayed. " We

[65] Ps. xxvii. 4.
[66] Ps. xxviii. 6.
[67] Ps. xxv. 4.
[68] Ps. xl. 8 (Heb. 9).
[69] Ps. cxix. 10.
[70] Ps. xxxi. 5 (Heb. 6).
[71] Ps. xxxi. 15 (Heb. 16).

do not present our supplications before Thee for our right-eousness, but for Thy great mercies." [72]

Nor will his petitions be marked by the spirit of selfish-ness alone. He will be reminded of the vast sweep of God's purposes. " I the Lord have called thee in righteousness, and will hold thy hand, and will keep thee and give thee for a covenant of the people, for a light of the Gentiles; to open the blind eyes, to bring out the prisoners from the dungeon, and them that sit in darkness out of the prison house." [73] He will enter into the yearning for the realiza-tion of that purpose. " Drop down, ye heavens, from above, and let the skies pour down righteousness: let the earth open, that they may bring forth salvation, and let her cause righteousness to spring up together." [74] " Sing unto the Lord, bless His name; Shew forth His salvation from day to day. Declare His glory among the nations, His marvellous works among all the peoples." [75] Nor will his cry be one of empty desire, or addressed to others alone. It will be ad-dressed to his own heart, for he will desire some share in carrying the praises of God to all men. " I will praise Thee, O Lord, among the nations, And will sing of Thy name." [76]

In these few passages we have gathered but a fraction of the vast contribution of the Old Testament to the spirit and content of worship. For it holds vast riches, unsurpassed in any literature in the world. And Judaism that gave this Book to us, and taught us to read and sing its words as one of the instruments of our worship, rendered us a service we should not forget. Much that it contains enlarges our knowledge of God and our understanding of His truth; much falls upon our ears with rebuke and challenge. But much moves our spirit with the impulse of worship, and lifts us into its own awareness of God and response to His presence.

[72] Dan. ix. 18.
[73] Isa. xlii. 6 f.
[74] Isa. xlv. 8.

[75] Ps. xcvi. 2 f.
[76] Ps. xviii. 49 (Heb. 50).

XI. THE GOAL OF HISTORY

MODERN STUDY of the Old Testament prophets has stressed
the ethical teaching addressed to the contemporaries of the
speakers, and has tended to pass more lightly over the predictive element in prophecy, and especially over the predictions of the more distant future in what is known as messianic prophecy. The early Christians were particularly
interested in these prophecies, and cherished a large number of passages which were regarded as direct and supernatural promises of the mission of Christ. On many of these
passages scholars to-day put a different interpretation, and
they are able to show that what the writers had in mind was
something quite other than what the early Christians hailed
as the fulfilment of their words. Hence interest in messianic
prophecy has waned, and discussion of it has tended to be
negative, emphasizing what it does not mean rather than
what it does.

It is undeniable that beyond their interest in the immediate future that should arise out of the present the prophets cherished the thought of a Golden Age that lay far off
in the future. Much of their prediction concerned itself
with the issue of the policies of their own day and the harvest of sorrow that men were laying up for themselves by
the follies in which they indulged, and by their indifference to the will of God. Yet they were not just gloomy pes-
simists, without hope for the world. Away on the far horizon they perceived the dawn of hope for men, and they
spoke of a distant future that they did not connect causally
with the present, a future that should be born of the grace
of God rather than of the acts of men. They placed that

future " in the latter end of the days," on the confines of history, and they did not endeavour to place it in any defined relation to the perspective of the present. Around them they saw human sin and folly, and immediately before them predominantly sorrow and judgement; but beyond that, though afar off, an age of glory which should be the consummation and crown of all history.

In itself this is a testimony to the deep-seated optimism of Old Testament thought. Its Golden Age was not placed far back in the infancy of the world. It is true that at the beginning of the Bible we have the idyllic picture of the Garden of Eden, but that is pictured as an age of innocence and simplicity rather than as a Golden Age. Man and woman were there alone, a solitary pair, living a life of naked savagery, without knowledge of good and evil, and therefore living a life that was morally neutral. It was not until they had left the Garden that their children were born, and the pain of childbirth is represented as the price of the fall from innocence. This is no Golden Age, and it will not compare with the prophetic pictures of the Golden Age that lies in the future, in which human society shall be infused with an abiding glory that is the fruit of its obedience to the will of God. In the Garden of Eden there was no human society, in any full meaning of the words. But the Golden Age of the prophets is a kingdom of God, whether the term figures in their prophecies or not.

It is also important to observe that their optimism did not rest on their trust in man, but on their trust in God. That is why it was so wisely based and so sure. Around them they found many who cherished an optimism that was born of their confidence in human wisdom, or who had a shallow trust in God and believed that whatever they did He would not let them down, but would see to it that things turned out all right in the end. In our own day we are familiar with these types, and especially with those who pervert the glorious truth of the love of God into the picture of a spineless Being, who is indifferent to all moral worth and who makes no moral demand on men. The prophets saw God as the embodiment in Himself of all moral worth, and therefore as being in Himself the supreme challenge to men to reflect that worth in their life. They were not blind to the sternness of God and were not afraid to speak of His burning anger, and of His visitation of men in judgement and wrath. For they understood the love of God far better than many in our day who talk so glibly of that love. They knew that a God who was indifferent to human sin could not love men, and that all His visitation in judgement was born essentially of His love. The anger of God was the expression of His love, for its purpose was to bring man to realize how his sin was cursing himself and destroying the glory that God had purposed for him. And just because the prophets saw the wrath of God as born of His love, they never saw the expression of that wrath as the final end of all things. The purpose of that expression was to open men's eyes to the folly of their way that they might turn from it to the better way of God's will, a way which they could never find of themselves or traverse of themselves, but into which God would transport them when they truly desired to walk in it. They were sure that that purpose of God would ultimately triumph, and His wrath dissolve into the love out of which it sprang.

The apocalyptists believed that the days of this great consummation were approaching, and they endeavoured to place it in the perspective of human history. This is what we find in the book of Daniel, which is the first great apocalyptic work of Judaism.[1] There had, indeed, been some preparation for apocalyptic in some passages in the

[1] For my justification of this statement, which some would dispute, I must refer the reader to what I have written in *The Relevance of Apocalyptic*, 1944, Chap. i, and Notes A and B.

prophetic books, such as Isa. xxiv–xxvii and some parts of the book of Joel, but the book of Daniel presents us with a fully apocalyptic work for the first time. The author not merely believed that the Golden Age of which men had so long dreamed was nigh at hand, but he indicates the precise date of the expected consummation. And it is his own day. For reasons which probably grew out of the history of the book he writes in the character of a Daniel who is placed in the sixth century B.C.,[2] though he himself lived in the second century B.C. He therefore furnished a bridge, in the form of a skeleton of the history of the intervening period, to convey the reader to his own day, in which the focus of his interest lay. The mingled iron and pottery of the divided fourth kingdom would be identified by his contemporaries with the Seleucid and Ptolemaic branches of the kingdom founded by Alexander, and the ten horns of the fourth beast would similarly be identified with the Seleucid line of rulers, with the upstart Antiochus Epiphanes as the Little Horn, that had a mouth speaking great things against the Most High and that made war on the saints. And the book of Daniel declared to men that in his day, in the day of this Antiochus, the God of Heaven would establish His enduring kingdom of righteousness. All of the stories of this book have relevance to the days of Antiochus, and the climax of all its visions is to be found in his day and in his policies, and in the sweeping away of all earthly empires in the judgement that is about to be executed on him. No longer is the Golden Age on the far horizon, or even merely near, illumining the present with its brightness, though lying beyond the present in an undefined and unrelated way. It is related to human history, in the precise sequence of events that are to lead to its establishment.

---

2 On the reasons for the pseudonymity of the book of Daniel, cf. *ibid.*, pp. 35 ff. and "The Bilingual Problem of Daniel," in *Zeitschrift für die alttestamentliche Wissenschaft*, N.F. ix, 1932, pp. 256 ff.

Nevertheless, it is still not represented as the mere issue of the present. It is the divine breaking into history, the act of God's grace in setting up His everlasting kingdom amongst men. It is the stone cut without hands that shall strike the brittle pottery and shatter it and bring down the whole statue that represents human history in the succession of world empires. And although the Maccabees and their supporters are probably referred to as " a little help," [3] which God in His graciousness does not disdain, there is no suggestion that the setting up of the kingdom is anything but God's act. Its authority is to be given to the saints, and not seized by them with God's approval and help. For the consummation shall be seen of all men to be the setting up of the divine throne of judgement amongst men, and His sweeping away of all that is opposed to Him in a final act.

That this was not fulfilled in the age of Antiochus Epiphanes needs not to be said. So completely mistaken was the author in his hopes that to some modern writers it was a mistake to include his work in the Canon. This is in part due to the effects of his mistaken hopes on the men of other days. For all down the ages men have cherished the hope of this author that they were about to witness the climax of history in their day. Many expressed this in fresh apocalyptic works, while more have done so in a re-interpretation of the book of Daniel in the terms of the events and conditions of their own day. The earliest re-interpretation of the book of Daniel is found in 2 Esdras (4 Ezra), where we read: " The eagle, which thou sawest come up from the sea, is the fourth kingdom which appeared in vision to thy brother Daniel. But it was not expounded unto him, as I now expound it unto thee." [4] And all down the centuries men have continued to suppose that every previous interpretation was wrong, while their own at last is right, and is

[3] Dan. xi. 34.   [4] 2 Esd. (4 Ezr.) xii. 11 f.

to be vindicated in the fulfilment of the expectations of the book of Daniel in their own day, only to find that their own interpretation inexorably goes to join the others that events have demonstrated to be wrong.

It is unfortunate that there is still too little appreciation of the real worth of these apocalyptic hopes and of the dreams of the Golden Age that are found in the prophets. For here as everywhere we should remember that the Old Testament is essentially a religious book, and for its religious message we should look. That many of the traditions recorded in the Old Testament cannot to-day be regarded as sober history does not mean that we sweep them aside as worthless; nor should the fact that these forecasts of the future, whether in detailed outlines of the sequence of events or in more general terms, have failed to correspond with fact lead us to cast them aside. In both cases we should remember that whether by tradition or by forecast the Biblical writers are delivering themselves of a religious message, and that what they write is charged with the word of God unto us. There was a time when men asked, " Can any good come out of Nazareth? " [5] and, " Doth any prophet arise in Galilee? " [6] and, " Is not this the carpenter's Son? " [7] We realize their folly in missing the supreme spiritual worth of the message that reached them, because they looked no farther than the commonplace conditions in which He who was the medium of that message lived. We repeat that folly when we miss the spiritual significance of what we read in the Old Testament because we are so conscious of the trappings in which that message is found.

To examine all the eschatological passages found in the prophetic and apocalyptic sections of the Old Testament,

---

[5] John i. 46.

[6] John vii. 52. My conversion of the categorical negative of the Pharisees into a rhetorical question that implies that negative does no violence to their thought.

[7] Matt. xiii. 55. Cf. Mark vi. 3.

and to try to recover the primary thought of the writer and the enduring message of what he wrote, would again require a separate treatise, and is far beyond the limits appropriate here. We can only endeavour to look at a few of the more outstanding ideas found in the principal passages, and go behind them to the religious essence of the message they enshrine.

It is necessary in the first place to make clear what we mean by the term messianic prophecy, and to distinguish between the use of the term Messiah and messianic prophecy. We are familiar with the term Messiah, or Christ, in the New Testament, where it is equated with the Son of David, and it therefore attaches to itself those passages in the Old Testament which look forward to the rise of a scion of the house of David, who shall restore the fortunes of Israel. Actually in the Old Testament the term Messiah is not used in these passages. The word which is transliterated Messiah is frequently found, but it is applied to the reigning king, or to the high priest, or even to Cyrus, the Persian king.[8] There is only one passage where the term Messiah is found as a *terminus technicus* in the Old Testament in the Authorized Version, and there the Revised Version substitutes for it " the anointed one." [9] For the reference there is probably to one who was contemporary with the author of the book, and not to the future Davidic leader. For it was in the period between the Testaments that the term Messiah became attached to the concept of this Davidic leader. And for a time, under the influence of the Hasmonaean combination of the kingly and priestly offices, a Levitical, rather than a Davidic, Messiah was awaited. But when the popularity of the Hasmonaean house waned and its fortunes fell, men returned to the hope of a Davidic leader. It is probable that the attachment of the term Messiah to the concept owed something to Ps. ii, where the rul-

[8] Isa. xlv. 1.   [9] Dan. ix. 25 f.

ers of the earth are represented as combining against Yahweh and His Anointed. This psalm has been traditionally interpreted of the future ideal Son of David, rather than of any historical event of the past, though this has not gone unchallenged. But whatever the reference in this passage, there is no evidence to show that in Old Testament times the term " Anointed One " was used as a technical synonym for the expected Davidic leader, though clearly that leader was expected to be an anointed one, since all kings were anointed. Nevertheless, we may for convenience use the later term, Messiah, for this expected royal leader.

Messianic prophecy, however, is much wider than prophecy of the coming of this Messiah. There are many passages which tell of the coming Golden Age in terms of the ideal quality of its life, but without any reference to the Messiah. This is true of the book of Daniel, though not only of that book. Here we find that the glorious and everlasting kingdom of God is one in which the dominion is given to the people of the saints of the Most High, but there is no reference to any Davidic, or royal, leader. It is true that we here find the term Son of Man, with which we are familiar in the New Testament, and since it is there applied by our Lord to Himself, and since He is also called by the name Messiah, we have come to equate " Son of Man " and " Messiah " as titles. A moment's reflexion should suffice to show us our error, however. For while our Lord is presented as referring to Himself continually as the Son of Man, He is not represented as welcoming the application of the term Messiah to Himself. That He regards Himself as both Messiah and Son of Man, indeed, need not be denied, and when at His trial He is asked, " I adjure Thee by the living God, that Thou tell us whether Thou be the Christ," He replies, " Thou hast said." But even here He turns immediately to express His mission in terms of the Son of Man:

" Nevertheless I say unto you, Henceforth ye shall see the Son of Man sitting at the right hand of power, and coming on the clouds of heaven," [10] where there is a clear reference to the Son of Man of Dan. vii. 13. That our Lord identified the Messiah and the Son of Man may be concluded from this passage, but that the identification had not been made by any before Him is equally clear. For why should He have been challenged to express His mission in terms of the Messiahship, if the term Son of Man, so freely applied to Himself, had been an acknowledged synonym? Moreover, His solemn charge to His disciples, after Peter's confession at Caesarea Philippi, to tell no man that He was the Messiah,[11] would have been utterly futile if everyone knew that the Son of Man and the Messiah were one and the same in their significance. For us to recognize in our Lord the fulfilment of the hopes that gathered around both of these terms is not to justify their equation, and still less to carry that equation back into the Old Testament and into the minds of its writers.

In the book of Daniel the term " Son of Man " is a figure for the kingdom of God, or for the saints as vested with the authority of the kingdom. The four successive earthly kingdoms which are to be swept away before the kingdom of God are represented by four beasts arising from the sea; the fifth and enduring kingdom is represented by one like a Son of Man coming with the clouds of heaven. This kingdom could not be represented as arising from below, for it arises not from the activity of man but by the intervention of God. From heaven therefore it must come. And similarly its character must be contrasted with the kingdoms that preceded it, by its symbolical representation by a human figure, rather than by a beast. It is not to be denied that the author of the book of Daniel would hardly have thought of the kingdom as without any leader, but the person of that

[10] Matt. xxvi. 63 f.   [11] Matt. xvi. 20.

leader is of no moment to him beside the thought of the kingdom as God's kingdom, in which the now persecuted saints of God shall be in the ascendant. At the time when he was writing the actual human leader of the saints was Judas the Maccabee, a member of a relatively humble priestly family. When that family attained the high priestly and royal rank, the conception of a Levitical Messiah might arise. But one would hardly expect such an idea to be coined by the author of the book of Daniel, who did not regard Judas the Maccabee as in any sense the instrument of the founding of the kingdom, but merely as " a little help," and a Davidic Messiah would be an even greater irrelevance to him. For no Davidic Messiah was on the horizon, but the kingdom seemed to him about to break into history. To him therefore the Son of Man stood for the kingdom in its manifestation, and there are passages in the New Testament where we may with probability find a similar meaning.[12] It is probable, however, that before the days of our Lord the term " Son of Man " had been individualized to stand for a divinely sent leader and establisher of the kingdom, though thought of as quite distinct from the Messiah. This development was probably due in no small measure to the book known as 1 Enoch, and in particular to the section of this book called " The Similitudes of Enoch." This development is here spoken of only as probable, because there are scholars of eminence who deny that the term Son of Man had been individualized prior to the ministry of our Lord.[13] For our present purpose this is not of importance, since such a view only goes farther than that here taken, that in the Old Testament the term Son of Man is associated with the messianic conception in its wider range, but not in its narrower limitation to an individual Davidic Messiah.

[12] Cf. my *Relevance of Apocalyptic*, pp. 114 ff.
[13] Cf. *ibid.*, pp. 28 ff., 114 ff.

The Suffering Servant of Deutero-Isaiah has also been given a messianic interpretation until modern times. But here again we must be careful to recognize that the Suffering Servant is not the Messiah in Old Testament thought. There are some who deny any messianic significance to the Suffering Servant in the thought of the writer, and who believe that his thought was either of the community of Israel or of some past or contemporary historical figure. But in so far as we find his thought to be of a future person who should through suffering richly serve his people and the world, we may treat the conception as messianic, in the wider sense of the term, provided we clearly distinguish between the figure of the Servant and the figure of the Messiah. It is true once more that our Lord owed much to the Servant passages, and that He interpreted His own mission in terms of the Servant even more than in terms of the Messiah. It is also true that He brought the concept of the Servant and that of the Son of Man into intimate relationship. "The Son of Man came not to be ministered unto, but to minister, and to give His life a ransom for many." [14] In the same way we read that immediately after Peter's confession at Caesarea Philippi, He began " to show unto His disciples that He . . . must suffer many things." [15] Messiah, Son of Man, and Suffering Servant were clearly thought of as coming together in Him, so that He could identify Himself equally with them all. Yet this is not to identify them in the thought of the Old Testament, or in our interpretation of the Old Testament. Before the days of our Lord it had not occurred to anyone to equate these figures. When, on the occasion above referred to, our Lord began to talk to His disciples of His coming sufferings, Peter rebuked Him for talking what he thought was nonsense. The Messiah was clearly not a concept associated with suffering in the minds of the disciples. Nor was it any better

[14] Mark x. 45.   [15] Matt. xvi. 21.

with the Son of Man. Hence they completely failed to understand all this side of His teaching, and we read that on the Resurrection Day, when He joined the two walking out to Emmaus, He deplored that still continued failure. " O fools, and slow of heart to believe all that the prophets have spoken: Ought not Christ to have suffered these things, and to enter into His glory? " [16]

In the next chapter we shall have to consider the fulfilment of Old Testament expectations in Christ. Here we are rather concerned with the nature of Old Testament expectations of the goal of history in the Golden Age. For though there is variety of idea as to the means whereby history shall reach its goal, there is no doubt whatever that it is to be a Golden Age, and a deep measure of agreement as to the character of that age. This will appear from a rapid review of a few of the passages in which these hopes of Israel are enshrined. Questions of date and authorship need not here concern us, since it is the character of the hopes rather than the date of their emergence and expression which is of present moment.

Familiar are the words: " The people that walked in darkness have seen a great light: they that dwell in the land of the shadow of death, upon them hath the light shined. . . . For unto us a child is born, unto us a son is given: and the government shall be upon his shoulder: and his name shall be called Wonderful, Counsellor, Mighty God, Everlasting Father, Prince of Peace. Of the increase of his government and of peace there shall be no end, upon the throne of David, and upon his kingdom, to establish it, and to uphold it with judgment and with righteousness from henceforth even for ever." [17] Here the reference to the throne of David makes it clear that it is the Davidic Messiah that is in mind, though he is depicted in exalted and superhuman terms. His kingdom is to be an everlasting

[16] Luke xxiv. 25 f.   [17] Isa. ix. 2 ff.

kingdom, and its supreme marks are to be the righteousness of its rule and its unbroken peace.

A similar picture, also associated with the Davidic Messiah, is found in another passage. " And there shall come
forth a shoot out of the stock of Jesse, and a branch out of
his roots shall bear fruit: And the spirit of Yahweh shall
rest upon him, the spirit of wisdom and understanding, the
spirit of counsel and might, the spirit of knowledge and of
the fear of Yahweh; And he shall not judge after the sight
of his eyes, neither reprove after the hearing of his ears: But
with righteousness shall he judge the poor, and reprove
with equity for the meek of the earth: and he shall smite
the oppressor with the rod of his mouth, and with the
breath of his lips shall he stay the wicked. And righteousness shall be the girdle of his loins, and faithfulness the
girdle of his reins. And the wolf shall dwell with the lamb,
and the leopard shall lie down with the kid; and the calf
and the young lion shall graze together; and a little child
shall lead them. And the cow and the bear shall be friends;
their young ones shall lie down together: and the lion shall
eat straw like the ox. And the sucking child shall play on
the hole of the asp, and the weaned child shall put his hand
on the viper's den. They shall not hurt nor destroy in all
my holy mountain: for the earth shall be full of the knowledge of Yahweh, as the waters cover the sea." [18] Whether the
final verse is a separate fragment, as some believe, is imma-
terial. It fits well into the thought of the whole, which
promises an age in which the royal rule shall be inflexibly
just, because divinely inspired, and the spirit of concord
shall not alone possess the hearts of men, but even extend
to wild beasts, whose nature shall be radically transformed,
and men everywhere shall find the spring of their life in
God. It is an earthly paradise that is depicted, but it is this
because it is wholly directed by the spirit of God.

[18] Isa. xi. 1 ff.

So again in a passage from the book of Micah: " But thou, Bethlehem Ephratah, which art little to be among the thousands of Judah, out of thee shall one come forth unto me that is to be ruler in Israel; whose goings forth are from of old, from everlasting. . . . And he shall stand and rule in the strength of Yahweh, in the majesty of the name of his God: and they shall abide. For now shall he be great unto the ends of the earth." [19] Here again, the Davidic leader is in mind, and his rule is conceived of as extending through all the earth. Yet it is less his rule than God's, whose instrument he is.

Or in Jeremiah we read: " Behold, the days come, saith Yahweh, that I will raise unto David a righteous Branch, and he shall reign as king and deal wisely, and shall execute judgment and justice in the land. In his days shall Judah be saved, and Israel shall dwell safely; and this is his name whereby he shall be called, Yahweh is our righteousness." [20] The emphasis is, as ever, less on the Davidic character of the ruler than on the beneficence and justice of his rule, and on the fact that this rests manifestly on the will of God.

In a great many passages where there is no reference to the house of David we find the Golden Age pictured in terms which agree in essence with these promises. For though there is no reference to the divinely established leader, it is precisely the same world fellowship of harmony and concord, based on man's obedience to the divine will, and not on the inherent goodness of the human heart, or on earthly wisdom. " It shall come to pass in the latter days that the mountain of Yahweh's house shall be established as the chief of the mountains, and shall be exalted above the hills; and all nations shall flow unto it. And many peoples shall go and say, Come ye, and let us go up to the mountain of Yahweh, to the house of the God of Jacob; and He will teach us of His ways, and we will walk in His

---

[19] Micah v. 2, 4 (Heb. 1, 3).   [20] Jer. xxiii. 5 f.

paths: for out of Zion shall go forth instruction, and the word of Yahweh from Jerusalem. And He shall judge between the nations, and shall reprove many peoples: and they shall beat their swords into ploughshares, and their spears into pruning-hooks: nation shall not lift up sword against nation, neither shall they learn war any more." [21] This is not the mere yearning of men for deliverance from war, but the recognition that that deliverance can only be found in the spread of the spirit of submission to God. The reconciliation of man with man and of nation with nation is only to be found in their common reconciliation with God and obedience to His law. In the form in which this oracle is preserved in the book of Micah there is added: " But they shall sit every man under his vine and under his fig-tree; and none shall make them afraid: for the mouth of Yahweh hath spoken it." [22] Yet here again it is to be noted that the economic bliss of this picture is but the corollary of obedience to the will of God.

Jeremiah, in a great passage where he is thinking only of his own nation, and not of the worldwide Golden Age, finds the spring of hope in the same place. " Behold the days come, saith Yahweh, that I will make a new covenant with the house of Israel, and with the house of Judah: . . . This is the covenant that I will make. . . . I will put My law in their inward parts, and in their heart will I write it; and I will be their God, and they shall be My people. And they shall teach no more every man his neighbour, and every man his brother, saying, Know Yahweh: for they shall all know Me, from the least of them to the greatest of them, saith Yahweh. For I will forgive their iniquity, and their sin will I remember no more." [23] There is here no description of outer conditions of life in the Golden Age, but only of its inner spring in loyalty to God. But it is clear that the prophet believed that when the law of God was written on

[21] Isa. ii. 2 ff.   [22] Micah iv. 4.   [23] Jer. xxxi. 31 ff.

the living tables of men's hearts and found its expression in every aspect of their lives, human society would be inexpressibly glorious, and the truest bliss would abound. So, too, perceived Deutero-Isaiah: " All thy children shall be taught of Yahweh; and great shall be the peace of thy children." [24] Peace is here something far more inclusive than the mere absence of war. It is positive well-being. And man's well-being in its highest degree is perceived to arise out of his willingness to be schooled of God.

This last passage is from Deutero-Isaiah, whose vision was certainly not limited to Israel, as we have already seen. " Look unto Me, and be ye saved, all the ends of the earth," he cried, " for I am God, and there is no other." [25] And when men should bring to Him their worship, they should find life rich with a richness that consisted in its reflexion of His will and His righteousness. " Attend unto Me, O My people; and give ear unto Me, O My nation; for instruction shall go forth from Me, and My judgment shall be the light of the peoples. In a moment My righteousness shall be near. My salvation is gone forth, and Mine arms shall judge the peoples; the isles shall wait for Me, and on Mine arm shall they trust. Lift up your eyes to the heavens, and look upon the earth beneath: for the heavens shall vanish away like smoke, and the earth shall wax old like a garment, and they that dwell therein shall die like flies: but My salvation shall be for ever, and my righteousness shall not be abolished." [26] Here the everlasting character of the Golden Age is once more brought out. It shall contain within itself no seed of decay, like the corrupt ages that precede it. For while all sin is self-destructive, and all that does not spring from God is sin, all that is born of His spirit is enduring in its goodness.

This appears in another oracle, from a later prophet. " For behold, I create new heavens and a new earth: and the former things shall not be remembered, nor come to

24 Isa. liv. 13.   25 Isa. xlv. 22.   26 Isa. li. 4 ff.

mind. But be ye glad and rejoice for ever in that which I create: for behold, I create Jerusalem a rejoicing, and her people a joy. . . . There shall be no more thence an infant of days, nor an old man that hath not filled his days: for the child shall die an hundred years old, and the sinner being an hundred years old shall be accursed. And they shall build houses, and inhabit them; and they shall plant vineyards, and eat the fruit thereof. They shall not build, and another inhabit; they shall not plant, and another eat: for as the days of a tree shall be the days of My people, and My chosen shall long enjoy the work of their hands." 27 " And it shall come to pass that from one new moon to another, and from one Sabbath to another, shall all flesh come to worship before Me, saith Yahweh." 28 All the richness and enduring quality of this beauteous world is the creation of God, and not of man, and it is capable of realization only when all flesh bows in worship before Him.

Of the psalms to which a messianic interpretation has been given we may be content with one, which almost certainly has the Davidic Messiah in mind though he is not described as such. This is Ps. lxxii, which is too long to cite, but which throughout describes the glory of the world which is united under the beneficent sway of the king whose rule is the instrument of the divine power. His dominion is from sea to sea, and from the River unto the ends of the earth. All kings bow down before him, and all nations are subject to his sway. But that sway does not consist in the harsh imposition of his will on the world, but in the exercise of justice to the poorest of the land, and the distribution unto all of the blessings of life. Once again there shall be no seed of decay in a state which so manifestly rests on the will of God, and whose righteousness is His gift. The king's name shall endure for ever, and shall be continued so long as the sun endures.

27 Isa. lxv. 17 ff.   28 Isa. lxvi. 23.

The same everlasting quality of its bliss is ascribed by the author of Daniel to the kingdom of God for which he looked. It should be set up not by man but by God, and therefore it should be secure against overthrow. " And in the days of those kings shall the God of heaven set up a kingdom, which shall never be destroyed, nor shall the sovereignty thereof be left to another people; but it shall break in pieces and consume all these kingdoms, and it shall stand for ever." [29] Similarly to the " one like unto a son of man " there was given " dominion, and glory, and a kingdom, that all the peoples, nations, and languages should serve him: his dominion is an everlasting kingdom, which shall not pass away, and his kingdom that which shall not be destroyed." [30] That the " one like unto a son of man " is a symbolic figure for the saints as invested with the authority of the kingdom has been said above, and is made quite clear in the interpretation of the chapter itself. " The time came that the saints possessed the kingdom," [31] and the kingdom and the dominion, and the greatness of the kingdoms under the whole heaven, shall be given to the people of the saints of the Most High: their kingdom is an everlasting kingdom, and all dominions shall serve and obey them." [32] Here there is the same general picture as in the previously noted passages. And that the thought is not just of a chauvinistic Jewish hegemony of the world, but of a genuine kingdom of God, in which righteousness shall be the basis of all life, is clear from the whole tenor of the book. " They that be wise shall shine as the brightness of the firmament; and they that turn many to righteousness as the stars for ever and ever." [33]

The relevance of the Suffering Servant to the messianic picture, in the wider sense of the term, is less direct. Here there is no description of the glories of the Golden Age, no

[29] Dan. ii. 44.   [31] Dan. vii. 22.   [33] Dan. xii. 3.
[30] Dan. vii. 14.   [32] Dan. vii. 27.

interest in the exaltation of the saints or the worldwide and everlasting sway of any Davidic leader in that age, but a focussing of interest on the means whereby the spirit of submission to the will of God and humble surrender of heart to Him is to be spread. And in all its varying forms we have found the common recognition that this is the sole basis of the glories to which Israel looked forward with such eagerness. The Servant is not just thrown up from below, born of the aspiration of the human heart. He is chosen of God, and commissioned to his task by the Lord of the universe. And his task is announced at the outset as the bringing forth " judgment to the Gentiles." [34] It is probable that the word *judgement* has here a more than forensic meaning, and that it includes both true religion, which is the spring of justice, and a spirit of judgement which expresses itself over the whole field of life. His mission is exercised in a gentleness that is surpassing, and a fortitude that triumphs over all discouragement. Though there are times when he says in his heart, " I have laboured in vain, I have spent my strength for nought," yet he does not lose heart, but adds, " Yet surely my cause is with Yahweh, and my recompense with my God." [35] And the full glory of his mission opens before his eyes: " It is too light a thing that though shouldest be My servant to raise up the tribes of Jacob, and to restore the preserved of Israel: I will also give thee for a light to the Gentiles, that My salvation may reach unto the end of the earth." [36] There is no need to describe the glories of the world that shall be in those days. The divine salvation brings the perfect well-being of man, and when that perfect well-being is universal and all life reflects the will of God, what more remains to be said? What more, save of the means whereby the Servant shall fulfil His mission? " I gave My back to the smiters, and My cheeks to them that plucked off the hair: I hid not My face from

---

[34] Isa. xlii. 1.   [35] Isa. xlix. 4.   [36] Isa. xlix. 6.

shame and spitting." [37] "He was wounded for our transgressions, He was bruised for our iniquities: the chastisement of our peace was upon Him; and with His stripes we
are healed." [38] It was by His suffering that He should accomplish His mission, a suffering that should be unto death
and that should serve as " an offering for sin " [39] whereby
He should " justify many." [40]

The book of Daniel was written in a time of great tribulation, when the saints were being persecuted, and apocalyptic hopes of the Golden Age have always flourished in
times of tribulation. The figure of Antiochus Epiphanes has
been matched by many another, who has seemed the incarnation of all that is opposed to the will of God, and who has
crushed the saints beneath his cruel heel. But here is something quite other than that. The sufferings of the saints at
the hands of Antichrist may be thought of as preceding the
breaking of the new age; but they are not thought of as inherently capable of creating the new age. But the sufferings
of the Servant are the organ whereby His mission of spreading light and salvation is fulfilled. The world is cleansed
in its soul and lifted to God, and hence the conditions that
all Israel's visionaries had seen to be indispensable to the
Golden Age are realized.

Beneath all the varying forms and emphases of these eschatological hopes of Israel there is a deep underlying unity
of conception, to which the world will come back when it is
wise for the inspiration of sober hope. The preternatural
lengthening of life and the transformation of animal nature may seem idle dreams to all but those who have literalistic minds, and the day when swords shall be beaten to
ploughshares may seem far off to a world which is devas-
tated by war to a degree never before known in history.
Yet no age has known a deeper yearning for the Golden

37 Isa. l. 6.   39 Isa. liii. 10.
38 Isa. liii. 5.   40 Isa. liii. 11.

Age than our own. It created the League of Nations as the expression of its desire to be freed from war, and its blue prints of Utopia, in which every sphere of human society is idealized, are presented to the public in swift succession. It is sure that the world was created for a higher destiny than it has yet achieved, and that life might be fairer for men than any they now know. But the Utopia it seeks is one which man designs for himself, and one which he desires to create for himself. Into its planning his highest wisdom is to go, and all the resources of science are to be devoted to its realization. It believes that there is a goal of history, separated from us by but a thin veil of mist, attainable by our effort, and able to make the highest glories of the past look pale and poor.

To such an age the Old Testament brings a message of the deepest import, a message urgent and vital and full of mingled hope and warning. It declares that man's assurance that he was created for a higher destiny than he has found is well-grounded. There is a goal of history, an age in which life shall know a fairness beyond the imagination of man. But it cannot arise out of the present by ordinary causation. Evil is evil and can only bring forth evil fruits. And the present, with all its sorrow and destruction, is evil. And the morrow that will be born of the present is evil, and delusive is every promise that out of the heart of man the nobler world of his dreams can be born. There was always a hiatus in prophecy between the future that should arise from the present and "the latter end of the days." And though to the author of Daniel there was little temporal hiatus to separate him from the kingdom of God, there was a causal hiatus. It was to come down from God on to the plane of history and to be established by His activity. Only the hand of God could break the causal nexus between sin and its fruit, which is more sin.

This does not mean that the way of wisdom for men is to

wait in slothful and fatalistic indifference until it shall
please God to intervene in history. Nor is it true that God
stands outside history until the great moment of the establishment of His kingdom. All history is under His control,
and He is active all the time in its affairs. But in the great
consummation of history, there will be no alien will strug-
gling against His will and marring the life of men. The divine activity will be the sole source of the life of that day,
and hence the divine control of history will be manifested
in a new way.

In another connexion it has been said that faith is the
condition of salvation, but not its organ. Man is saved by
the power of God and by no activity of his own; yet is he
saved only when he yields himself to be saved. In a similar
way the Golden Age will be the divine creation, yet God
will not create it until the conditions for its creation are
ready. Man has not just to sit down idly and wait for it.
The author of the book of Daniel desired to encourage men
to such loyalty to God as Daniel and the three youths in the
fire showed, a loyalty that could not be diverted by threats
and pains, nor even by being apparently abandoned by
God. " They that turn many to righteousness," he said, shall
shine " as the stars for ever and ever." [41] Clearly he thought
it a good thing to be active not alone in loyalty but in winning men to loyalty, for though that activity could not itself bring the kingdom, it could help to provide the conditions in which God would bring it.

But it is significant that man's activity is assigned this
part. Man is ever eager to be the builder and founder of the
kingdom. And the Old Testament says he cannot be. Instead of seeking to usurp what God has reserved for Himself, he is wise if he plays the part that God in His wisdom
has assigned him. And that part is just to be loyal to the
will of God, and to spread that spirit of loyalty amongst

41 Dan. xii. 3.

men. This is not to say that all the legislative plans that are proposed for the post-war world are evil, but to say that far more fundamental than any of them is the spirit of loyalty to the will of God, and that he who seeks to infuse men with that spirit of loyalty is doing something of far deeper significance than any legislator can do.

The Golden Age is the age in which the will of God will be the sole basis of life, when all life will blossom with a fairness that springs from this root. God has a will for the world, a will that embraces all nations and all men, and that is not without purpose for every aspect of man's life and activity. Loyalty to God, and the execution of His purpose, can alone ensure the enduring good of men. That is why the Golden Age is only for the saints of the Most High. Men who will not have their lives ordered by the will of God cannot express that will in their lives. And therefore they cannot know the Golden Age. And neither can anyone else. For the Golden Age is only for all.

When the Old Testament depicts the kingdom of the Messiah as worldwide, it is not just Jewish megalomania, and imperialistic nationalism. It simply means that the Old Testament writers realized that we are parts one of another, and that no man or nation lives to himself or itself alone. It is a commonplace that in Hebrew thought a man was not merely an individual, but a member of a community, and that the unit of its thought was often the community and not the individual. It is less seldom noted that in her eschatological dreams Israel testified to a much more remarkable faith, that the single nation was a fragment of a yet larger whole. Israel knew that the individual is often swept in the current of the life of the community, and involved in experiences which he does not bring on himself. But here is the recognition that no frontiers can isolate the life of a nation, and that it, too, may be swept in the current of the wider life of the peoples, and that until the will of God is done in all the earth, that will is imperilled in every part. The universalizing of the kingdom of God is essential to its character.

And similarly the sweeping away of the enemies of God in the great judgement that heralds the founding of the kingdom is not just fierce desire for vengeance on the persecutors of the saints. It is but the simple recognition that so long as there are enemies of God amongst men, so long His kingdom cannot come in all its glory. Every man who resists the will of God in his own life is the enemy of God and of himself, and also the enemy of all mankind. It has already been said that all sin is sin against God, and yet no sin is merely a private matter between a man and God. And the same truth comes out again here. In all his sin a man makes himself the enemy of mankind, and before the Golden Age can dawn sinners must either be consumed or saved.

For it is to be observed that the expectation of the book of Daniel that the evil should be destroyed by the power of God is to be synthesized with the thought of the Servant Songs, which is of a salvation from sin which may fit men for the kingdom of God. There is nothing in the Bible to favour the view that by steady evolution and upward progress, arising out of his own heart, man will attain the perfection of his nature. There is nothing to suggest that all men will necessarily and automatically become good. In the Golden Age there will be only men who reflect the will of God in their lives, but that will be because they have been saved by the power of God and transmuted by His touch, while all others have been consumed. And until they who finally and irrevocably resist the will of God are consumed, the kingdom of God cannot come in all its glory.

This does not mean that we should be eager for the destruction of the wicked. So long as the patience of God lasts, we cannot reflect His will by our impatience. But if we are sincere in our desire for the Golden Age, our sincerity should express itself in our eagerness to let our life be in harmony with the will of God, so far as that is possible in a world in which His will is not universally done. Yet again it is not by our effort that our lives may be brought into harmony with His will. The Servant Songs add an element that is vital to the completion of the picture, with their indication that it is by the sacrificial offering which God Himself provides in His Servant that men are transmuted and prepared to be citizens of the kingdom. If we would hasten the coming of the Golden Age, it must be by yielding ourselves to the hand of God that He may make us as He wills, and by seeking to turn many to righteousness and to spread the spirit of humble submission unto His will.

While it is idle to deny the diversity of level and standpoint found in the Old Testament, which covers so long a period of development, it is equally idle to ignore the fundamental unity which runs through so much of its teaching. The universalism which was the corollary of its recognition of the unity of God was also the necessary ground of its hope for the future of the world, and the missionary purpose which was born of its monotheism was the *sine qua non* of the fulfilment of its dreams. For the world will be really one only when it is one in religion, and when the foundations of its life rest on a religious basis, when the unity of the will of God is the source of its unity.

XII. THE FULFILMENT OF THE
OLD TESTAMENT IN THE NEW

THAT THE OLD and New Testaments belong indissolubly together has been more than once affirmed in the foregoing pages. Certainly the early Christians believed that the Old Testament was intimately relevant to the message with which they were charged, and found the testimony to Christ within its pages. We read in the New Testament that the Risen Lord " beginning from Moses and from all the prophets interpreted in all the Scriptures the things concerning Himself." [1] And with diligence the Christians searched the Scriptures, and found therein important weapons of their armoury for debate with the Jews. Until modern times Old Testament passages continued to be connected with their fulfilment in Christ in such a way as to give the impression that the primary meaning of the Old Testament texts was that which appeared in the light of Christ, and they were read as direct and supernatural predictions of His life and work.

All of this has receded into the background in modern study of the Bible. For to whatever extent the hand of God has been found in the Old Testament, and in whatever sense it has continued to be read as the word of God, the human factors in its creation have occupied a large share of interest. Its writings have been studied in the setting of their times, and every effort has been made to get into the mind of the writer, and into the outlook of his contemporaries, so as to see just what he is likely to have meant by his words, and just how they are likely to have been understood by men. It has been agreed in the present book that

1 Luke xxiv. 27.

this is not enough. Yet there is no disposition to deny that in all our interpretation we should begin from this point. But since the significance of ideas lies no less in what grows from them than in what they are in themselves we should not end there. In the preceding chapters there has been frequent effort to see the significance of the religious ideas expressed by Israel's teachers in the light of what they led to in the period of the Old Testament. And more than once this process has been carried farther, and we have found ourselves in the New Testament.

This is to imply that what the early Christians did is not regarded as a historical curiosity of interpretation, to be cast aside as worthless. Nor is it regarded as something that is spiritually and devotionally profitable so long as it is carried on entirely without relation to the primary, historical interpretation of the text of the Old Testament. The Old Testament should be read both historically and dynamically, and both in intimate relation. All that grew out of the ideas there expressed should be seen in relation to those ideas, and traced back to them, but without being read back, in all its explicit fullness, into the thought of the writers.

The predictive element in the Old Testament has been largely neglected in modern study. The familiar cliché that the prophets were forthtellers rather than foretellers has concentrated attention on them as preachers and social reformers. It has been agreed above that this emphasis needs correcting, and that prediction entered deeply into all prophecy. Yet most of that prediction concerned the immediate future, and was, as has been said, the unveiling of the future as arising out of the present, the unfolding to men of the issue of the policies and sins of their day. Of all the elements of prophecy prediction, speaking generally, was that which was most definitely addressed to the prophet's own generation, and its interest for us is largely historical.

Much of that prediction was never literally fulfilled. Nor was it ever intended to be. When Deutero-Isaiah sang, " Every valley shall be exalted, and every mountain and hill shall be made low; and the crooked shall be made straight, and the rough places plain," [2] he was using the language of poetry, and not seriously suggesting that this transformation should take place at the time of the return from captivity. Similarly, when we read in another passage: " The wilderness and the parched land shall be glad; and the desert shall rejoice, and blossom as the rose," and all the words that follow,[3] we need find nothing more than a poetic ascription to Nature of a mood that corresponds to the writer's spirit, and of a transformation that seems to him appropriate for so notable an occasion as the return of the exiles.

In the book of Joel we read: " And it shall come to pass afterward, that I will pour out My spirit upon all flesh; and your sons and your daughters shall prophesy, your old men shall dream dreams, your young men shall see visions: and also upon the servants and upon the handmaids in those days will I pour out My spirit. And I will show wonders in the heavens and in the earth, blood, and fire, and pillars of smoke. The sun shall be turned into darkness, and the moon into blood, before the great and terrible day of Yahweh come." [4] The New Testament declares that this was fulfilled on the day of Pentecost,[5] and yet there is nothing to suggest that it was fulfilled in any literal sense. No mention is made of any turning of the sun into darkness or of the moon into blood. The fulfilment claimed was in the accession of spiritual power, and the contagious ecstasy of that great day. With such a clear example from the Early Church of indifference to details, we may be delivered from the spirit that comes to the prophecies of the Old Testament

2 Isa. xl. 4.
3 Isa. xxxv. 1 ff.
4 Joel ii. 28 ff. (Heb. iii. 1 ff.).
5 Acts ii. 16.

with the preconceived idea that every detail must be fulfilled in literal fashion.

Of a different order was the failure of Jeremiah's prophecies to find the fulfilment Jeremiah himself expected. In the time of the Scythian peril he predicted doom upon Judah. Yet though Judah may have suffered to some extent, it was slight compared with the disaster he expected. Again twenty years later he re-issued his prophecies, revised to fit the circumstances of the time when the Chaldaeans were pursuing the Egyptians in their flight back to Egypt. And once more nothing comparable with his expectations came to pass. For there were no half-tones in Jeremiah's pictures. " I beheld the earth, and lo! it was void; and the heavens and they had no light. I beheld the mountains, and lo! they trembled, and all the hills moved to and fro. I beheld, and lo! there was no man, and all the birds of the heavens were fled. I beheld, and lo! the fruitful field was a wilderness, and all the cities were broken down at the presence of Yahweh, before His fierce anger." [6] It is impossible not to feel the impressiveness of that picture of disaster, unrelieved and immeasurable. So too with that other great and moving poem, in which Death the Reaper is depicted with such terrifying brilliance: " Thus saith Yahweh of hosts, Call for the mourning women to come, and send for the wise ones in haste; and let them raise a wailing for us, that our eyes may run with tears, and our eyelids gush forth waters. . . . Yet hear, O ye women, the word of Yahweh, and let your ear receive the word of His mouth; and teach your daughters wailing, and each her friend a dirge: Death is come up through our windows, has entered our palaces, to cut off the children without, and the young men from the streets. . . . And the corpses of men shall fall on the open field, as the sheaf behind the reaper, and none shall gather

[6] Jer. iv. 23 ff.

them." [7] When we remember that these were the words of a prophet, and not merely of a poet, and that therefore his hearers would feel that they were charged with power that would work for the realization of what they described, we may the better enter into their impressiveness. And certain it is that Jeremiah believed the things he spoke with all his heart. He was therefore completely non-plussed when the event proved so widely different from his expectation. He cursed the day of his birth, and cried, " Wherefore came I forth out of the womb to see labour and sorrow, that my days should be consumed with shame? " [8] For the non-fulfilment of his word made him the laughing-stock of men. And he carried his perplexity to God and roundly complained of the way He had let him down. " O Yahweh, Thou hast deceived me, and I was deceived: Thou art stronger than I, and has prevailed: I am become a laughing-stock all the day, every one mocketh me. For as often as I speak, I cry out; I cry, Violence and spoil: because the word of Yahweh is made a reproach unto me, and a derision all the day." [9] Yet ultimately his words were fulfilled, and more than fulfilled. The accidents of time and agent were different, but the essence and content of the disasters came fully upon his generation. But again we may be warned against a too literal reading of prophecy.

In predicting the fall of Babylon, a passage which stands in the book of Jeremiah, but which is commonly ascribed to another hand, says: " Yahweh hath stirred up the spirit of the kings of the Medes; because His device is against Babylon, to destroy it." [10] Later in the same chapter we read: " Prepare against her the nations, the kings of the Medes, the governors thereof, and all the deputies thereof. . . . For the purposes of Yahweh against Babylon do stand,

[7] Jer. ix. 17 ff. (Heb. 16 ff.) .   [9] Jer. xx. 7 f.
[8] Jer. xx. 18.   [10] Jer. li. 11.

to make the land of Babylon a desolation, without inhabitant." [11] The writer of these words clearly expected Babylon to fall to the Medes and to suffer destruction at their hands. A passage now found in the book of Isaiah presents a similar picture: " Behold I will stir up the Medes against them [sc. the Babylonians], which shall not regard silver, and as for gold, they shall not delight in it." [12] Of the sufferings of the men of the city this passage says: " Their infants also shall be dashed in pieces before their eyes, their houses shall be spoiled, and their wives ravished. . . . And their bows shall dash the young men in pieces; and they shall have no pity on the fruit of the womb; their eye shall not spare children. And Babylon, the glory of kingdoms, the beauty of the Chaldaeans' pride, shall be as when God overthrew Sodom and Gomorrah." [13] These circumstantial prophecies were not exactly fulfilled. The Median kingdom had itself been swallowed up by the Persian ere Babylon fell, and when it fell it surrendered peacefully to the conqueror. There was no sack of the city and no destruction. The conqueror made it a royal residence, and it continued to exist for many centuries. It is true that then it became a memory of the past, and ceased to exist as a living city. But that was through no attack of the Medes, and in no sense a fulfilment of this ancient prophecy. Yet again, while we can find no literal fulfilment of this expectation, we can find its substantial fulfilment. For Babylon, the proud ruler of kingdoms, exercised but a short-lived sway, and her empire was swallowed up in the Persian empire. As the mistress of Israel's world she ceased to be, and whether she fell to Mede or to Persian was not the vital matter.

That some prophecies were not fulfilled might be explained by the contingent element in prophecy. For in all prophecy there is an implied contingent element. This is made quite clear in the book of Jonah. That book is unlike

[11] Jer. li. 28.   [12] Isa. xiii. 17.   [13] Isa. xiii. 16, 18.

all the other books of the prophetic canon in that it delivers its prophetic message through a story, and not through a series of oracles. In this it is like the first half of the book of Daniel, which does not stand in the prophetic canon. It tells the story of a prophet who was sent to Nineveh; and who promised it destruction as the price of its sins. And when Nineveh repented, it was spared that destruction, to the chagrin of the prophet. It is clear that to the author prophecy, even when expressed in absolute terms, is really contingent, and by repentance and return to God the promised disasters may be avoided.

This is made even more explicit in some other passages. "Yet even now, saith Yahweh, turn ye unto Me with all your heart, and with fasting, and with weeping, and with mourning: And rend your heart, and not your garments, and turn unto Yahweh your God: for He is gracious and full of compassion, slow to anger, and plenteous in mercy, and repenteth Him of the evil. Who knoweth whether He will turn and repent, and leave a blessing behind Him? " [14] " At what instant I shall speak concerning a nation . . . to pluck up and to break down and to destroy it; if that nation . . . turn from their evil, I will repent of the evil that I thought to do unto them." [15]

Few of the prophecies were unfulfilled for this reason, however, for it was rarely the lot of a prophet to be heeded in his own day. It is more widely true to say that many prophecies were not strictly fulfilled because the infallible word of God came to men through the fallible organ of human personality. In the intangible realm of the spirit that word was given unto them, but it was translated and given form, and clothed in images, by the prophets. Hence there is no reason for us to be unduly disturbed by the predictions that were not fulfilled, or by those that were but partially fulfilled, for we can see prophecy as something

[14] Joel ii. 12 ff.   [15] Jer. xviii. 7 f.

richer, profounder and more spiritual than mere prediction. The prophet did not minister to idle curiosity as to
the hidden events of the future. He proclaimed great spiritual principles and uttered the clear call of God, and to
this all his predictions ministered. If we are undisturbed
by prophecies that were not literally fulfilled, therefore, it
is not because we regard prophecy as some common thing,
with no deeper origin than the human spirit, but because
we see it as a precious gift of God given in earthen vessels.

This does not mean that the fulfilment of prophecy is a
negligible study. It has already been agreed that it is not,
and that the interest of the Early Church rested on a sound
instinct. They were unconcerned with the academic study
of the subject, and in no way troubled to find out how far
the details of the prophecies found fulfilment. They were
looking for testimonies unto Christ, and they ignored all
that was of no use for their purpose, and often treated what
they used in a rabbinical way, lifting words out of their
context and interpreting them in a forced way that offends
our exegetical sense. Yet they were profoundly convinced
that Christ was the fulfilment of the highest hopes of the
prophets. And in this they were following our Lord Himself. In the synagogue at Nazareth He read the words: " The
Spirit of the Lord is upon Me, because He anointed Me to
preach good tidings to the poor; He hath sent Me to proclaim release to the captives, and recovering of sight to the
blind, to set at liberty them that are bruised, to proclaim
the acceptable year of the Lord." [16] And He followed this
reading with the calm announcement, " To-day hath this
Scripture been fulfilled in your ears."

In some cases it is possible to say prophecies which were
uttered with no direct reference to our Lord, and whose
primary and specific meaning had no relation to Him, were
taken up and filled with a new meaning in Him. The New

[16] Luke iv. 18 f.

Testament use of the Immanuel prophecy is a case in point. The First Gospel says that the birth of Jesus was a fulfilment of the prophecy of Isaiah. Attention is commonly centred on the word " virgin " in the verse as quoted in the New Testament, and modern writers point out that Isaiah did not really prophesy a Virgin Birth at all. The Hebrew word which he used simply means a mature young woman, whether she be a virgin or married. But more important than any philological study is the whole import of Isaiah's prophecy. When King Ahaz was filled with terror through the attack of Ephraim and Syria, he assured him that they were not to be feared, and then gave him a sign from God, whereby he might know that his word was to be believed. If that sign was one which could only be tested in something over seven hundred years, it would have been quite futile for its purpose. It is not even clear what it does mean. It is commonly taken to be a promise of deliverance for Judah, though there are some who find in it a threat of disaster. The young woman is sometimes thought to be the king's wife, and sometimes the prophet's, and sometimes any young woman of the time who might give birth to a child and call him by this name. By yet others the whole incident is connected with the old Canaanite fertility rites, and the young woman is supposed to be one whom the king had married, or should marry, at the annual festival of the cult that year, and the name to be one of good omen which should be given to the child she should bear, but a good omen that should be falsified by the event. But whatever the prophet's meaning, it clearly had reference to the immediate future, and it was a prophecy of things that should happen in his own day. To suppose that our Lord's birth of the Virgin Mary validated Isaiah's prophecy to Ahaz that the king of Assyria would come upon Judah is to make nonsense of the prophet's words. Not in that sense was his word fulfilled in Christ.

Yet we may recognize that no child born in the history of
man better deserved the name Immanuel than did our
Lord. Whether the Immanuel of Isaiah's prophecy was so
named in recognition of an achieved deliverance from the
Syro-Ephraimitish alliance, or as an omen of a deliverance
which did not mature, no child of that day could so fittingly
be named Immanuel as the Child that was born of Mary.
He lifted up into Himself the hope of a child who should
symbolize in his name the divine presence amongst His
people just because it was not in His name alone, but in
Himself, that He fulfilled the hope. In Matt. i. 21 the Evan-
gelist says that His name is to be called Jesus, a fitting symbol of His saving work; and then adds that He fulfilled the
hope of the coming of One who should be called Immanuel, for Immanuel — God with us — He was in His Person. He gathered up into Himself the noblest hopes and
dreams of the prophets, and gave them a richer fulfilment
than any could have conceived, save in the light of that
fulfilment.

Of other prophecies we may say that they so deeply influenced our Lord that He entered into their spirit, and so
embodied their mission and message in Himself, and became their fulfilment. Yet it is a fulfilment which was not
without reflex influence on the prophecies themselves, and
we see them in a new light when we look at them in the
light of Christ.

Of outstanding importance here is the great conception
of the Suffering Servant in Deutero-Isaiah. Very familiar
was our Lord with the passages that deal with the Servant,
and deeply did He drink of their spirit. They seem to have
influenced His conception of His mission, and therefore
He fulfilled their hope. Not every detail is fulfilled in Him,
indeed. There is no indication in the Gospels that He was
unattractive and even repulsive in appearance, lacking form
and comeliness, and with a face so disfigured that men could

not bear even to look at Him. Yet viewed as a whole, it cannot be denied that the fourth Servant Song finds its amazingly close realization in Him. In the conception of the Servant it has been above suggested that the prophet began with the thought of Israel and her mission to the nations, but by the time he penned the fourth Song he was thinking of an individual in whom that mission should find its supreme expression. It was to be a mission of service through suffering, redemptive through the spirit in which the suffering should be endured. If this great creative idea were not merely born of the prophet's own thought, but kindled in his mind by the spirit of God, it is not surprising that it found its fulfilment in such a Person as it envisaged. For of all the promises of a future Person who should be the agent of God's activity amongst men, this is the most deeply spiritual. The measure of its fulfilment in Christ is therefore greater than that of any other prophecy. Yet even here it does not mean that the prophet was thinking specifically of our Lord, or had any idea how long it would be ere his vision found its realization. He was charged with a great creative idea, which came from God, and was taken up into God's purpose in Christ — an idea which was not merely an anticipation of that which should be, but whose expression was to play an active part in its realization.

Nor should we forget that while our Lord has given this vision its fulfilment *par excellence,* it has found partial fulfilment in others. For many prophecies, just because they embody eternal principles or ideas, have found repeated but partial fulfilment. There have been others who have manifested a love that was unmoved by hatred and persecution, who have served with a love that knew no bounds, and who have been potent to bless the very society at whose hands they have suffered and died. The Christian martyrs were such partial illustrations of this principle, and embodiments of the spirit of the Suffering Servant. They found their inspiration in Christ, the supreme embodiment of the Suffering Servant, and sought to manifest His spirit, and by their patient nobility in suffering they won those who tormented and killed them. They too " saw of the travail of their soul " and were satisfied. Yet Jesus is clearly the supreme example of that principle, far transcending the martyrs and all others in His manifestation of the spirit of the Servant, and in the significance and power of His obedience to its whole conception. It is therefore wholly legitimate to find in Him the fulfilment of the prophecy, without claiming that it was written consciously and specifically of Him. And whatever view is taken of the primary reference of the Songs, it is quite inadequate to think of them only in terms of that reference. Even those scholars who think of the Suffering Servant as Jeremiah, or Zerubbabel, or Jehoiachin, or any other figure of history, have failed to bring out the real spiritual or historical significance of the prophecy, until they have unfolded the creative power of the ideas it enshrines, and their effect on our Lord in the conception and execution of His mission. Nothing is completely understood merely in terms of that out of which it arises. That unto which it issues must also be borne in mind. Whoso would understand the prophets must study them in the setting of their own times. But he must also see the significance of their great ideas, and of the figures in which they clothed those ideas, in the light of all they have led to.

Amongst His followers the most familiar title for our Lord is Christ, which is merely a Greek translation of the title Messiah. It therefore links Him at once with those Old Testament prophecies of the future Davidic leaders, and claims that He is the fulfilment of those promises. His own favourite term for Himself was Son of Man, and this links Him with the promise that figures in the book of Daniel. In the preceding chapter it has been said that Suffering Servant, Messiah, and Son of Man were in the Old Testament three quite separate and distinct conceptions, and that they first came together in Him in whom they found their fulfilment. Yet if we recognize in Him Messiah and Son of Man, it can be in no literal and exact way. For both conceptions have been modified by being brought into association with the figure of the Suffering Servant. In taking up into Himself the hopes that gathered around these terms, our Lord has profoundly modified them. There were nationalistic and political elements in these hopes, which He rejected, and all that he retained He spiritualized and enriched by the association with the Suffering Servant idea. The Davidic Messiah was depicted as one who should restore the political fortunes of Israel, and in the time of our Lord it was the political subjection to Rome which resulted in the intense eagerness of men for the coming of the Messiah. Similarly the Son of Man was a symbol for an earthly kingdom of the saints. It is sometimes suggested that our Lord cherished the political side of the hopes associated with these figures. That is extremely hard to believe. For it is clear beyond a peradventure that He interpreted His Messiahship in terms of the Suffering Servant, and equally understood His mission as Son of Man in similar terms. It was quite impossible to bring the Suffering Servant into association with these other terms without their transformation. For this meant that by suffering His mission was to be fulfilled, and by bitter humiliation at the hands of men. Not so was a messianic kingdom to be established, in the same sphere as the world empires that had preceded it, though founded on justice and superior to them in character. The concept of the Davidic Messiah had fostered hopes of a successful revolt against Rome, and it was only slowly that the disciples of our Lord could be lifted out of such hopes. They could see no relevance in the Suffering Servant idea to these hopes. For it meant that the beneficent sway of the Messiah was one to which men must

bring the willing dedication of themselves, and the authority of the kingdom which He had come to establish was the
authority of the spirit. It is this bringing together of three
orginally distinct streams for their mutual modification,
and for the spiritualization of the whole, which constitutes
one aspect of that reflex influence of Christ on prophecy,
comparable to the influence of the sea in the tidal estuary
of a river. In Him the hopes of the prophets were not so
much realized as transmuted, and given a higher realization
than their authors dreamed.

In the previous chapter it has been said that in their eschatological passages the prophets leapt across the undefined chasm that separated the present from " the latter end
of the days," with no indication of time perspective. There
are some instances of a similar leap within the limits of a
single oracle or series of oracles. The artist who paints the
stars on a flat canvas, or even on a dome, has no more means
of indicating perspective than the eye itself has of perceiving it. Stars that lie side by side may differ in their dis-
tances from the earth beyond the power of the mind to
grasp, yet the eye cannot tell which is near and which far
merely by looking. In the same way the prophet who looks
into the future often loses his perspective, and tends to relate together what may be separated far in time. He is describing the near future and he passes over to the distant
without knowing it.

An illustration of this is probably to be found in the
New Testament in Mark xiii and its parallels. Often this
chapter is analysed into two separate discourses, the one
having reference to the fall of Jerusalem and the other to
the end of the age. It is possible that the transitions might
be less baffling if we had the full discourse, but it does not
seem unlikely that our Lord passed from the one to the
other, though events have shown that they are separated

far from one another. He expressly disclaimed any knowledge of the time perspective involved.

Similar baffling transitions are found in the book of Joel. Here again we are often offered an analysis of the book into sections that have to do with the locusts and the situation of the moment, and sections of eschatological import, which are attributed to another author. But again it may be that to the prophet perspective was lost as he leapt from the near to the distant future.

The same consideration may be useful in studying the Servant Songs of Isaiah. The author believed that the Israel of his day was called to be the missionary nation, to carry the knowledge of the One True God to all men. Yet the Israel of his day did not rise to her high vocation, and in the centuries that followed the exile she was more concerned to preserve her own life than to spread her faith. Nevertheless, though Israel never rose to the heights of the exuberance of Deutero-Isaiah, she was not wholly faithless to her mission, and she did win some Gentiles to share her faith. Despite all her particularism she made proselytes, and the New Testament declared that there were men who were ready to compass sea and land to make proselytes. Deutero-Isaiah's hopes were fulfilled to some degree, though only slightly compared with the grandeur of those hopes. But in the fourth Song he passed over from the corporate to the individual Servant, in whom the mission should be more deeply expressed. There is nothing to indicate that he was aware that he was leaping over a gulf of time, or that the Servant in whom the mission of Israel should reach its climax was any less of his own age and the immediate future than the Israel to whom he brought the call to be missionaries of their faith. The time perspective is lost.

For all this variety of reasons the fulfilment of prophecy must not be looked for in any literalistic way, yet at the

same time we may find a real fulfilment in the taking of
the great hopes of the prophets, and their finest ideas, and
in the cleansing of them from their less spiritual trappings,
and the clothing with reality of their purified hopes and
dreams. For any true understanding of prophecy we must
have a clear historical sense. Yet beyond that we must have
spiritual penetration.

We do not find the fulfilment of the Old Testament in
the New, however, merely in the fulfilment of prophecy in
Christ. In a far wider sense the New Testament gathers into
itself the mission and message of the Old. But just as prophecies are transformed in the process of fulfilment, so in the
wider field, the full significance of the Old is only seen in
the light of the New. All the meaning of sacrifice is only to
be seen in the light of the sacrifice in which all other is done
away, and all the real effectiveness of such offerings, after
which the religion of the Old Testament was ever feeling,
is only found when they are transcended.

Of further illustrations of this principle we must confine
ourselves to but one or two. When Israel came out of Egypt,
the Passover gained a new significance for her. That the
Passover is older in its origin than the time of Moses has
been allowed to be probable, but its significance for Israel
was not. Whatever meaning it might have had before, from
this time on it stood as a memorial of the deliverance from
Egypt and of the Covenant made with God. In the New
Testament we find that the Synoptic Gospels represent our
Lord's Last Supper with His disciples as a Passover, whereas
the Fourth Gospel represents His death as taking place before the Passover night. There have been many attempts to
resolve this conflict, and it would carry us much too far to
attempt to examine them. Where there is no attempt to resolve the conflict, New Testament scholars must choose between these two accounts, and a number of scholars, including some of the highest eminence, have in recent years

expressed a preference for that of the Fourth Gospel. That that Gospel is later than the others does not mean that it is necessarily inferior historically, and that the testimony of the others is threefold does not increase its weight, since two of the three rest on the third. It is with some diffidence that the present writer ventures to express a view on a problem which is admittedly difficult. Yet he feels that if a choice must be made, probability favours the Synoptic Gospels.

That the death of Christ took place at the Passover season, whether actually after the Passover meal or before it, is beyond controversy. Hence in either case, there was reason to link that death in thought with the Passover. Paul says, " For our Passover also hath been sacrificed, even Christ." [17] This offers no particular support to the Fourth Gospel, since if He were crucified actually on the Passover day, this would be an intelligible observation. But once the observation had been made, it offered a theological reason for representing the death of Jesus as taking place at the very hour when Passover lambs were being slain. On the other hand no obvious reason can be suggested to account for the Synoptic writers' account, if it is unhistorical. The Fourth Gospel is more interested in the theological significance of the things it records than are the Synoptic Gospels, and is more likely to have been influenced by such a consideration. Moreover, the Epistle to the Hebrews shows no knowledge of this tradition. It unfolds the sacrificial significance of the death of Christ, but in terms of the ritual of the Day of Atonement, and not of the Passover.

Accepting, then, the Synoptic tradition, we may observe that the Egyptian Passover was designed to protect the Israelite households, but that succeeding Passovers were memorials. But they were not intended to keep alive the memory of the slaughter of the first Passover lambs, but the

[17] 1 Cor. v. 7.

protection of Israelite households from the slayer of the
firstborn and the deliverance from Egypt to which it led.
They were therefore designed to remember a deliverance
which followed the Egyptian Passover. In the same way the
Lord's Supper is represented as a memorial feast instituted
to remember a deliverance which Christ should effect after
its first celebration. The new feast like the old, pointed to
a definite date in history and a definite event of history,
and its message is the completion and fulfilment of the
promise of the old one.

The old deliverance was from the physical bondage in
Egypt. But Israel had learned to recognize her need for a
deeper deliverance from sin, and the new Deliverer brought
"the remission of sins." The old deliverance was marked
by the death of the firstborn of the Egyptians, but the new
by the death of the only-begotten Son of God; the old was
purchased by the divinely exacted sacrifice of the enemies of
Israel, the new by the divinely offered sacrifice of Him who
represented the new Israel of God. Into all the complex of
ideas that gather round the Last Supper and the Crucifixion, the Passover had no little place.

Moreover, the Last Supper was called a Covenant by our
Lord. And again He was linking it to Old Testament
thought, and declaring it to be the crown and completion
of so much that is found in the Old Testament. The old deliverance was followed by the Covenant of Sinai, when Israel pledged herself to God in gratitude for the deliverance
that had been wrought. And the Lord's Supper that was instituted on that Passover night was to be an ever-renewed
Covenant in which the redeemed should pledge themselves
in loyalty and gratitude to Him by whom the new deliverance was to be wrought. "This cup is the new covenant in
My blood," [18] "which is shed for many unto remission of
sins." [19] Here it was linked not alone with the Covenant of

[18] Luke xxii. 20.   [19] Matt. xxvi. 28.

Sinai, but with that New Covenant, of which Jeremiah had spoken, the New Covenant that should have its law inscribed on the tables of human personality and not on tables of stone, when God would forgive men their iniquity and remember their sin no more. There is no mere going back in thought to the Egyptian Passover and to Sinai, but a gathering together of rich streams of thought which had marked the development of Old Testament religion through all its long course, and the bringing of them here to their climax. There was fulfilment, but more than fulfilment. Without the Old Testament and all the divine discipline of Israel that had gone into its making this could never be understood. Yet from the Old Testament alone this could never have been deduced as its inevitable fulfilment. It was in Christ that all its meaning was to be seen, for He showed Himself to be the goal of all its dynamic.

Again, in the Last Supper our Lord called for the identification of His followers with Himself. " Take, eat; this is My body." [20] " Drink ye all of it; for this is My blood." [21] And the Fourth Gospel offers its interpretation in the address attributed to our Lord in the Capernaum synagogue: " He that eateth My flesh and drinketh My blood abideth in Me, and I in him." [22] It has already been said that in the initial act of surrender to Christ, and in the sacrament of the Lord's Supper, the believer becomes by faith one with Christ, and so is both lifted to God and enriched by God in Him. But there is a further consequence of this union with Christ. It was Israel's mission to be the light of the nations, and the purpose of her election was to share its fruit with all the world. And the Suffering Servant was to take her mission into Himself, and lift it to its highest point. And since in Christ the vision of the Suffering Servant finds its realization, He could rightly say: " I am the light of the world." [23] But in our identification with Him we must be lifted into His spirit and His purpose, so that He can say to us, " Ye are the light of the world." [24] Israel's mission gathered into Himself is communicated unto us, so that we are not alone the heirs of the promises, but the heirs of the tasks committed unto her. That is why the Christian Church was essentially missionary from the start. For there was here a further fulfilment of the Old Testament. And in so far as men are truly one with Christ, and in so far as they truly partake of the sacrament which is so central to Christian worship, they must be filled with holy purpose to spread to all men the knowledge of God's grace in Christ.

[23] John viii. 12.   [24] Matt. v. 14.

INDEX

(a) GENERAL

AARON, 141
Abaddon, 224
Abel, 104, 182
Abiathar, 73
Abraham (Abram), 51, 67, 85, 220
Accession Festival, 179 f., 247
Achan, 210, 216, 220
Ackerman, H. C., 116 n.
Adonis, 69 ff.
Ahab, 40, 100, 138 f., 153, 214
Ahijah, 137
Ahikar, 78
Ahiram, 47
Ai, 116
Aijalon, 96
Albright, W. F., 34 n., 40, 46 n., 52, 54 f., 64, 70, 72, 75, 115, 142
Alexander, 165 f., 263
Aleyin, 69 f.
Amalekites, 187
Amarna letters, 47 ff., 53, 55, 60, 61 n., 63, 110, 112 f.
Amaziah, 145
Amen, 48; Cairo Hymn to, 77
Amen-em-ope, 78 f.
Amenhotep III, 59
Ammon, 123
Amos, 41, 121, 129, 139, 144, 154 f., 172, 191 f., 219, 245
Anat, 69 f.
Anath-bethel, 75
Anath-yahu, 75
Anathoth, 71
Anthropomorphism, 188
Antichrist, 279
Antiochus Epiphanes, 227, 263 f., 279
'Aperu, 63
Aphek, Battle of, 101
Apocalyptists, 262 ff., 265
Apocrypha, 13
Archaeology and O.T., 16 ff., 33 ff., 59 ff.
Ark, 101, 127, 144, 179, 187, 232, 247
Armageddon, 134
Arrapha, 54
Artaxerxes I, 45
Artaxerxes II, 45
Ashdod, 52
Asher, 54, 60, 79
Asherat, 69 f.
Asherat of the Sea, 69

Ashima, 75
Ashtarte, 40, 69, 71
Asia Minor, 39, 49, 67, 72
Assuan, 44
Assyria, 38, 44, 49, 98 f., 102 ff., 129, 153 f.
Assyrian archaeology, 34 f., 53
Aton, 48
Augustine, 230
Avaris-Tanis, 113
Azekah, 43

BAAL, 69, 86, 125 ff., 135 f.
Baalzebub, 54
Babel und Bibel, 17
Babylon, 38, 49, 75, 102 ff., 153 f., 161 f., 173 f., 243, 289 f.
Babylonian archaeology, 34 f.
Babylonian culture, 51 f., 67 ff., 72, 75 ff.
Babylonian Job, 76 f.
Balaam, 135
Barak, 96
Barnabas, 242
Bathsheba, 138, 153, 214, 217 f.
Bauer, H., 50
Beelzeboul, 54
Benenima, 63
Benjamin, 63
Beth-anath, 71
Bethel, 138 f., 147
Bethlehem-judah, 115, 117
Bethshean, 36 f., 71, 73
Beth-shemesh, 47, 73
Boghaz Keui, 47, 49
Box, G. H., 250
Buddhism, 122
Burrows, M., 33 n., 65
Byblos, 47

CAESAREA PHILIPPI, 268, 270
Calves, Golden, 72
Cambyses, 44
Canaan (see also Palestine), 48, 53, 63, 66 f.
Canaanite culture, 17, 53, 72 f.
Canaanites, 125
Canon, 172, 174 ff., 250, 264
Capernaum, 303
Carchemish, 48

INDEX
(b) TEXTS
(English references only)